Association American Art

Art Collection Formed by the Late Mrs. Mary J. Morgan

Association American Art

Art Collection Formed by the Late Mrs. Mary J. Morgan

ISBN/EAN: 9783744673211

Printed in Europe, USA, Canada, Australia, Japan

Cover: Foto ©Thomas Meinert / pixelio.de

More available books at **www.hansebooks.com**

Index and Biographical Notes

MODERN PAINTINGS

INDEX TO ARTISTS REPRESENTED,

TOGETHER

WITH BIOGRAPHICAL NOTES, LISTS OF HONORS, AND OTHER INFORMATION.

ALMA-TADEMA (Laurenz), R. A., . . . London

Born at Dronryn, West Friesland, Holland, 1836. First studied in the Gymnasium of Leinwarden, where he devoted much of his time to the study of Roman and Egyptian antiquities. Entered the Academy at Antwerp in 1852, and studied under Leys. In 1870 fixed his residence in London. Medals, Paris, 1864–1867 (Exposition Universelle)–*1878* (Exposition Universelle). *Grand Gold Medal, Berlin, 1874. Legion of Honor, 1873; Officer of the same, 1878. Order of Merit, Berlin, 1881. Knight of the Order of Leopold; of the Order of the Dutch Lion; of the Order of St. Michael of Bavaria; of the Gold Lion of the House of Nassau; of the Königliche Kronen-Orden of Prussia. Member of the Royal Academy of Amsterdam; of the Royal Academy of Munich; of the Royal Academy of Berlin, and of the Royal Academy of London. Member of the English Society of Painters in Water Colors. Honorary Professor of the Royal Institute of Fine Arts, Naples, and Corresponding Member of the Academy of the* Beaux Arts, *France.*

AUBERT (Jean Ernest), ... Paris

Born at Paris, 1824. Entered l'École des Beaux Arts *in 1841, as a pupil of Paul Delaroche and Achille—Louis Martinet. Awarded the* Prix de Rome, *1844, after which he studied five years in Italy. Medals, Paris, 1857–1859–1861–1878.*

No. 179—Love Quenching His Thirst, . . Page 73

ARTZ (ADOLPHE), ... Hague

Pupil of Mollinger and Israels.

No. 159—The Frugal Meal, ... Page 67

BARGUE (CHAS.), deceased, ... Paris

No. 164—The Sentinel, ... Page 69

BAUGNIET (CHARLES), ... Sèvres

Born at Brussels, 1814. First known as a lithographer. In 1841 appointed draughtsman to the King of the Belgians; 1843, Knight of the Order of Leopold. Went to England, where he painted portraits for eighteen years. Later went to Paris, where he established himself as a genre-painter. Knight of the Orders of Leopold; of La Branche Ernestine de Saxe; of Christ of Portugal, and of Isabella the Catholic, of Spain. Pupil of Drölling and Cabat.

No. 110—The Bride's Toilet, ... Page 58

BECKER (ERNST ALBERT), ... Berlin

(Commonly called "Q. Becker.") Born October 22, 1830, at Berlin. From his frequently painting cows, he came to be called Kuh-Becker (Cow-Becker), a jest which he himself accepted by signing his pictures "Q. Becker." (H. A. Müller: Künsthe-Lexikon.)

No. 18—Head of Peasant Woman, . . . Page 38

BENEDICTER (A.), ... Munich

BERANGER (ANTOINE ÉMILE), deceased, . Paris

Born at Sèvres, August 30, 1814. Began life as a painter on porcelain under his father, after whom he was named. Pupil of Paul Delaroche. Medals, 1846-1848. Died, 1882.

BERNE-BELLECOUR (ETIENNE PROSPER), Paris

Born at Boulogne-sur-Mer. Pupil of Picot and of F. Barrias. Medals, Paris, 1869-1872-1878 (at Salon and Exposition Universelle). *Legion of Honor, 1878.*

BEYLE (PIERRE M.), ... Paris

Medal, Paris, 1884.

BONHEUR (MARIE ROSA), ... Paris

Born at Bordeaux, 1822. Pupil of her father, Raymond Bonheur. Medals, 1845-1848-1855-1867 (Exposition Universelle). *Legion of Honor, 1865.*

BLOMMERS (B. J.), ... Hague

No. 64—Departure of the Fisher's Boat, . . Page 48

No. 95—Shoveling Snow, ... Page 55

BONVIN (FRANÇOIS-SAINT), ... Paris

Born at Vaugirard, Paris, 1817. Medals, Paris, 1849–1851. Chevalier of the Legion of Honor, 1870.

No. 30—A Pinch of Snuff, ... Page 41

BONNAT (LÉON JOSEPH FLORENTIN), . . Paris

Born at Bayonne, 1833. Studied under Madrazo, at Madrid, and afterward under Léon Cogniet, in Paris. He took the second grand Prix de Rome, *which did not entitle him to enter the Villa Medicis, but by the aid of friends in Bayonne he was able to spend four years in study in Italy. Medals, Paris, 1861–1863–1867. Medal of Honor, 1869. Paris Legion of Honor, 1869; Officer of the same, 1874; Commander, 1882. Knight of the Order of Leopold and Member of the Institute of France.*

No. 152—An Arab Chief, ... Page 66

BOUGHTON (GEORGE H.), N.A., and A.R.A., London

Born in England, 1834. Brought to Albany, N. Y., by his parents in 1837, where, when a youth, he began the study of Art. Afterward he studied in London and Paris. Elected member of the National Academy, New York, 1871; Associate of the Royal Academy, England, 1879.

No. 84—The Finishing Touch, ... Page 52

BOUGUEREAU (WILLIAM ADOLPHE), . . Paris

Born at La Rochelle, 1825. When very young, after passing

through the College at Pons, where he showed an aptitude for drawing, Bouguereau was placed in a business house in Bordeaux. While there he attended, two hours a day, the drawing-school of M. Alaux. Treated contemptuously by his fellow students on account of his unaristocratic business connections, Bouguereau nevertheless took the first prize at the end of the year, the award causing such excitement in the school that a riot was the consequence. Bouguereau then resolved to turn his attention to art, and after he had earned sufficient money by painting portraits at Saintouge, where his uncle was a priest, he went to Paris and entered the studio of Picot, and later l'École des Beaux Arts, *where his progress was rapid. He gained the* Prix de Rome *in 1850, and then studied in Rome. Medals, Paris, 1855* (Exposition Universelle)-*1857-1867* (Exposition Universelle). *Legion of Honor, 1859. Member of the Institute of France,* 1876. *Officer of the Legion of Honor, 1876. Medal of Honor* (Exposition Universelle), *1878. Knight of the Order of Leopold, 1881. Grand Medal of Honor, Paris, 1885. Medal of Honor, Antwerp, 1885.*

BOUCHARD (Louis P.), ... Paris

Pupil of Lefebvre.

BÖEHM (Palik), ... Munich

Medal, Vienna, 1882.

BOSBOOM (Johannes), ... Hague

Born at the Hague, 1817. Pupil of B. J. Van Bree. Knight of the Order of the Lion of Netherland; of the Crown of Oak, and the Order of Leopold. Medals, At the Paris Exposition of 1855, and Centennial Exhibition, Philadelphia, 1876.

No. 85—Church Interior, ... Page 53

BROZIK (Vacslav), ... Paris

Born at Pilsen, 1852. Pupil of the School of Fine Arts at Prague, of Piloty and Munkacsy. Medal, at the Salon, 1878.

No. 49—The Falconer's Recital, . . . Page 45

BRÉTON (Jules Adolphe), ... Paris

Born at Courrieres, France, 1827. Pupil of Drölling and of Devigne. Medals, London, Vienna and Brussels, and at Paris in 1855-1857-1859-1861. Legion of Honor, 1861. Medal of the First Class, and officer of the Legion of Honor (at Exposition Universelle), *1867. Medal of Honor (Salon), 1872. Knight of the Order of Leopold, 1881. Ribbon of St. Stanislaus of Russia. Corresponding Member of the Academies of Vienna, Stockholm and Madrid.*

No. 55—The Bird Nest, ... Page 46

No. 158—Returning from the Fields, ... 67

No. 235—Communicants, ... 85

BRIDGMAN (Frederick A.), N.A., . . . Paris

Born in Alabama, 1847. At an early age began his professional work as an engraver with the American Bank Note Company, New York, studying in his leisure hours in the schools of the Brooklyn Art Association. Later, studied with Jean Léon Gérôme, of whom he was a favorite pupil in Paris. Medals, Paris, 1877–1878 (Exposition Universelle). *Legion of Honor, 1878.*

CABANEL (Alexandre), ... Paris

Born at Montpellier, 1823. Pupil of Picot. Prix de Rome, 1845. Medals, Paris, 1852–1855 (Exposition Universelle). *Legion of Honor, 1855. Member of the Institute of France, 1863. Officer of the Legion of Honor, 1864. Medals of Honor, 1865–1867* (Exposition Universelle). *Medal of Honor, 1868* (Exposition Universelle). *Professor in l'Ecole des Beaux Arts.*

CAMERON (Hugh), ... London

Born in Edinburgh, October, 1835. He was educated in the Trustees Academy, working at his profession in that city until his removal to London, in 1876. Member of Royal Scottish Academy.

CASANOVA (Antonio), ... Paris

Pupil of Madrazo.

CEDERSTRÖM (Theo), ... Munich

CHURCH (Frederick Edwin), . . . New York

Born at Hartford, Conn., March 14, 1826. Member of National Academy of Design, New York.

No. 148—"Al Ayn"—The Fountain, . . . Page 65

CLAYS (Paul Jean), ... Brussels

Born at Bruges, Belgium, 1819. Pupil of Gudin, Paris. Medals, Paris, 1867 (Exposition Universelle). *Legion of Honor, 1875. Medal, 1878* (Exposition Universelle). *Officer of the Legion of Honor, 1881.*

No. 139—On the Thames, ... Page 63

CONRAD (Albert), ... Munich

Born at Torgau, February, 1837. Followed at first the profession of his father, who was a sculptor, but in Berlin turned his attention to painting.

No. 44—A Tyrolese Inn, ... Page 44

No. 78—The Old, Old Story, . . 50

CONSTABLE (John), dec'd, ... London

Born at Bergholt, in Suffolk, June 11, 1776. Died in London, April 1, 1837.

No. 184—English Landscape, ... Page 74

COROT (Jean Baptiste Camille), dec'd, . . Paris

Born at Paris, 1796. Studied art against the wishes of his family. Instructed first by Michallon, afterward by Victor Bertin, and then spent several years in Italy. At first unsuccessful in obtaining recognition, Corot's works afterward became so popular that his income for several years averaged over two hundred thousand francs from his profession alone. Medals, Paris, 1838–1848–1855–1867 (Exposition Universelle). *Legion of Honor, 1846; officer of the same, 1867. Died, 1875. Diploma to the memory of Deceased Artists* (Exposition Universelle), *1878.*

COUTURE (Thomas). Paris

Born at Senlis, December 21, 1815. Studied with Gros, later with Paul Delaroche. Medals, 1844–1849–1855. Died, March 31, 1879.

DAGNAN-BOUVERET (Pascal Adol. Jean), Paris

Born at Paris. Pupil of Jean Léon Gérôme. Medals, Paris, 1878–1880.

DAUBIGNY (Charles François), dec'd, . . Paris

Born at Paris, 1817. Pupil of his father and Paul Delaroche, and for three years studied in Italy. Medals, 1848–1853–1855–1857–1859–1867. Legion of Honor, 1859; officer of the same, 1874. Died, 1878. Diploma to the Memory of Deceased Artists (Exposition Universelle), *1878.*

DECAMPS (Alexandre-Gabriel), dec'd, . Paris

Born at Paris, 1803. Pupil of Abel de Pujol. Medals, Paris, 1831–1834. Legion of Honor, 1839; officer of the same, 1851. Died, 1860.

DELACROIX (Ferd'd Victor Eugene), dec'd, Paris

Born at Charenton-Saint Meurice, near Paris, April 26, 1798. Pupil of Guerin. Medals, Paris, 1824–1848. Legion of Honor, 1831; officer of the same, 1846; commander of the same, 1855. Medal of Honor (Exposition Universelle), *1855. Member of the Institute of France, 1857. Died, August 13, 1863.*

DELORT (CHARLES EDOUARD), ... Paris

Born at Nîmes, France. Pupil of Gleyre and of Gérôme. Medals, 1875–1882.

DE NEUVILLE (ALPHONSE MARIE), dec'd, Paris

Born at Saint Omer, France, 1836. A member of a wealthy family, his parents intended him for an official career, but he was only willing to join the army, and entered the school at Lorient. Here his astonishing skill in drawing was remarked. In order to make peace with his family he went to Paris and entered the law-school, but he spent more time at the military school and in the Champs-de-Mars, *sketching and becoming familiar with all the details of a soldier's life. He returned home, declaring he would be a painter or nothing. His friends endeavored to discourage his determination, and the artists upon whom he called in Paris advised him to go back home. Delacroix, however, became his friend, and with him De Neuville spent many hours. He studied also with Picot. De Neuville's first pictures were not particularly remarkable, but the Franco-Prussian war gave him inspiration and subjects almost without limit, and since that time the artist has produced some of the greatest battle-pictures of any time. Medals, Paris, 1859–1861. Legion of Honor, 1873; officer of the same, 1881. Died 1885.*

DÉTAILLE (JEAN BAPTISTE EDOUARD), . . Paris

Born at Paris, 1848. Favorite pupil of Meissonier. Medals, Paris, 1869-1870-1872. Legion of Honor, 1873; officer of the same, 1881.

DIAZ (NARCISSE VIRGILE, DE LA PENA) dec., . Paris

Born at Bordeaux, 1807. His parents were banished from Spain on account of political troubles, and at ten years of age Diaz was left an orphan in a strange country. At fifteen years of age he was apprenticed to a maker of porcelain, where his talent first displayed itself. He quarreled with and left his master, and subsequently spent several years in most bitter poverty. After his ability as a most wonderful colorist was recognized, Diaz painted and sold many pictures, working even too constantly, as if endeavoring by the accumulation of a vast fortune to avenge the poverty of his youth. Medals, 1844-1846-1848. Legion of Honor, 1851. Died, 1876. Diploma to the Memory of Deceased Artists (Exposition Universelle), *1878.*

DOMINGO (J.), ... Madrid

Born in Spain. Pupil of Meissonier, Paris, and friend of the late M. Fortuny, who greatly admired his work and criticised and encouraged him in his student days.

DUPRÉ (JULES), ... Paris

Born in Nantes, 1812. As a boy he studied design in the porcelain manufactory of his father, but soon turned his attention to landscape painting, and made his début in the Salon of 1831. Medals, Paris, 1833. Legion of Honor, 1849. Medals (Exposition Universelle), *1867. Officer of the Legion of Honor, 1870.*

EPP (RUDOLF), ... Munich

Born at Eberbach in Baden, July, 1834.

ESCOSURA (LEON Y), ... Paris

Born in Asturias. Pupil of Jean Léon Gérôme, Paris. Commander of the Order of Isabel, the Catholic. Chevalier of the Order of Charles III. of Spain, and of the Order of Christ of Portugal.

FAED (THOMAS), R. A., ... London

Born in Scotland, 1826. Studied with his brother, John, and in the School of Design, Edinburgh, under Sir William Allan. Was made an Associate of the Royal Scottish Academy in 1849. Went to London in 1852, and was made an Associate of the Royal Academy in 1861, and an Academician in 1866.

No. 161—In Doubt, ... Page 69

FORTUNY (MARIANO), deceased, ... Rome

Born in Reus, Catalonia, June 11, 1839. Pupil of the Barcelona Academy, Chevalier of the Order of Charles III., Prize of Rome from Spain, 1858. Died in Rome, November 21, 1874. Diploma to the Memory of Deceased Artists (Exposition Universelle), *1878.*

No. 115—Italian Woman, ... Page 59

No. 165—Spanish Lady with Fan, ... 70

No. 199—The Rare Vase, ... 77

FRÈRE (EDOUARD), ... Paris

Born at Paris, 1819. Pupil of Paul Delaroche. Medals at Paris, 1851-1852-1855. Chevalier of the Legion of Honor, 1855.

No. 171—Prayer, ... Page 71

FROMENTIN (EUGÈNE), deceased, . . . Paris

Born at La Rochelle, France, 1820. Studied landscape-painting under Cabat, and traveled in the East from 1842 to 1846, making many studies of Oriental subjects. Medals, Paris, 1849-1857-1859. Legion of Honor, 1859. Medal (Exposition Universelle), *1867. Officer of the Legion of Honor, 1869. Died, 1876. Diploma to the Memory of Deceased Artists, 1878.*

GALLAIT (Louis), ... Brussels

Born at Tournai, March 10, 1810. Medals, 1835–1848. Legion of Honor, 1841; Chevalier of the Order of the Cross of Oak, Holland; Honorary Member of the Royal Academy, London. Grand Cordon of the Order of Leopold, 1881.

GÉRÔME (Jean Léon), ... Paris

Born at Vesoul, France, 1824. Went to Paris in 1841, and entered the studio of Paul Delaroche, at the same time following the course of l'École des Beaux Arts. *In 1844 he accompanied Delaroche to Italy. He made his début at the Salon of 1847. In 1853 and 1856 he traveled in Egypt and Turkey, studying closely the history and customs of those countries. Medals, Paris, 1847–1848–1855* (Exposition Universelle). *Medal of the Institute, 1865. Medal of Honor,* Exposition Universelle, *1867. Medals of Honor, 1874. Medal for Sculpture and one of the eight Grand Medals of Honor,* Exposition Universelle, *1878. Legion of Honor, 1855; Officer of the same, 1867; Commander, 1878; Chevalier of the* Order de l'Aigle Rouge, *and Member of the Institute of France (1878). Professor in* l'École des Beaux Arts.

GREÜTZNER (E.), ... Munich

No. 124—The Puzzled Priest, ... Page 60

GUNTHER (OTTO EDMUND), dec'd, . . Munich

Born at Halle, September 30, 1838. Professor at the Academy, Königsberg. Gold Medal, Berlin, 1876. Died, 1884.

No. 219—The Pastor's Visit, ... Page 81

HAQUETTE (GEORGES), ... Paris

Born at Paris. Pupil of Jean François Millet and Alexander Cabanel. Medal, Paris, 1880.

No. 1—The Signal, ... Page 35

HARBURGER (EDMOND), ... Munich

Born at Eichstadt, Bavaria. Pupil of W. Lindenschmidt, Munich.

No. 97—Dutch Peasant, ... Page 55

HÉBERT (ANTOINE AUGUSTE ERNEST), . . Paris

Born at Grenoble, 1817. Studied at the Lycée of Grenoble. Entered l'École de Droit, *in Paris, in deference to the wishes of his family, but at the same time he worked in the studio of David d'Angers, the sculptor, and was often with Paul Delaroche, who urged him to become an artist. He worked by himself and sent a picture to the Salon of 1839, which was purchased by the Government. This encouraged him to enter* l'École des Beaux Arts, *and there he gained the* Prix de Rome. *Medals, Paris, 1851-1855* (Exposition Universelle)—*1867* (Exposition Universelle). *Legion of Honor, 1853; Officer of the same, 1867; Commander, 1874. Director of the Academy of France, at Rome, 1866. Member of the Institute of France, 1874.*

No. 12—Madonna and Child, ... Page 37

HENNER (JEAN JACQUES), ... Paris

Born at Bernailler (Alsace). Pupil of Drölling, of Picot, and of l'Ecole des Beaux Arts. Prix de Rome, *1858. Medals, Paris, 1863-1865-1866-1878* (Exposition Universelle). *Legion of Honor, 1873; Officer of the same, 1878.*

No. 77—Sleeping Nymph, ... Page 50

No. 149—Repose, ... 65

No. 177—Fabiola, ... 72

No. 229—La Source, ... 83

HERVIER (ADOLPHE LOUIS), ... Paris

Pupil of E. Osabey.

No. 10—Kitchen Interior, ... Page 37

HOGUET (CHARLES), deceased, ... Berlin

Born at Berlin in 1813. Finished his studies at Paris under Bertin and Paul Delaroche. Has painted in England, Germany, and Holland. Member of the Berlin Academy. Medal, Paris, 1848. Died, 1870.

No. 35—Landscape, ... Page 42

JACQUE (CHARLES ÉMILE), ... Paris

Born at Paris, 1813. Early in life studied with a geographical engraver; later, spent seven years in the army, and worked two years in England as an engraver on wood. Is famous for his etchings as well as his paintings. Medals, Paris, 1861-1863-1864-1867. Legion of Honor, 1867.

No. 94—Shepherdess and Sheep, ... Page 54

JACQUET (J. G.), ... Paris

Born at Paris, 1846. Pupil of Bouguereau. Medals, 1868–1875–1878 (Exposition Universelle), *Legion of Honor, 1879.*

JIMINEZ (JOSE-Y-ARANDA), ... Paris

Born at Seville, Spain. Pupil of the Academy of Fine Arts, Seville.

KAEMMERER (FREDERIC HENRI), . . . Paris

Born at the Hague. Pupil of Jean Léon Gérôme, Paris. Medal, Paris, 1874.

KNAUS (PROFESSOR LUDWIG), ... Berlin

Born at Wiesbaden, 1829. Pupil of Jacobi, and the Academy of Düsseldorf under Sohn and Schadow. Afterward he allied himself with Lessing, Leutze, and Weber. Member of the Academies of Berlin, Vienna, Munich, Amsterdam, Antwerp, and Christiana, and Knight of the Order of Merit. Medals, Paris, 1853–1855 (Exposition Universelle)—*1859. Medal of Honor, 1867* (Exposition Universelle). *Legion of Honor, 1859; Officer of the same, 1867. Medals, Vienna, 1882; Munich, 1883. Professor in the Academy at Berlin. Medal of Honor, Antwerp, 1885.*

KNIGHT (Daniel Ridgeway), ... Paris

Born at Philadelphia. Pupil of l'École des Beaux Arts, *Gleyre and Meissonier, Paris.*

KOEK-KOEK (Barend-Cornelis),dec., Amsterdam

Born at Middelsbourg, Holland, 1803. Pupil of Schelfont. Medals, Paris, 1840–1843, Chevalier of the Order of the Lion of Netherlands, and Leopold of Belgium. Died, 1862.

KOWALSKI (Alfred Wieruz), ... Paris

Born at Warsaw, Poland. Pupil of Brandt.

LEFEBVRE (Jules Joseph), ... Paris

Born at Tournau, 1836. Pupil of Léon Cogniet, Grand Prix de Rome, *1861, Chevalier of the Legion of Honor.*

LHERMITTE (L.), ... Paris

LELOIR (LOUIS ALEXANDRE), deceased . . Paris

Born at Paris. Pupil of his father, Jean Baptiste Auguste Leloir. Medals, Paris, 1864–1868–1870–1878 (Exposition Universelle). *Legion of Honor, 1876.*

LEROUX (HECTOR), ... Paris

Born at Verdun, December 29, 1829. Pupil of Picot. Medals, Paris, 1863–1864–1874. Cross of the Legion of Honor, 1877. Medal (Exposition Universelle), *1878. His best known picture, "The Vestal Tuccia," is in the Corcoran gallery in Washington.*

LYMAN (JOSEPH, JR.), ... New York

Born at Ravenna, Ohio. Studied in Europe, 1864-1866, and afterward with J. H. Dolph, A.N.A., and Samuel Colman, N.A. First exhibited, 1876, at the National Academy, New York.

LÖFFTZ (LUDWIG), ... Munich

Born at Darmstadt, June 21, 1845. Professor in the Academy of Fine Arts at Munich.

MARIS (MATTHEW), ... London

Born at the Hague, 1835. Has long lived in London.

MEISSONIER (JEAN LOUIS ERNEST), . . . Paris

Born at Lyons, 1813. He went to Paris when quite young, and was, for a time, a pupil of Léon Cogniet. First exhibited at the Salon in 1836. His picture "A Dream" (1855) was purchased by Napoleon III. and presented to the late Prince Albert, of England. Medals, Paris, 1840–1841–1843–1848. Grand Medal of Honor, 1855 (Exposition Universelle). *One of the eight Grand Medals of Honor* (Exposition Universelle), *1867; Grand Medal of Honor* (Exposition Universelle), *1878; Legion of Honor, 1846; Officer of the same, 1856; Commander, 1867; Grand Officer of the Legion, 1878. Member of the Institute of France, 1861. Honorary Member of the Royal Academy, London.*

No. 75—In the Library, ... Page 50

No. 150—A Standard Bearer, ... 66

No. 227—The Vidette, 1812, ... 83

MEISSONIER (CHARLES), ... Paris

Pupil of his Father. Medal, 1866.

No. 151—The Musician, ... Page 66

MERLE (HUGHES), dec'd, ... Paris

Born at Saint-Marcellin, France, 1822. Pupil of Léon Cogniet. Medals, 1861–1863. Legion of Honor, 1866. Died, 1881.

No. 88—St. Elizabeth of Hungary, ... Page 53

METTLING (LOUIS), ... Paris

Pupil of the Lyons Fine Art School.

No. 16—Domestic Interior, ... Page 38

No. 90—Street Sweeper at Lunch, ... 54

MEYER (JOHANN GEORG), ... Berlin

Called from his birth-place Meyer Von Bremen. Born October 28, 1813. Pupil of Sohn. Member of the Amsterdam Academy. Gold Medal of Prussia, 1850. Medals at Berlin and Philadelphia.

MILLER (FRANCIS), ... New York

Born in Columbia, Ohio, 1854. Pupil of the Pennsylvania Academy of Fine Arts, Philadelphia, and of Carolus Duran, Paris.

MILLET (JEAN FRANÇOIS), dec'd, ... Paris

Born at Greville, France, 1814. Pupil of Langlois, at Cherbourg. His progress there was so remarkable that the Municipality of Cherbourg gave him a small pension that he might go to study in Paris. In 1837 he became a pupil of Paul Delaroche and the friend of Corot, Theodore Rousseau, Dupré and Diaz. Medals, Paris, 1853-1864-1867 (Exposition Universelle). *Legion of Honor, 1868. Died, 1875. Diploma to the Memory of Deceased Artists* (Exposition Universelle), *1878. In his whole artistic career Millet only finished about eighty oil paintings, many of which he retained in his studio for a long time, returning to them again and again, in order to satisfy himself.*

MONTICELLI, ... Paris

NEUHUYS (Albert), ... The Hague

Born at Utrecht.

NICOL (Erskine), A.R.A., ... London

Born at Edinburgh, Scotland, 1825. Was apprenticed to a house-painter in his native city, but studied art in his leisure hours in the "Trustees' Academy." Afterward taught drawing in the

High School at Leith, and later in Dublin. Member of the Royal Scottish Academy and Associate Member of the Royal Academy of England. Many of his paintings, cleverly depicting Scotch or Irish character, have been engraved. Medal (Exposition Universelle), *Paris, 1867.*

PASINI (ALBERTO), ... Paris

Born at Busseto, Italy. Pupil of Ciceri. Medals, Paris, 1859–1863–1864. Grand Medal of Honor (Exposition Universelle), *1878. Legion of Honor, 1868; Officer of the same, 1878. Medal at Vienna Exposition, 1873. Knight of the Order of Saints Maurice and Lazarus, and Officer of the Orders of Turkey and Persia. Honorary Professor of the Academies of Parma and Turin.*

PASSINI (LUDWIG), ... Vienna

Born at Vienna, July 9, 1832. Pupil of the Academy of Vienna. Medal at Paris, 1870. Legion of Honor, 1878.

PELEZ (FERNAND), ... Paris

Pupil of Cabanel. Medals at Paris, 1876–1879–1880.

PERRAULT (Léon), ... Paris

Born at Poitiers. Pupil of Picot and Bouguereau. Medals, Paris, 1864-1865; Philadelphia, Centennial Exposition, 1876.

No. 42—A Young Gleaner, ... Page 43

No. 218—A Flower Girl, ... 81

PIOT (Adolphe), ... Paris

Pupil of Cogniet.

No. 66—Adoration, ... Page 48

No. 206—The Young Wanderer, ... 78

POKITONOW (J.), ... Paris

No. 6—Landscape, ... Page 36

RÉNOUF (Émile), ... Paris

Born at Paris. Pupil of G. Boulanger, J. Lefebvre, and Carolus Duran. Medal, Paris, 1880.

No. 80—Repairing the Old Boat, ... Page 51

RENTAL (Max), ... Munich

Medal, Munich, 1881.

No. 207—Norwegian Fisher's Dance, ... Page 78

RICHET (Léon), ... Paris

Born at Solesmes. Pupil of Diaz, of Lefebvre, and of Boulanger.

No. 155—Coming from Labor, ... Page 67

ROBIE (Jean Baptiste), ... Paris

Born at Brussels, 1821. Gold Medal at Brussels, 1848. Medals at Paris, 1851–1863. Gold Medal, Hague, 1861. Officer of the Order of Leopold, 1869.

ROUSSEAU (Théodore), deceased, . . . Paris

Born at Paris, 1812. Pupil of Guillon-Lethiere. First exhibited, Salon, 1834. Medals, 1834–1849–1855. Legion of Honor, 1852. One of the eight Grand Medals of Honor (Exposition Universelle), *Paris, 1867. Died, 1867. Diploma to the Memory of Deceased Artists, 1868.*

ROYBET (Ferdinand), ... Paris

Born at Uzes. Medal, Paris, 1866.

RYDER (A. P.), ... New York

Born at New Bedford, Mass., March 20, 1847.

No. 86—Landscape and Figure, ... Page 53

No. 168—The Resurrection, ... 70

RYDER (P. P.), ... New York

Born Brooklyn, N. Y. Began his profession by painting portraits. In 1869 became a pupil of Léon Bonnat, Paris. Also studied in Belgium and Holland. Member of the Artists' Fund Society. Associate Member of the National Academy of Design, New York.

No. 68—Shelling Peas, ... Page 48

SCHEFFER (Ary), deceased, ... Paris

Born at Dordrecht in 1795. Pupil of Guérin, Grand Prize for painting at Antwerp, 1816. Medals, Paris, 1824–1832. Legion of Honor, 1837. Died, 1858.

No. 125—Christ in the Garden, ... Page 61

SCHREYER (Adolphe), ... Paris

Born at Frankfort-on-the-Main, 1828. Belonging to a distinguished family, this artist enjoyed every advantage of travel and instruction. In 1855 he followed the regiment commanded by Prince Taxis to the Crimea, making many spirited studies. Medals, Paris, 1864–1865–1867 (Exposition Universelle); *Brussels Exposition, 1863, and Vienna Exposition, 1873. Cross of the Order of Leopold, 1864. In 1862 he was made Painter to the Court of the Grand Duke of Mecklenbeurg-Schwerin. Member of the Academies of Antwerp and Rotterdam, and Honorary Member of the Deutsches Nochstift.*

SEITZ (Antoine), ... Munich

Born at Rotham-Sand, near Nuremberg, January 23, 1829. Pupil of Munich Academy. Professor and Honorary Member of the Royal Academy of Munich. Gold Medals at Munich and Vienna. Chevalier of the Bavarian Order of St. Michael.

SEIFERT (A.), ... Munich

STEVENS (Alfred), ... Paris

Born at Brussels, 1828. Pupil of Navez in Belgium, and Roqueplan at Paris. Medals, Paris, 1853, and at Expositions Universelle *of 1855–1867 and 1878. Legion of Honor, 1863; officer of same, 1867; commander, 1878. Officer of the Order of Leopold. Commander of the Order of St. Michael, of Bavaria. Commander of the Order of Ferdinand, of Austria.*

TEYSSONNIÈRES (P.), ... Paris

TISSOT (James), ... Paris

Born at Nantes. Pupil of Baron Leys. Medal at Paris, 1866.

TROYON (Constantine), deceased, . . . Paris

Born at Sèvres, 1810. His parents wished him to be a painter of porcelain, but after a time spent in the manufactory at Sèvres, he studied under Riocreux, and became a painter of landscapes and animals. Medals, Paris, 1838–1840–1846–1848–1855. Legion of Honor, 1849. Member of the Amsterdam Academy. Died, 1865. Diploma to the Memory of Deceased Artists, Exposition Universelle, *1878.*

VALTON (E.), ... Paris

VAN MARCKE (Émile), ... Paris

Born at Sèvres, France. Pupil of Troyon. Medals, 1867–1869–1870. Legion of Honor, 1872. First-class Medal (Exposition Universelle), *1878.*

VAUTIER (BENJAMIN), ... Paris

Born at Morges, Switzerland, 1830. Pupil of Rudolphe Jordan, Düsseldorf, Member of the Academies of Berlin, Munich, Antwerp, and Amsterdam. Medals, Paris, 1865–1866, and at Exposition Universelle, *1867–1878. Legion of Honor, 1878.*

VERBOECKHOVEN (EUGENE J.), dec'd, Brussels

Born at Warneton (West Flanders), July 8, 1799. Medals at Paris, 1824–1841–1855. Legion of Honor, 1845. Chevalier of the Orders of Leopold, St. Michael of Bavaria, and Christ of Portugal. Decoration of the Iron Cross, Member of the Royal Academies of Belgium, Antwerp, and St. Petersburg. Died, 1881.

VIBERT (JEAN GEORGES), ... Paris

Born at Paris, 1840. Pupil of l'École des Beaux Arts, *and of Barrias, Paris. Medals, Paris, 1864–1867–1868–1878* (Exposition Universelle). *Legion of Honor, 1870.*

VIRY (PAUL), ... Paris

Born at Pocé. Pupil of Picot.

No. 112—My Lady's Page, ... Page 58

VOLLON (ANTOINE), ... Paris

Born at Lyon, April 20, 1833. Pupil of the Academy at Lyons. Medals, 1865–1868–1869. Chevalier of the Legion of Honor, 1870. Medal (Exposition Universelle), *1878. Officer's Cross of the Legion of Honor, 1878.*

No. 20—Study of a Donkey, ... Page 39

VOLTZ (FRIEDRICH JOHANN), ... Berlin

Born at Nordlingen, October 31, 1817. Pupil of the Munich Academy, Royal Bavarian Professor. Medal at Berlin. Great Würtemberg Art Medal. Member of the Academies of Berlin and Munich.

No. 83—The Watering Place, ... Page 52

WILLEMS (FLORENT), ... Paris

Born at Lüttich, January 8, 1823. Medals at Paris, 1844–1846–1855, at Brussels, 1843. Chevalier and officer of the Order of Leopold and Legion of Honor. Medal at Exposition Universelle, *1867. First-class Medal* (Exposition Universelle), *1878.*

No. 25—The Music Lesson, ... Page 40

WORMS (JULES), ... Paris

Born at Paris, 1837. Pupil of Lafosse. Medals, Paris, 1867–1868–1869–1878 (Exposition Universelle). *Legion of Honor, 1878.*

ZAMAÇOIS (ÉDOUARD), dec'd, ... Paris

Born at Bilboa, Spain, 1843. Pupil of Meissonier. Made his début at the Salon of 1863. Medal, Paris, 1867. Died, 1871. Diploma to the Memory of Deceased Artists (Exposition Universelle), *1878.*

ZIEM (FELIX FRANÇOIS, GEORGE PHILIBERT), . Paris

Born at Beauns (Côte d'Or), February 25, 1821. Medals at Paris, 1851–1852–1855. Cross of the Legion of Honor, 1857.

CATALOGUE.

FIRST NIGHT'S SALE.

WEDNESDAY, MARCH 3D, 1886, BEGINNING AT 7.30 P.M.

AT CHICKERING HALL.

*** Measurements given are in inches, the first figures indicating the *width* of the canvas.

1

GEORGE HAQUETTE.

The Signal. *$575*

28 x 34.—Dated 1884.

H. S. Wilson

2

A. SEIFERT.

Head of Young Girl. *300*

11 x 16.

H. J. Williams

3

RUDOLF EPP.

Knitting. *800*

20 x 30.

H. S. Wilson

4

P. M. BEYLE.

$1,050 **Fishing for Sole.**

28 x 40.

5

E. VALTON.

125 **Girl and Parrot.**

8½ x 10½.—Dated 1876.

6

J. POKITONOW.

875 **Landscape.**

12 x 7½.—Dated 1884.

7

P. TEYSSONNIÈRES.

350 **Gathering Mussels.**

22 x 15.

8

EUGÈNE FROMENTIN (deceased).

725 **In Pursuit.**

Water Color.

10 x 13.

9

EUGÈNE FROMENTIN (deceased).

Hawking. $550

Water Color.

10 x 13.

10

A. L. HERVIER.

Kitchen Interior. 475

12 x 14.—Dated 1856.

11

CONSTANTINE TROYON (deceased).

Cattle and Horses. 1,050

18 x 12.

12

A. A. E. HÉBERT.

Madonna and Child. 950

11 x 16.

13

J. G. MEYER VON BREMEN.

Gathering Wild Flowers. 2,100

22 x 11.—Dated 1884.

14

FRANCIS MILLER.

$250 **Return of the Fishing Boats.—North Sea.**

13 x 16.

15

J. G. JACQUET.

1,075 **Susanne.**

36 x 54.

16

LOUIS METTLING.

800 **Domestic Interior.**

30 x 25.—Dated 1877.

17

N. V. DIAZ (deceased).

1,550 **Oriental Woman.**

11 x 17.—Dated 1865.

18

Q. BECKER.

475 **Head of Peasant Woman.**

11 x 16.

19

J. B. C. COROT (deceased).

Landscape. *$9,000*

31 x 21.

Knoedler

20

A. VOLLON.

Study of a Donkey. *500*

16 x 13.

Newcomb

21

L. LHERMITTE.

Spinning. *1,000*

14½ x 18.

Sutton X

22

ÉMILE VAN MARCKE.

Cows Drinking. *1,325*

19 x 13.

Mr. Woodward

23

ANTOINE SEITZ.

Mother and Infant. *725*

6 x 8. Conrad Smith

24

J. G. MEYER VON BREMEN.

$925 The Wonder Book.

6 x 7.—Dated 1869.

Phelps

25

F. WILLEMS.

1,250 The Music Lesson.

27 x 39.—Knoedler

26

MATTHEW MARIS.

1,000 The Trysting Place.

17 x 13. Inglis

27

N. V. DIAZ (deceased).

2,500 Lane Near Fontainebleau.

25 x 19.—Dated 1865.

Miss D. P. Kimball

28

A. NEWHUYS.

725 The Reading Lesson.

13 x 18.—Dated 1874. Sexton

29

JEAN FRANÇOIS MILLET (deceased).

Shepherdess and Sheep. *$1,525*

Pastel.
10 x 15. H. O. Havemeyer

30

FRANÇOIS S. BONVIN.

A Pinch of Snuff. *2,550*

13 x 20.—Dated 1859. J. T. Williams

31

D. RIDGEWAY KNIGHT.

Noonday Repast. *1,350*

25 x 20.—Dated 1884. J. A. Kernochan

32

JULES WORMS.

The Proposal. *1,175*

14 x 17. Schaus

33

HUGH CAMERON.

Carrying Little Sister. *600*

11 x 15. Donald Smith

34

LEON Y. ESCOSURA.

$550 **End of the Game.**

6 x 4.—Dated 1884.

35

CHARLES HOGUET (deceased).

250 **Landscape.**

5 x 7.

36

LUDWIG KNAUS.

2,300 **A Farmer's Daughter.**

9 x 7.—Dated 1884.

37

A. BENEDICTER.

475 **Mother and Child.**

12 x 15.—Dated 1884.

38

LOUIS LELOIR.

1,900 **Three Stages of Life.**

Water color design for a Fan.

13 x 11.

39

C. F. DAUBIGNY (deceased).

Boats on the Shore. $1,325

21 x 12. H. Williams

40

A. W. KOWALSKI.

Hunting. 2,225

40 x 31. Williams

41

HECTOR LE ROUX.

Sleeping Vestal. 1,675

27 x 54. Newcomb

42

LÉON PERRAULT.

A Young Gleaner. 2,500

36 x 50.—Dated 1882. S. V. White

43

MONTICELLI.

A Garden Party. 450

30 x 17. L. D. Warren

44

ALBERT CONRAD.

$1,025 A Tyrolese Inn.

30 x 36.

45

JULES DUPRÉ.

1,700 Stormy Weather.

18 x 21.

46

THEODORE CEDERSTRÖM.

725 A Tight Cork.

7 x 9.

47

LOUIS P. BOUCHARD.

725 The Pet Kid.

28 x 45.

48

PALIK BÖEHM.

1,600 Wayside Fountain.—Hungary.

47 x 30.

49

VACSLAV BROZIK.

The Falconer's Recital. $2,600

54 x 36.

50

JIMINEZ-Y-ARANDA.

Interesting News. 4,100

27 x 22.—Dated 1884.

51

ÉDOUARD ZAMAÇOIS (deceased).

The Singing Lesson. 5,300

18 x 15.—Dated 1866.

52

N. V. DIAZ (deceased).

Study of the Nude. 1,375

10 x 14.

53

J. DOMINGO.

A Spanish Inn. 2,550

6 x 8.—Dated 1876.

54

ÉMILE VAN MARCKE.

$4,275 **Spring Time.**

26 x 32. M. J. Williams

55

JULES BRÉTON.

3,600 **The Bird Nest.**

14½ x 21.—Dated 1884. Knoedler

56

J. B. C. COROT (deceased).

4,800 **Nymphs Bathing.**

29 x 39. J. A. Garland

57

THÉODORE ROUSSEAU (deceased).

3,300 **Landscape and Cottages.**

12 x 8. Knoedler

58

J. G. MEYER VON BREMEN.

2,100 **Bread and Milk.**

9 x 11.—Dated 1884. J. H. Corbet

59

JULES WORMS.

Spanish Market Day. $2,300

31 x 24. G. H. Halsted

60

ADOLPHE SCHREYER.

Wallachian Post Station. 1,150

6 x 8. E. W. Bass

61

JEAN LÉON GÉRÔME.

Vase Seller.—Cairo. 4,600

14 x 18. J. A. Garland

62

N. V. DIAZ (deceased).

Edge of a Wood. 2,750

16 x 12. G. J. Williams

63

ERSKINE NICOL.

Bachelor Life. 2,025

23 x 17.—Dated 1860. [illegible]

64

B. J. BLOMMERS.

$825 **Departure of the Fisher's Boat.**

25 x 18.

65

FELIX ZIEM.

1,350 **Fishing Boats.—Bay of Venice.**

31 x 19.

66

ADOLPHE PIOT.

1,300 **Adoration.**

17 x 21.

67

L. LÖEFFTZ.

4,100 **Money Changers.**

39 x 31.—Dated 1884.

68

P. P. RYDER.

275 **Shelling Peas.**

20 x 16.—Dated 1883.

69

B. C. KOEK KOEK (deceased).

Winter in Holland. *$1,875*

28 x 23.—Dated 1842. Mrs M. A. Ogden

70

N. V. DIAZ (deceased).

Moonlight Concert. *2,400*

19 x 16. Sutton

71

JEAN FRANÇOIS MILLET (deceased).

Gathering Apples. *2,575*

11 x 14. Jas. J. Hill

72

CONSTANTINE TROYON (deceased).

Coast Near Villiers. *8,100*

37 x 26. Sutton

73

J. G. VIBERT.

Palm Sunday. *2,000*

16 x 21.—Dated 1873. R. E. Moore

74

W. A. BOUGUEREAU.

$6,500 Cupid.

22 x 25. H. J. Williams

75

J. L. E. MEISSONIER.

16,525 In the Library.

12 x 18.—Dated 1876. Knoedler

76

J. G. MEYER VON BREMEN.

3,700 Return from the Vintage.

23 x 43.—Dated 1883. Donald Smith

77

JEAN J. HENNER.

2,075 Sleeping Nymph.

26 x 16 Blakeslee

78

ALBERT CONRAD.

1,650 The Old Old Story.

36 x 30. Phelps

79

JULES LEFEBVRE.

Sappho.

$4,500

45 x 78.—Dated 1884. Donald Smith

80

ÉMILE RÉNOUF.

Repairing the Old Boat.

5,050

80 x 56.—Dated 1879. F. O. Matthiesen

SECOND NIGHT'S SALE.

THURSDAY, MARCH 4TH, 1886, BEGINNING AT 7.30 P.M.

AT CHICKERING HALL.

81

P. A. J. DAGNAN-BOUVERET.

$1,000 Violinist.

8 x 10.—Dated 1884. Walters

82

FERNAND PELEZ.

2,100 Without a Home.

26 x 36.—Dated 1880. Halsted

83

FR. VOLTZ.

525 The Watering Place.

16 x 9.—Dated 1881. J. A. Young

84

GEORGE H. BOUGHTON.

625 The Finishing Touch.

11 x 17. Donald Smith

85

JOHANNES BOSBOOM.

Church Interior. $775

10 x 16.—Dated 1868. Phelps

86

A. P. RYDER.

Landscape and Figure. 225

6 x 11½.—Dated 1885. Cottier

87

JULES DUPRÉ.

Driving Cows to Water. 1,850

16 x 18. Phelps.

88

HUGHES MERLE (deceased).

St. Elizabeth of Hungary. 725

18 x 22.—Dated 1876. J. E. Scripps

89

ÉMILE BERANGER (deceased).

Arranging Flowers. 500

9 x 12.—Dated 1880. L. L. Wilson

90

LOUIS METTLING.

$875 **Street Sweeper at Lunch.**

17 x 14.

91

THÉODORE ROUSSEAU (deceased).

1,100 **A Waterfall.**

13 x 8.

92

J. G. MEYER VON BREMEN.

2,025 **The Lesson.**

10 x 14.—Dated 1880.

93

N. V. DIAZ (deceased).

2,600 **A Pool in the Woods.**

14 x 10.—Dated 1873.

94

CHARLES ÉMILE JACQUE.

1,850 **Shepherdess and Sheep.**

17 x 23.

95

B. J. BLOMMERS.

Shoveling Snow.

$725

14 x 10. Newcomb

96

E. P. BERNE-BELLECOUR.

The Last Drop.

625

5 x 6. McCrosky Butt

97

E. HARBURGER.

Dutch Peasant.

200

4 x 5. V. H. Rothschild

98

JEAN FRANÇOIS MILLET (deceased).

The Wool Carder.

3,650

14 x 17. Knoedler

99

N. V. DIAZ (deceased).

Toilet of Venus.

3,300

16 x 18.—Dated 1877. Knoedler

100

J. B. C. COROT (deceased).

$4,050 **Evening on a River.**

23 x 18.

101

LEON Y. ESCOSURA.

2,600 **Convalescent Prince.**

24 x 19.—Dated 1872.

102

EUGÉNE DELACROIX (deceased).

1,250 **Cleopatra.**

13 x 10.

103

LUDWIG KNAUS.

3,150 **A Young Satyr.**

10 x 8.

104

THÉODORE ROUSSEAU (deceased).

3,650 **St. Michael's Mount.**

13 x 9.

105

L. PASSINI.

Young Girl of Venice. *$1,650*

Water Color.
13 x 17. Garland

106

N. V. DIAZ (deceased).

Flowers. *500*

8 x 6. Sutton x

107

J. G. VIBERT.

Eyes and Ears. *3,500*

12 x 19. L. King

108

ANTONIO CASANOVA.

The Gourmand. *1,750*

15 x 19.—Dated 1883. Halsted

109

FREDERICK A. BRIDGMAN.

Afternoon Hours.—Algiers. *1,750*

36 x 25.—Dated 1883. D. W. Powers

110

CHARLES BAUGNIET.

$900 **The Bride's Toilet.**

18 x 27.

111

EUGÈNE VERBOECKHOVEN (deceased).

4,050 **Sheep Leaving the Barn.**

35 x 24.—Dated 1880.

112

PAUL VIRY.

750 **My Lady's Page.**

21 x 17.—Dated 1880.

113

JOSEPH LYMAN, JR.

1,550 **Waiting for the Tide.**

31 x 36.—Dated 1883.

114

THOMAS COUTURE (deceased).

975 **Faust and Mephistopheles.**

10 x 14.

115

MARIANO FORTUNY (deceased)

Italian Woman. $450

Water Color. Knoedler

6 x 9.

116

JEAN FRANÇOIS MILLET (deceased).

Feeding Poultry. 4,000

14 x 17. Henry Field

117

JULES DUPRÉ.

A Cloudy Day. 2,500

14 x 18. Garland

118

EUGÈNE FROMENTIN (deceased).

Arab Horseman. 4,050

16 x 12.—Dated 1875. A. B. Darling

119

J. G. MEYER VON BREMEN.

Decorating the Shrine. 2,550

16 x 20.—Dated 1868. L. Stern

120

N. V. DIAZ (deceased).

$3,900 **L'Ile Des Amours.**

24 x 16.—Dated 1857. Garland

121

THÉODORE ROUSSEAU (deceased).

4,500 **A Quiet Pool.**

10 x 8. S. P. Avery

From the collection of Jules Lefébvre.

122

EDOUARD DÉTAILLE.

1,950 **A French Lancer.**

8 x 12.—Dated 1880. Wilson

123

ÉMILE VAN MARCKE.

2,650 **Cattle Reposing.**

20 x 13. Wysong

124

E. GREÜTZNER.

2,575 **The Puzzled Priest.**

27 x 34.—Dated 1883. R. E. Moore

125

ARY SCHEFFER (deceased).

Christ in the Garden. *$975*

12 x 17. J. E. Scripps

126

EUGÉNE DELACROIX (deceased).

Landscape. *950*

13 x 8. C. S. Bradley

127

MATTHEW MARIS.

Village in Holland. *675*

13 x 10. Mrs D. P. Kimball

128

J. DOMINGO.

Head of a Spanish Cavalier. *1,225*

6 x 8.—Dated 1883. N. Q. Pope.

129

A. DE NEUVILLE (deceased).

French Cuirassier. *6,000*

19 x 23.—Dated 1884. P. Van Volkenburgh

130

JEAN FRANÇOIS MILLET (deceased).

$4,975 **Dressing Flax.**

17 x 21.—Dated 1854. R. E. Moore

131

MONTICELLI.

1,300 **Adoration of the Magi.**

25 x 13. Sutton +

132

ALEXANDRE CABANEL.

1,400 **Desdemona.**

17 x 21.—Dated 1880. Donald Smith

133

J. B. C. COROT (deceased).

4,200 **Landscape and Cattle.**

23 x 15. C. H. Sears

134

CONSTANTINE TROYON (deceased).

6,550 **Return from the Farm.**

30 x 19.—Dated 1852. Knoedler

From the Laurent Richard collection.

135

ADOLPHE SCHREYER.

Arab at Fountain. *$3,100*

28 x 23. Wilson

136

MLLE. ROSA BONHEUR.

Calf and Cow—Scotch Highlands. *12,200*

32 x 25.—Dated 1876. R. G. Dun

137

N. V. DIAZ (deceased).

Children Playing with a Kid. *2,750*

18 x 22.—Dated 1860. Donald Smith

138

PIERRE M. BEYLE.

Gathering Mussels. *750*

14 x 21. Sexton

139

PAUL JEAN CLAYS.

On the Thames. *1,150*

20 x 25.—Dated 1877. Warren

140

CHARLES E. DELORT.

$675 "My Neighbor."

8 x 12. J. H. Lindsey

141

CHARLES E. DELORT.

675 "Across the Way."

8 x 12. J. H. Lindsey

142

THÉODORE ROUSSEAU (deceased).

5,100 Landscape.

11 x 8. Garland

143

J. B. C. COROT (deceased).

3,500 Near Ville D'Avray.

15 x 19. W. J. Williams

144

LOUIS GALLAIT.

3,050 A Young Mother.

8 x 10.—Dated 1863. E. D. Warren

145

FERDINAND ROYBET.

Return from the Chase. $2,000

26 x 36. Havemeyer

146

RUDOLF EPP.

Saying Grace. 1,400

36 x 30. Phelps

147

N. V. DIAZ (deceased).

Group of Persian Women. 2,925

25 x 17.—Dated 1860. Schaus

148

FREDERICK E. CHURCH.

"Al Ayn"—The Fountain. 2,050

35 x 23.—Dated 1882. Reichard

149

JEAN J. HENNER.

Repose. 3,100

36 x 27. Halsted.

150

J. L. E. MEISSONIER.

$15,000 A Standard Bearer.

10 x 14.—Dated 1857. Knoedler

151

CHARLES MEISSONIER.

1,300 The Musician.

12 x 17. D. Smith

152

LÉON BONNAT.

2,350 An Arab Chief.

27 x 33. Walters

153

J. G. VIBERT.

12,500 The Cardinal's Menu.

28 x 22. M. H. Arnot

154

W. A. BOUGUEREAU.

7,250 Nut Gatherers.

52 x 34.—Dated 1882. Scripps

155

LÉON RICHET.

Coming from Labor. *$1,025*

32 x 24.—Dated 1882. J. Belden

156

JEAN LÉON GÉRÔME.

The Tulip Folly. *6,000*

38 x 25. Sutton x

157

L. ALMA-TADEMA.

Roman Lady Feeding Fish. *5,000*

28 x 13 J. J. Hill

158

JULES BRÉTON.

Returning from the Fields. *9,500*

40 x 27.—Dated 1878. Walters

159

ADOLPHE ARTZ.

The Frugal Meal. *1,800*

51 x 34. Quintard

160

CHARLES FRANÇOIS DAUBIGNY (deceased).

$5,300 A Cooper's Shop.

64 x 44.—Dated 1872. S. M. Ford

THIRD NIGHT'S SALE.

FRIDAY, MARCH 5TH, 1886, BEGINNING AT 7.30 P.M.

AT CHICKERING HALL.

161

THOMAS FAED.

In Doubt. $2,000

21 x 31.—Dated 1869. Schaus

162

THOMAS COUTURE (deceased).

A French Republican, 1795. 825

14 x 17. Sutton x

163

A. G. DECAMPS (deceased).

Bazaars in Cairo. 2,450

9 x 11. Warren

164

CHARLES BARGUE (deceased).

The Sentinel. 12,300

From the collection of Mr. John W. Wilson, Paris.

8 x 11.—Dated 1876. Jno. T. Martin

165

MARIANO FORTUNY (deceased).

$575 **Spanish Lady with Fan.**

Water Color.

8½ x 12.

166

J. G. MEYER VON BREMEN.

1,000 **Woman's Head.**

6 x 9.—Dated 1880.

167

J. DOMINGO.

2,450 **Card Players.**

4 x 5.—Dated 1882.

168

A. P. RYDER.

375 **The Resurrection.**

13 x 18.—Dated 1885.

169

N. V. DIAZ (deceased).

1,600 **Repose after the Bath.**

13 x 8.

170

JEAN FRANÇOIS MILLET (deceased).

The Churner. $8,100

From the collection of Laurent Richard.

14 x 22. Knoedler

171

EDOUARD FRÈRE.

Prayer. 2,150

15 x 18.—Dated 1861. D. Smith

172

LUDWIG KNAUS.

St. Martin's Day. 5,700

16 x 21.—Dated 1877. Knoedler

173

ÉMILE VAN MARCKE.

Cows in a Pool. 4,550

24 x 19. J. S. Barnes

174

ERSKINE NICOL.

Pills for the Saxon. 2,500

27 x 19.—Dated 1868. Knoedler

175

JULES WORMS.

$2,050 **Spanish Fortune Teller.**

31 x 23. Knoedler

176

EDOUARD DÉTAILLE.

7,150 **A Flag-Officer.**

14 x 17.—Dated 1883. Knoedler

177

JEAN J. HENNER.

4,100 **Fabiola.** Huntington

13 x 16½.

Fabiola, the heroine of the late Cardinal Wiseman's story, was the daughter of Fabius, a wealthy Roman living in the fourth century of our era. Her name, according to Roman custom, was softened from that of her father into the diminutive, and, the author tells us, is to be pronounced with the accent on the second syllable. The story narrates the development of Fabiola's character, born and brought up under pagan influences, and gradually brought into sympathy with the new principles of Christianity by the example of the converts whom she met in her own household and in the society in which she moved. Her slave Miriam first taught her the lesson of charity and forgiveness, while in her patrician friends Agnes and Cecilia she saw the new life reflected in its noblest and most heroic aspect. When the persecution was ended, in which both Agnes and Cecilia perished, Fabiola retired from the world, and after many years of charity and holiness withdrew to rest in peace by the side of her martyred friends.

178

J. TISSOT.

In the Louvre. $1,600

18 x 28. Sutton x

179

JEAN AUBERT.

Love Quenching his Thirst. 4,500

28 x 40.—Dated 1875. Huntington

180

N. V. DIAZ (deceased).

Boy with Hunting Dogs. 4,500

25 x 21.—Dated 1855. Knoedler

181

P. A. J. DAGNAN-BOUVERET.

An Orphan in Church. 2,300

21 x 17.—Dated 1880. J. M. Beecham

182

CONSTANTINE TROYON (deceased).

The Pasture. 7,100

15 x 11. Knoedler

183

J. B. C. COROT (deceased).

$3,300 **Landscape.**

20 x 15. Phelps

184

JOHN CONSTABLE (deceased).

3,350 **English Landscape.**

24 x 26. F. Layton

185

E. BERNE-BELLECOUR.

3,900 **The Prisoner.**

25 x 39.—Dated 1882. Halsted

186

W. A. BOUGUEREAU.

3,050 **Italian Mother and Child.**

17 x 22. Knoedler

187

JEAN FRANÇOIS MILLET (deceased).

6,300 **Gathering Beans.**

(The artist's mother, and cottage where he was born.)

12 x 15. Mrs D. P. Kimball

188

EUGÈNE DELACROIX (deceased).

Tiger and Serpent. $4,450

16 x 12.—Dated 1862. Knoedler

189

LUDWIG KNAUS.

The Hunter's Repast. 16,400

19 x 24.—Dated 1867. Mrs Ogden

190

N. V. DIAZ (deceased).

Holy Family. 4,100

20 x 27.—Dated 1853. R E Moore

191

JEAN BAPTISTE ROBIE.

Flowers and Strawberries. 2,100

20 x 28. Holchter

192

FERDINAND ROYBET.

The Connoisseurs. 3,000

26 x 32.—Dated 1883. Sutton +

193

CONSTANTINE TROYON (deceased).

$2,550 Going to the Fair.

34 x 24.

194

ALFRED STEVENS.

3,500 Conversation.

20 x 29.—Dated 1881.

195

ÉMILE VAN MARCKE.

4,050 On the Cliffs.

38 x 28.

196

EUGÈNE FROMENTIN (deceased).

925 Turkish Washer-Women.

13 x 10.

197

CHARLES F. DAUBIGNY (deceased).

6,200 On the Seine.

23 x 13.—Dated 1873.

198

CHARLES F. DAUBIGNY (deceased).

On the Marne. *$5,500*

23 x 13.—Dated 1873. Halsted

199

MARIANO FORTUNY (deceased).

The Rare Vase. *7,100*

Water Color.

9½ x 13.—Dated 1870. Walters

From the collection of the late John W. Wilson, of Paris.

200

J. G. MEYER VON BREMEN.

Evening Prayers. *2,700*

15 x 20.—Dated 1883. Sutton x

201

N. V. DIAZ (deceased).

Sunset after a Storm. *8,650*

34 x 36.—Dated 1871. Newcomb

202

JEAN FRANÇOIS MILLET (deceased).

Wood-Cutters. *5,000*

25 x 32. Knoedler

203

MLLE. ROSA BONHEUR.

$7,150 **Deer in Forest.**

31 x 39.—Dated 1867.

204

ALBERTO PASINI.

1,025 **Court Yard in Constantinople.**

7 x 9.—Dated 1871.

205

JIMINEZ-Y-ARANDA.

4,000 **Gossip.**

27 x 19.—Dated 1883.

206

ADOLPHE PIOT.

2,850 **The Young Wanderer.**

34 x 51.

207

MAX RENTAL.

1,750 **Norwegian Fisher's Dance.**

41 x 30.

208

THÉODORE ROUSSEAU (deceased).

A Mound, "Jean De Paris."—Autumn in the Forest of Fontainebleau. $9,700

20 x 25. Knoedler

From the collection of Baron Crabbe, Didier, and Laurent Richard.

209

L. ALMA-TADEMA.

Spring. 7,000

21 x 35.

When Winter's rage abates, when cheerful hours
Awake the Spring and Spring awakes the flowers,
On the green turf they careless limbs display,
And celebrate the mighty mother's day;
For then the hills with pleasing shades are crown'd
And sleeps are sweeter on the silken ground;
With milder beams the sun securely shines,
Fat are the lambs and luscious are the wines.

Let every swain adore her power divine,
And milk and honey mix with sparkling wine;
Let all the choir of clowns attend the show,
In long procession, shouting as they go;
Invoking her to bless their yearly stores,
Inviting plenty to their crowded floors.

Thus in the Spring, and thus in Summer's heat,
Before the sickles touch the ripening wheat,
On Ceres' call; and let the laboring hind
With oaken wreaths his hollow temples bind;
On Ceres let him call, and Ceres praise,
With uncouth dances and with country lays.

(*Georgics—Translated by John Dryden.*)

210

N. V. DIAZ (deceased).

$2,400 **The Bathers.**

16 x 10. Sutton

211

JEAN FRANÇOIS MILLET (deceased).

650 **Woman in Kitchen.**

3 x 4½. L. J. Leiter

212

JULES DUPRE.

8,050 **Morning.**

28 x 21. Knoedler

213

CONSTANTINE TROYON (deceased).

6,350 **Pasturage in Normandy.**

33 x 24. Mrs Kimball

214

ALBERTO PASINI.

2,300 **Barracks at Constantinople.**

31 x 25.—Dated 1882. Sutton

215

A. DE NEUVILLE (deceased).

Infantry. $5,300

16 x 20.—Dated 1884. Knoedler

216

J. B. C. COROT (deceased).

Lake Nemi. 14,000

52 x 38.—Dated 1865 Newcomb

217

ADOLPHE SCHREYER.

An Arab Scout. 3,500

27 x 32. W. J. Williams

218

LÉON PERRAULT.

A Flower Girl. 3,000

31 x 44.—Dated 1880. J. [illegible]

219

OTTO GUNTHER (deceased).

The Pastor's Visit. 2,500

45 x 32. Cohnfeld

220

JEAN FRANÇOIS MILLET (deceased).

$3,800 **The Spaders.**

38 x 30. Knoedler

221

JEAN LÉON GÉRÔME.

4,800 **Coffee-House.—Cairo.**

Bashi-Bazouks casting balls.

26 x 21. F. H. Cook

222

ADOLPHE SCHREYER.

4,300 **Wallachian Pack Horses.**

36 x 25. D. Smith

223

EUGÈNE FROMENTIN (deceased).

5,000 **On the Nile, near Philæ.**

43 x 24.—Dated 1871. R. E. Moore

224

N. V. DIAZ (deceased).

3,500 **Persian Woman and Child.**

9 x 12. Dehaus

225

A. G. DECAMPS (deceased).

The Walk to Emmæus. *$3,100*

18 x 12. Havemeyer

226

LUDWIG KNAUS.

The Country Store. *10,400*

30 x 25.—Dated 1883. W. W. Sevans

227

J. L. E. MEISSONIER.

The Vidette, 1812. *15,000*

20 x 17.—Dated 1883. S. P. A.

228

THÉODORE ROUSSEAU (deceased).

Twilight. *15,500*

24 x 16. Schaus

229

JEAN J. HENNER.

La Source. *10,100*

28 x 39. J. Smith

From the Paris Salon, 1881.

230

ÉMILE VAN MARCKE.

$8,600 **Going to Pasture.**

39 x 26.

From the collection of Laurent Richard.

231

J. G. VIBERT.

25,500 **The Missionary's Story.**

52 x 39.

From Paris Triennial Exhibition, 1883.

232

JULES DUPRÉ.

8,100 **A Symphony.**

39 x 27.

From the collection of M. Faure.

233

BENJAMIN VAUTIER.

4,500 **Botanist at Lunch.**

32 x 24.—Dated 1882.

234

JEAN FRANÇOIS MILLET (deceased).

14,000 **The Spinner.**

28 x 36.

235

JULES BRÉTON.

Communicants.

74 x 48. Donald Smith $45,500

Exhibited at the Paris Salon, 1884.

TRANSLATION OF A POEM BY JULES BRETON, ILLUSTRATING THIS PAINTING.

Among the fresh lilacs, and the new budding leaves,
In this spring-time that hums and smiles through the trees,
On this bright Sabbath day, maids with heavenly brows,
Marching onward to mass, beneath the young boughs:
Did you take from the sky, to commune for God's pleasure,
Your robes of pure white where quivers the azure?

Thus so would I think from your costumes so light
That bloom with the day, like the snow and as bright;
By the vapory veil, with its misty-like flounces,
By your virginal lips, and your sweet modest glances;
By your nosegays of gold, attached to your tapers,
And the heavenly light that illumines your faces.

How each thing around both greets you and blesses;
The mossy thatched roofs have enameled their ridges;
They curve rounding down to contours most supple;
The soft, tender grass does everywhere sparkle:
Still wet by the morn, its white dew breathing odors,
It unrolls to your feet its velvety borders.

Your folds of gauze in the breeze make angelic pinions,
Less white are the doves on the barn's lofty crestings;
Less pure is the hawthorn, with its balmy branches;
Thus onward you go to the old chapel's porches;
Where girdled by lindens the church bell is tolling,
While the sun on the tower its corners is gilding.

And spotless you go. The portal unfolds,
Your heart stronger beats, the bell louder tolls;
The aged, quite moved, at the tower's base centre;
The door opens wide. Go, gentle maids, enter;
And then from the burning ends of your nun's tapers,
Let bright stars of love float out with its vapors.

Ecstasy! holy fear of mystical raptures
When with your fingers quiver the hymnal's pages
In singing! O sweet tender Jesus, descend!
Ah! come, Divine Spouse, and with our soul blend.
The Host seems to tremble in the hands of the priest,
As seen through the whirl of the incense's mist.

Receive in his body the Lord of the earth;
Daughters, you ignore his mysterious worth;
And to him prefer, resuscitated being
The beautiful crucifix, on the hill dying;
You love its fair forehead, that's torn by the thorn,
And the bleeding wound on its holy side shown.

And above all, you love the child's rosy face,
Bathed, as the fair lamb, in the gold of its fleece;
Who came with its smiles, at the side of your cribs,
And its little clear eyes, when you were all babes:
'Tis for this that you beam, is it not, maiden, say?
And palpitate in the church aisles while you stay.

Vainly all reason succeeds to dead faith,
And no recollection goes forth with your breath
That does not vibrate like a ray from the skies,
So sing, virgins, sing! The glad summer close lies;
Then autumn, whose ripe fruits will fall to the ground;
So to dying spring, let your first chant resound.

236

J. B. C. COROT (deceased).

Wood Gatherers. $15,000

63 x 44.—Dated 1875. Corcoran Gallery

237

F. H. KAEMMERER.

Toast to the Bride. 4,100

42 x 29. Knoedler

238

W. A. BOUGUEREAU.

Madonna, Infant Saviour, and St. John.

42 x 74.—Dated 1882. Sutton x 9,000

239

CONSTANTINE TROYON (deceased).

Cow Chased by a Dog. 9,100

46 x 31. Knoedler

240

ÉMILE VAN MARCKE.

The Mill Farm. 11,500

76 x 54. Lanthard

ORIENTAL ART

CHINESE AND JAPANESE OBJECTS

SALE MONDAY AFTERNOON, MARCH 8,

BEGINNING AT 2.30 O'CLOCK.

AT THE AMERICAN ART GALLERIES.

OLD CHINESE PORCELAINS.

DECORATED IN BLUE, UNDER THE GLAZE.

242 LOTUS-SHAPED CUP, with bulb and figure inside, used by the Chinese in drinking a toast; when filled the figure rises above the surface, and disappears as the liquid diminishes. *$10 00*

243 SMALL VASE, bottled shaped, fluted in six compartments, painted in two shades of blue, melon vine bearing the fruit. Mark of the Yung-ching period, 1723–1736. Height 3½ inches. *35 00*

244 SMALL VASE, bottle shape, with slender neck, symbolical designs painted in a light and dark shade of blue, crackled texture. Mark of the Kea-tsing period, 1522–1567. Height 4 inches, has carved stand. *27 50*

245 TEA BOWL, painted inside and out, with dark blue, band extending around bowl of pierced ornaments, filled in with glaze, "Grains of Rice" effect. Seal-mark of the Keen-lung period, 1736–1795. *50 00*

246 SMALL BOTTLE, with lizard in relief on neck, flowers and vines painted in dark blue. *12 50*

247 SMALL COUPE, soft, creamy white texture, floral and vine designs painted in pale blue. *17 50*

248 VERY SMALL BOTTLE, decorated similar to the above. Mark of the Yung-ching period, 1723–1736. *27 50*

249 TALL CUP, semi-egg-shell texture, painting of landscape scene, figures, palaces, etc., in pale and dark blue. Mark of the
$17 50 Taou-Kwang period, 1821–1851.

250 SMALL BOTTLE, straight, octagonal shape, painted in dark blue, mandarin and other figures making offering to Deity, and clouds. Mark of the Keen-lung period, 1736–1795. Height
40 00 4½ inches.

251 TEA BOWL, semi-egg-shell texture, outside painted with delicate vine designs in pale blue and Arabic inscription in a darker
15 00 shade. Mark of Yung-ching period, 1723–1736.

252 BOTTLE SHAPE VASE, landscape and mountain scenery, painted
32 50 in deep blue. Height 8 inches, has carved stand.

253 CYLINDRICAL JAR, painted with dark blue arabesques and flowers, pierced designs filled in with glaze, "Rice Grains" effect.
65 00 Height 6¾ inches, diameter 4½ inches.

254 LARGE BOWL, fluted lotus pattern, outer surface painted with figures, garden and interior scenes, and various plants in two shades of blue, figure of philosopher inside in medallion, border of floral designs and symbols. Mark of the Ching-Hwa period,
37 50 1465–1488.

255 CYLINDRICAL JAR AND COVER, painted in dark and light blue, floral, vine and mottled designs. Show mark. Height 8 inches,
72 50 diameter 6 inches.

256 SMALL VASE, cylindrical bottle shape, with small neck, painted with fruit in dark blue, bands of flowers and arabesque designs.
37 50 Height 5½ inches, has carved stand.

257 SMALL GINGER JAR, painted with dark opaque blue "hawthorn blossoms" in white reserve; has silver lid with the blossoms
90 00 engraved and in relief. Height and diameter 6 x 4 inches.

258 SMALL VASE, straight beaker shape, with swelling centre and spreading at neck, painted with floral, leaf and other designs in
20 00 pale blue. Height 3½ inches, has carved stand.

259 "HAWTHORN" GINGER JAR, deep blue ground with branches of hawthorn blossoms in white reserve, running up and down the jar. Height and diameter 9½ x 7½ inches, has carved teak-
205 00 wood stand and lid.

260 LARGE "HAWTHORN" JAR, tall, ovoid shape, pale blue ground, with branches of hawthorn blossoms in white reserve, running up and down the jar. Ring mark of the Kang-he period, 1661–1722. Height and diameter 15½ x 10½ inches, has carved teak-wood stand and lid. *$260 00*

261 VERY LARGE VASE, flat pilgrim bottle shape, bulging in centre of each face, painted with symbolical, floral and other designs in dark blue. Mark of the Keen-lung period, 1736–1795. Height and diameter 20 x 15 inches, has carved teak-wood stand. *285 00*

OLD CHINESE PORCELAINS.

SINGLE OR "SOLID COLOR" SPECIMENS.

262 PLATE, fluted pattern, in design of chrysanthemum flower, rose color glaze covering entire surface, except where mark appears on bottom. Mark of Yung-ching period, 1723–1736. Diameter 7 inches, has stand made of fabric. *32 50*

263 PLATE, similar in shape as above, powdered blue glaze of a deep hue. Mark of the Yung-ching period, 1723–1736. Diameter 7 inches, has stand made of Chinese fabric. *22 50*

264 SMALL JAR, globular shape, *sang de bœuf* glaze, with lustrous over-glaze. Long-Yao specimen. Height and diameter 3½ x 5 inches, has stand. *90 00*

265 VASE, gourd shape, with two lobes and slightly spreading neck, mirror black glaze. Height 9 inches, has carved stand. *215 00*

266 GOURD-SHAPED VASE, lion head and ring handles in relief at side of lower lobe, tea color glaze of a light shade. Seal mark of the Keen-lung period, 1736–1795. Height and diameter 8½ x 7 inches, has carved stand. *92 50*

267 BOTTLE VASE, globular body with tall slender neck, ribbed design, metallic or "iron rust" glaze. Height 9 inches, diameter 5 inches, has carved stand. *130 00*

268 SMALL VASE, bottle shape, light turquoise glaze with metallic spots, small crackle beneath glaze. Height 6 inches, has carved stand. *32 50*

269 Ovoid Bottle-shaped Vase, spreading neck, pinkish glaze of the "peach blow" family. Seal mark of the Keen-lung period, 1736–1795. Height and diameter 8 x 4½ inches, has carved stand.
$87 50

270 Vase, shape of three gourds adhering, triple neck, celadon glaze beneath lustrous over-glaze. Height and diameter 7 x 4 inches, has teak stand finely carved.
57 50

271 Teapot, graceful ovoid shape, coral red glaze of even quality. Height 6½ inches, has carved stand.
37 50

272 Vase, flat ovoid shape, with slender neck of fluted design, leaf ornaments for handles, turquoise blue glaze, minute crackle beneath. Height and diameter 10 x 6 inches, has carved stand.
80 00

273 Ovoid Bottle-shaped Vase, lemon yellow glaze, with surface in imitation of lemon peel. Height and diameter 7½ x 5 inches.
190 00

274 Bowl and Cover, semi-egg-shell texture, both bowl and cover covered with coral red glaze, lustrous over-glaze. Height and diameter 4 x 4¾ inches.
35 00

275 Vase, straight ovoid form, covered with a red glaze running into garnet and purple, edges being uncovered and showing crackle beneath over-glaze. Elephant heads and rings in relief for handles. Height and diameter 6 x 4½ inches, has carved stand.
60 00

276 Bottle Vase, cylindrical shape with small low neck, apple-green glaze, with bold crackle beneath. Height and diameter 7¾ x 4 inches, has carved stand.
200 00

277 Ovoid Shape Vase, with low neck slightly spreading at top, covered with "peach-blow" glaze, running into a darker shade on reverse side. Height and diameter 11½ x 5 inches.
205 00

278 Cylindrical Vase, slightly ovoid, *sang de bœuf* glaze running down body and leaving neck almost devoid of the color, very lustrous over-glaze with iridescent effects. Height 6¾ inches, has carved stand.
67 50

279 Bottle Vase, ovoid shape with small neck, covered with tea-color glaze of a dark-green shade. Height and diameter 8 x 5½ inches, has fine stand.
67 50

280 LONG-YAO FIRE BOWL, *sang de bœuf* glaze on outer surface, showing white splashes with crackle beneath, metallic brown glaze inside with bold crackle beneath, has carved teak-wood high stand and cover, the latter having carved white jade stone ornament for handle. Height and diameter of coupe 3¾ x 6 inches. *$420 00*

From the collection of I Wang-ye, a Mandarin Prince.

281 SMALL BOTTLE, with fluted lobe at neck, glazed with color of veal's liver. Height 5 inches, has carved stand. *25 00*

282 OVOID BOTTLE VASE, covered with a rich garnet color beneath a lustrous over-glaze, the low neck showing a brown crackle beneath the outer or lustrous glaze. Height and diameter 6 x 3½ inches, has carved stand. *50 00*

283 LOW FAT BOTTLE, semi-globular shape, with three engraved crests in low relief, and covered with a yellow metallic glaze, showing iridescent effects. Mark of the Seuen-tih period, 1426–1436. Height and diameter 3½ x 4½ inches, has teak-wood stand. *100 00*

284 LARGE BOTTLE VASE, globular shape body with tall slender neck slightly spreading at top, entire outer surface of vase covered with a powdered blue glaze. Height and diameter 11½ x 8 inches, has carved stand. *147 50*

285 VASE, globular shaped bottle with tall neck, covered with *soufflé* glaze of chicken's blood color, very lustrous over-glaze. Height and diameter 12 x 6 inches, has carved stand. *180 00*

286 VASE, with globular body and spreading neck, covered with tea-color glaze, ornamentation of scroll and other designs carved in relief and applied with gold and bronze, double ring handles at neck. Has gold seal mark of the Keen-lung period, 1736–1795. Height and diameter 9 x 6 inches. *185 00*

From the collection of Comte de Semallé, member of the French Legation at Pekin from 1873 to 1885.

287 TALL BOTTLE VASE, ovoid shaped with low neck, imperial yellow glaze, beneath which is a profuse incised ornamentation of birds, flowers, archaic designs, etc., has iridescent lustre. Height and diameter 14 x 8 inches. *255 00*

288 **Ovoid Vase**, with slender base spreading at bottom, celadon glaze with bold crackle beneath, and beneath which is two medallions of floral designs incised. Height 11 inches, diameter
$55 00 3 inches.

289 **Large Vase**, fluted design, globular shaped body with bold flaring neck and base, the entire outer and inner surface covered with turquoise blue glaze, beneath which is a minute crackle.
130 00 Height and diameter 10 x 8½ inches.

290 **Covered Jar**, imperial yellow glaze, showing iridescent effects, ornamentation of jar and cover carved in low relief, bands of diaper, vine, trellis and other designs, griffin heads for handles and leaf-shaped ornaments for feet. Height and diameter
190 00 11 x 8 inches, has carved stand.

291 **Jar-shaped Vase**, of ovoid form with wide mouth, glazed with a dark mottled red color, shading into *sang de bœuf.* Height
130 00 11 inches, diameter 7 inches.

292 **Bottle-shaped Vase**, globular body with tall, slender neck, outer surface covered with a *soufflé* glaze of pinkish hue of light and dark shades, running down and leaving top of neck white.
352 50 Height and diameter 11½ x 6½ inches, has carved stand.

293 **Pilgrim Vase**, flat, circular, bottle-shaped, with handles at neck, tea-color glaze of a dark green shade. Seal mark of the Keen-lung period, 1736–1795. Height and diameter 10½ x 8½ inches,
120 00 has carved stand.

294 **Ovoid Jar**, the outer and inner surface covered with a translucent celadon glaze, running around the neck of jar is a boldly modeled dragon in high relief. Height 8¾ inches, diameter
630 00 6 inches, has carved stand.

295 **Jar-shaped Vase**, globular body, with low, wide mouth neck, around the body carved in relief are flowers and vines, and on neck, leaf designs running upwards, entire outer and inner surface covered with turquoise blue glaze of light and dark shades. Seal mark of the Keen-lung period, 1736–1795.
185 00 Height and diameter 9 x 9 inches.

296 **Vase**, bamboo design, celadon glaze of light translucent texture.
70 00 Height 9½ inches.

297 BOTTLE-SHAPED VASE, globular body with tall neck spreading at top, light texture, covered with turquoise blue glaze, showing very minute crackle beneath. Height and diameter 14 x 8 inches, has carved stand. *$350 00*

298 TALL CYLINDRICAL VASE, Long-Yao specimen, covered with *sang de bœuf* glaze of exceptional quality. Height and diameter 18 x 7 inches, has carved teak-wood stand and cover. *560 00*

299 BOTTLE VASE, with slender neck, gray pearl glaze with streaks of lavender, running around the neck and body of vase is a finely modeled lizard or dragon in bold relief and glazed in rose color. Height and diameter 11 x 5½ inches. *1,000 00*

From the collection of Comte de Semalle, member of the French Legation at Pekin from 1873 to 1885.

300 LOW FAT BOTTLE, semi-globular shape, with three incised medallions or crests, verdigris green glaze with cloudings and mottles of red. Mark of Kang-he period, 1661–1722. Height and diameter 4 x 5 inches, has stand. *500 00*

301 OVOID-SHAPED VASE, covered with a deep *sang de bœuf* glaze, neck of Oriental metal work in silver and gold. Height and diameter 9 x 4½ inches, including carved stand. *300 00*

302 STRAIGHT CYLINDRICAL VASE, with slightly spreading neck and head of mythological beast in relief for handles, mustard yellow glaze with fine crackle, iridescent over-glaze. Height 8 inches, diameter 3½ inches, has carved stand. *210 00*

303 LARGE BOTTLE VASE, globular body with long neck gracefully spreading at mouth, outer surface covered with mirror black glaze of great depth. Ring mark of Kang-he period, 1661–1722. Height and diameter 18 x 10 inches. *800 00*

From the collection of Comte de Semalle, member of the French Legation at Pekin from 1873 to 1885.

304 BOTTLE VASE, similar shape as above, gray pearl glaze of very even quality. Height and diameter 15 x 9 inches. *305 00*

From the collection of Count Kleczkowski of France.

305 SMALL VASE, ovoid shape with wide mouth, metallic or iron rust glaze. Height with stand 7½ inches. *40 00*

306 BOTTLE VASE, globular form with very tall slender neck, outer surface covered with an olive green glaze of great iridescence.
$260 00 Height and diameter 12¾ x 5 inches.

307 LARGE VASE, ovoid shape with low flaring neck, glazed with turquoise blue, relief and incised ornamentation of figures of fish, mouse, Seal of happiness, flying bats, etc., ribs running around vase in black, pierced band around neck. Height and
300 00 diameter, including carved stand, 16 x 8 inches.

From the collection of Comte de Semalle, member of the French Legation at Pekin from 1873 to 1885.

308 GOURD-SHAPED VASE, double lobe, imperial yellow glaze, with incised ornamentation of vine in green, and the gourds in white reserve. Height and diameter 9 x 4½ inches, has fine carved
260 00 stand.

From the collection of Comte de Semalle, member of the French Legation at Pekin.

309 OVOID BOTTLE VASE, with low neck, and ornaments in imitation of bronze for handles, celadon glaze with bold crackle beneath.
120 00 Height and diameter, with stand, 9 x 4 inches.

From the collection of Comte de Semalle, member of the French Legation at Pekin.

310 JAR-SHAPED VASE, basket-work pattern, with designs of coins in relief, celadon glaze. Mark of the Kea-King period, 1796–
32 50 1821. Height and diameter 4½ x 7 inches.

311 LARGE BOTTLE VASE, graceful ovoid shape, with tall slender neck, covered with turquoise blue glaze, archaic floral and other designs incised and carved in low relief. Rams' heads for handles and raised ornaments as division lines dividing the ornamentation into four panels. Height 15 inches, diameter
395 00 10¾ inches, has carved stand.

From the collection of Comte de Semalle, member of the French Legation at Pekin from 1873 to 1885.

312 VASE, globular shaped body, with tall cylindrical neck, imperial yellow glaze with incised ornamentation of plum tree in blossom, in green and purple glaze, on reverse side bamboo
165 00 branches in green. Height and diameter 12½ x 8 inches.

CABINET OBJECTS IN CHINESE PORCELAINS.

313 TEA BOWL, semi-egg-shell texture, outer surface covered with apple green glaze. Seal mark of Kea-King period, 1796–1821. $17 50

314 SMALL COUPE, round form, outer surface covered with *sang de bœuf* glaze, has carved stand. 27 50

315 PERFUME BURNER, globular shape on three slender feet, scroll handles, covered with a gray crackle glaze, has carved teak-wood stand and cover. Height of all, 5½ inches. 37 50

316 WINE CUP, with fluted corners, outer surface of engraved white glaze, figure of Deity, storks, flowers, and deer painted in colors. Seal mark. 22 50

317 SMALL BOTTLE VASE, ovoid shape, with low neck, brown glaze, with metallic or iron rust effects. Height with stand, 5½ inches. 27 50

318 CUP AND SAUCER, egg-shell texture, with pink, "rose-back" glaze, ornamentation of flowers and butterfly in natural color enamels on inner surface. 60 00

319 VASE, double diamond shape, one lozenge decorated with dragon, floral, and other designs in *bleu de Nankin* beneath glaze, the other with similar designs in coral red applied over glaze. Height 5½ inches. 25 00

320 BOTTLE VASE, globular body with long neck, apple green glaze, with faint crackle beneath at neck. Height 5 inches. 82 50

321 WINE CUP, semi-egg-shell texture, white glaze with ornamentation of crests in various colors of enamels applied over glaze. Seal mark of Taou-Kwang period, 1821–1851. 30 00

322 SNUFF BOTTLE, pure white texture, cylindrical shape, with low neck, decoration of five claw dragon and clouds, painted in coral red over glaze. Mark of Ching-Hwa period, 1465–1488. 22 50

323 BOTTLE VASE, semi-ovoid body with tall slender neck, outer surface covered with coral red glaze. Height 5½ inches, has carved stand. 50 00

324 OVOID BOTTLE, with low neck, outer surface covered with lavender color glaze. Height 5 inches, has carved teak-wood stand. 40 00

325 VASE, of turquoise blue glaze, ovoid shape with flaring neck.
$70 00 Height and diameter 8 x 4 inches.

326 PERFUME BURNER, Chinese porcelain, globular shape, on three legs, lion heads with rings in relief for handles, imperial yellow glaze with incised ornamentation of dragons and clouds, in green. Height, including carved teak-wood stand and cover,
47 50 6½ inches.

327 TEA BOWL, outer surface painted and enameled with deities, symbols, and inscriptions in various delicate colors. Mon-
17 50 golian seal mark.

328 COUPE, globular shape with wide mouth, scroll, arabesque and floral designs in gold and colors, on sea-green glaze. Keen-lung period, 1736–1795. Height and diameter, including
25 00 carved stand, 3¼ x 3 inches.

329 BOTTLE VASE, *flambe* glaze in reds, brown, purple, etc. Height
22 50 4 inches, exclusive of stand.

330 WINE CUP, outer surface of red glaze, with enameled ornamentation of branches of hawthorn blossoms, in white and other
10 00 colors. Seal mark of Yung-ching period, 1723–1736.

331 BOTTLE VASE with cover, white glaze with basket design in
7 50 green, and text panels in black. Height 3½ inches.

332 OVOID BOTTLE VASE, with slender neck, outer surface of mus-
50 00 tard crackle glaze. Height and diameter 6½ x 3½ inches.

333 GLOBULAR JAR, with indented circle at top around neck, outer surface covered with gray pearl glaze. Mark of Kang-he pe-riod, 1661–1722. Height and diameter, including stand, 4 x 4
160 00 inches.

334 SMALL VASE, hexagonal shape, after the design of a Chinese garden seat, turquoise glaze with incised and relief ornamen-
30 00 tation. Height 4¼ inches, has carved stand.

335 STRAIGHT VASE, with slight spreading neck, outer surface cov-
205 00 ered with rose *souffle* glaze. Height 5¼ inches, has carved stand.

336 GOURD-SHAPED VASE, dark blue glaze with gourd vine, gourds and flying bats carved in relief and painted in coral red, green
52 50 and other colors. Height and diameter 6 x 3 inches.

337 SMALL BOWL, egg-shell texture, rose color, *soufflé* glaze on outer surface, medallion of enameled fruit inside. "Rose-back" specimen. *$82 50*

338 DIMINUTIVE VASE, bottle shape, chrysanthemum flowers painted in blue beneath glaze. *17 50*

339 WINE CUP, semi-egg-shell texture and pure white glaze. Mark of Taou-Kwang period, 1821–1851. *7 50*

340 —— Another similar, same period. *5 00*

SERIES OF CHINESE PORCELAINS.

"PEACH BLOW" OR "CRUSHED STRAWBERRY" COLOR.

341 VASE, of graceful ovoid shape with slender neck, slightly spreading at top, perfection in form, color and texture. Height, exclusive of carved stand, 8 inches, diameter 3 inches. Mark of the Kang-he period, 1661–1722. *18,000 00*

The above from the private collection of I Wang-ye, a Mandarin Prince, has a world-wide reputation as being the finest specimen of its class in existence.

342 VASE, same shape and size as above specimen, glaze running into a darker shade. Height 8 inches, diameter 3 inches. Mark of Kang-he period, 1661–1722, has carved stand. *6,000 00*

Companion to No. 341, and from the same private collection.

343 ROUGE BOX, with cover, round flat shape, mellow glaze and clear texture. Mark of Kang-he period, 1661–1722, has carved teakwood stand. *350 00*

344 —— Similar Box, of same shape and size, equal quality of glaze and porcelain, slight difference in diffusion of color. Mark of Kang-he period, 1661–1722, has carved stand. *375 00*

345 BOTTLE VASE, semi-globular shape with three incised medallions or crests, light shade of color, with dark specks. Mark of Kang-he period, 1661–1722. Height and diameter 3½ x 5 inches, has carved stand. *675 00*

From the private collection of the Mandarin Prince, I Wang-ye.

346 VASE, ovoid shaped body, with tall slender neck, top of which is mounted in silver and gold of Oriental design and workmanship, relief corrugated design at base of vase. Mark of Kang-he period, 1661–1722. Height 8½ inches, diameter 3½ inches, has carved teak-wood high stand. *$1,200 00*

347 BOTTLE-SHAPED VASE, with tall slender neck, dark shade of glaze covering the outer surface, dragon in green and in bold relief runing around lower part of neck. Height and diameter 8¾ x 3 inches. Mark of the Kang-he period, 1661–1722. *250 00*

348 OVOID VASE, with tall slender neck, flaring at top, corrugated or chrysanthemum design at base of vase, glaze of crushed strawberry color of the light and dark shade. Mark of the Kang-he period, 1661–1722. Height and diameter 8¼ x 3½ inches, has carved stand. *1,000 00*

349 VASE, similar shape as above, but neck made of gold and silver of Oriental design and workmanship; dragon in solid gold encircling neck, cloudings of greenish hue visible in glaze. Mark of the Kang-he period, 1661–1722. Height 8 inches, diameter 3½ inches. *1,000 00*

350 SMALL VASE, of amphora shape, very even quality mellow glaze. Mark of the Kang-he period, 1661–1722. Height, exclusive of stand, 6 inches, diameter 2¼ inches. *1,150 00*

From the private collection of the Mandarin Prince, I Wang-ye.

OLD CHINESE CLOISONNÉ ENAMELS.

351 SMALL VASE, with flaring base and neck, floral designs in Indian red, white and black enamels on blue ground, gilt-bronze dragons for handles, and carved gilt bands. Keen-lung period, 1736–1795. Height 7½ inches. *40 00*

352 FIRE VASE, OR INCENSE BURNER, on tripod, floral and crest designs in Indian red, yellow, brown, green and white enamels on turquoise blue ground. Ming period. Height and diameter 3 x 5½ inches, has carved teak stand. *62 50*

353 Gourd-shaped Vase, with handles shape of sceptre of longevity, floral designs in various old colors on blue ground, over which are distributed flakes of gold. Early Ming specimen. Height and diameter 11 x 8 inches. *$335 00*

354 Pair of Vases, tall ovoid shape with spreading necks, designs of flowers and fruits in red, green, blue, yellow, white and other colors of enamel on light blue ground, gilt bands top and bottom, and running around neck. Keen-lung period. Height and diameter 15 x 7½ inches. 2 pieces. *150 00*

355 Fire Vase, quadrangular shape, on feet, symbolic and floral designs in bright enamels in light green panels, and on turquoise ground, gilt divisions and engraved band at top. Keen-lung period, 1736–1795. Height and diameter 3¼ x 9 inches. *67 50*

356 Pair Vases, bottle shape, with fine tall slender necks, chocolate enamel ground, with vine designs running upwards, in blue, green and white enamels. Engraved mark of Ching-Hwa period, 1465–1488. Height and diameter 14 x 8 inches. 2 pieces. *360 00*

357 Small Beaker, archaic and floral designs in Indian red, yellow, dark green and blue, on turquoise ground, gilt-bronze ornaments on swelling centre. Ming period. Height and diameter 7¾ x 5 inches, has carved stand. *75 00*

358 Bottle Vase, three gilt bronze lizards in bold relief running around body of vase, flower and vine designs in red, green, yellow and white enamels, on turquoise ground. Height and diameter 8½ x 7 inches, has carved stand. *125 00*

359 Incense Burner, with gilt elephant-head feet and handles, gilt and incrusted enamel stand and open work, and incrusted enamel cover. Mark of Keen-lung period, 1736–1795. Height and diameter, including stand, 14 x 7½ inches. *180 00*

From the collection of Count Kleczkowski, of France. Stand *50 00*

360 Wall Vase, gourd design, turquoise blue enamel ground, with inscription in black, and flowers and symbols in red, green, yellow, white and dark blue. Height 9½ inches. Keen-lung period, 1736–1795. *132 50*

361 Ovoid Vase, with tall, slender neck and spreading base, gilt handles at neck, floral designs in old colors on a turquoise blue ground. Ming period. Height and diameter 13 x 4½ inches. *160 00*

362 INCENSE BURNER, gilt and incrusted enamel, globular shape, with three feet and scroll handles, open work and gilt cover. Height and diameter 10 x 10½ inches, has carved teak-wood stand.
$310 00

From the collection of Count Kleczkowski, of France.

363 SMALL VASE, ovoid form with low neck, three gilt rams' heads in relief on neck, floral designs in various colors of enamels on a base of very heavy gold bronze. Engraved mark of the Keen-lung period, 1736–1795. Height and diameter 5½ x 4 inches, has carved teak-wood stand.
455 00

From the collection of Comte de Semallé, member of the French Legation at Pekin from 1873 to 1885.

364 BEAKER VASE, with swelling centre and gilt bronze ornaments, archaic and floral designs in dark green, blue, black, yellow and red enamels on turquoise ground. Height and diameter 12 x 7 inches, has carved teak stand.
180 00

365 BUDDHISTIC COMMUNION SERVICE, tall wine tankard, and a cup and saucer, stork, water scene, crest, vine and other designs in gray enamel, gilt ornaments.
450 00

366 PAIR TALL CYLINDRICAL VASES, with low spreading necks, turquoise enamel ground with flowers, vases and other ornaments in various colors. Height and diameter 19 x 8 inches.
170 00 2 pieces.

367 LARGE INCENSE BURNER OR SACRED VESSEL, globular shape, on three feet, with cover, gilt handles and ornaments in relief, light blue enamel ground with archaic and other designs in Indian red, dark blue, black and white enamels. Ming period. Height and diameter 12 x 11 inches, including teak-wood stand.
355 00

368 VERY LARGE BEAKER VASE, with swelling body and bold flaring neck, groundwork of turquoise blue enamel, designs of five-claw dragons in red, yellow and white enamels. Height 30 inches, diameter 12 inches. Keen-lung period, 1736–1795.
290 00

---

369 PAIR MODERN VASES, Japanese *cloisonné* enamel on copper, tall ovoid shape with spreading necks; on body of vase, designs of storks, chrysanthemum flowers, grasses, etc., in various enamels on turquoise blue ground, black necks with crests, vines, flowers and birds in bright colors. Height and diameter 18 x 8 inches.
130 00 2 pieces.

ANTIQUE AND MODERN BRONZES.

CHINESE AND JAPANESE SPECIMENS.

370 VASE, old Japanese, cylindrical shape on tripod, lizard handles, four figures of Deities in bold relief. Height and diameter 8½ x 3½ inches. *$30 00*

371 STATUETTE, old Japanese bronze, figure of boy on conch shell. Height 9½ inches. *22 50*

372 VASE, old Chinese gold bronze, ovoid bottle shape with tall neck, dragon in bold relief encircling neck. Height and diameter 13½ x 6 inches. *185 00*

373 TRAY, oblong shape, modern Japanese specimen, *repoussé* and incised ornamentation of leaves, flowers and butterfly, 9½ x 14 inches. *7 50*

374 JAR, globular shape, with lacquered cover. Old Japanese specimen by Gorosa, *repoussé* and chiseled ornamentation, turtle of longevity, water, etc., brown *patine*. Height and diameter 5½ x 7 inches. *57 50*

375 JAR AND COVER, cylindrical shape, spreading at neck. Old Japanese specimen, two bands running around jar, on which are the Mikado's private crest and imperial seal, dark brown *patine*. Height and diameter 8 x 7½ inches. *110 00*

376 FLOWER VASE, globular shape, with spreading base and wide mouth, modern Japanese specimen, inlaid and ornamented in relief with gold, silver, and other metals, bold design of pine tree, aquatic bird, etc. Bronze shows interesting effect of mixture of lacquer with the molten metal. Height and diameter 11 x 12 inches. *205 00*

377 JAR AND COVER, Japanese specimen, *repoussé* and incised designs of dragon, crests and archaic patterns, light brown *patine*. Height and diameter 6 x 7 inches. *85 00*

378 TALL CYLINDRICAL VASE, modern Japanese silver bronze, relief and inlaid ornamentation in gold, silver, Gorosa bronze, and enamel, in one upright panel figure of Japanese philosopher, frog dancing, etc., on reverse side aquatic birds, grasses, etc., bands of archaic designs, flowers and arabesques. Height and diameter 17 x 10 inches. *725 00*

379 BEAKER-SHAPED VASE, modern Japanese specimen of Gorosa bronze with avanturine *patine*, around body of vase is bold open-work design of dragon and clouds in Shakudo. Vase ornamented in relief with gold, silver, Shibu-ichi and Shakudo, designs of birds, turtles, symbols of longevity, flowers, etc. Height and diameter 22½ x 10 inches, including stand, which is wrought of same material as vase.

$560 00

380 PAIR VERY LARGE VASES, modern Japanese bronze, tall ovoid shape with spreading neck and bases, ornamentation of chrysanthemum and other flowers in bold relief, in gold, silver, and other metals and lacquer, Damascened designs in gold on bands running around body of vases. Height and diameter 36 x 16 inches. 2 pieces.

5,300 00

These vases were designed by the late Christian Herter, Esq., of Herter Brothers, and made in Tokio under the personal supervision of the late K. Yaye of Japan, the highest artistic skill being engaged in their production, which occupied four years.

381 PAIR PEDESTALS, for above vases, carved rosewood with octagon shaped tops, which are inlaid with panels of metal work of Japanese designs. Height and diameter 42 x 15 inches. 2 pieces.

1,250 00

Designed and made to order by Messrs. Herter Brothers. Panels of metal work by Messrs. Tiffany & Co.

SPECIMENS OF JADE, AGATE, CRYSTAL, ETC.

382 CUP AND COVER, mottled white jade, with emerald green spots. Height and diameter 3½ x 4½ inches.

30 00

383 SMALL VASE OR ORNAMENT, agate of clouded white color, carved design of fungus and persimmon fruit; has stand.

25 00

384 ORNAMENT, in white jade stone. Two mandarin ducks, eating lotus flowers; has carved stand. 3 x 3 inches.

42 50

385 SMALL COUPE, of agate, globular shape, fluted design. 2 x 2½ inches.

50 00

386 CUP, of smoky brown rock crystal, two birds and branch of blossoms carved in relief. 2 x 3 inches. Has carved teak-wood stand.

82 50

From the collection of Count Kleczkowski, France.

387 SNUFF BOTTLE, of smoky brown agate, flat shape. 2 x 2 inches. Has stand. *$25 00*

From the collection of Count Kleczkowski, France.

388 VERY SMALL ORNAMENT, in jade, frog in *Feï-tsoueï* on lotus leaf. *15 00*

389 CUP, with two handles, in white jade, outer and inner surface carved in low relief with floral designs, thin texture. Height and diameter 2 x 4 inches, has carved teak stand. *102 50*

390 SMALL VASE, of carnelian, carved bamboo design, with relief ornamentation of flowers and bamboo leaves. Height 2½ inches, has stand. *42 50*

391 BOX AND COVER, round, flat shape, dark green jade, with light and darker veins. 1½ x 2½ inches, has carved stand. *30 00*

392 BOWL, of gray jade, design of lotus leaf, with turtle in bold relief inside. 2½ x 7 inches. *57 50*

393 ORNAMENT, in agate, pomegranate fruit. 2 x 1½ inches, has carved stand. *37 50*

394 CUP, of lapis-lazuli, heavy texture. 2 x 2½ inches. *72 50*

395 ORNAMENT, or ancestral tablet, of milky-white jade, specimen of intricate carving, suspended in teak-wood frame. *37 50*

396 CUP, of red and white agate, designs of fungus carved in bold relief. 4 x 2 inches, has carved stand of teak wood. *70 00*

397 SAUCER, of highly-polished agate. Diameter 4¾ inches. *25 00*

398 KI-LEN, carved in gray white jade. 3 x 3 inches, has carved teak stand. *55 00*

399 SMALL ORNAMENT, of white and pink carnelian, fungus design, with peach fruit carved in relief, with stand. *75 00*

400 ORNAMENT, fish carved in red and white carnelian. 4 x 2 inches. *32 50*

401 BOWL AND COVER, on stand, all of milky-white jade stone. Bowl of carved fluted design, stand of leaf design, elaborately carved. Height and diameter of all, 6½ x 4½ inches. *710 00*

From the collection of Count Kleczkowski, France.

402 CUP, of agate, shape of Chinese peach, stem forming handle, milky-white and amber color. 2 x 4½ inches, has carved teak stand with plush mat. $95 00

403 VASE, of white and red carnelian, fungus design, with fruit and other ornamentation cut in relief. 4 inches high, has carved teak-wood stand. 97 50

404 SMALL VASE, or ornamental piece, carved in red Oriental amber, of dark tone, design of flower and fruit, carved ivory and teak-wood stand. 42 50

From the collection of Count Kleczkowski, France.

405 SMALL ORNAMENTAL PIECE, in gray-white jade. Vase with cover, stork and pine tree in relief. 4½ x 3 inches, with stand. 85 00

406 TABLET, of agate, gray pearl and lavender color. 4 x 5 inches. 12 50

407 FLOWER VASE, of greenish-white jade, lotus leaf design, with bud and stem in relief. 6 x 5 inches, has carved teak stand. 80 00

408 CUP AND SAUCER, of Oriental gold agate, delicate texture, highly polished. 90 00

From the collection of Count Kleczkowski, France.

409 FRAGMENT OF JADE STONE, specimen known as *Fei-tsouei* or jewel green jade, has carved teak-wood stand. 55 00

From the collection of Count Kleczkowski, France.

410 ORNAMENTAL PIECE, specimen of lapis-lazuli, carved in strong relief, and showing various metallic veins. 4½ x 3½ inches, has carved teak stand. 175 00

411 VASE, of milky-white jade, flat beaker shape, archaic and other designs carved in low relief. Height and diameter 4½ x 4½ inches, has stand. 132 50

412 SACRIFICIAL VESSEL, of carved rhinoceros horn, square spreading cup-shape, on four feet, lizards in relief for handles. 3½ x 5½ inches. 45 00

413 COVERED VASE, of white jade, square shape, with round corners, dragon head and ring handles, dragon and dragon crests in relief on cover. 4½ x 4 inches, exclusive of teak stand. 145 00

414 ORNAMENTAL PIECE, in crystal, frog on green jade leaf. 115 00

415 BOX AND COVER, of light green jade, circular shape, ornamentation of incised and pierced designs, inside of box spray of flowers carved in high relief. Height and diameter 2 x 4 inches, has carved teak-wood and plush stand. *$510 00*

From the collection of Count Kleczkowski, France.

416 TABLET, of serpentine or dark green jade, both sides carved in bold relief with mountain scenery, figures, rocks, water, etc., a scene from Chinese mythology. 6 x 8 inches, has carved teak-wood mounting and stand. *385 00*

From the collection of Count Kleczkowski, France.

417 SHRINE GARNITURE, of carved Pekin or cinnabar lacquer, comprises incense burner, perfume box on stand, and two vases, all on oblong pedestal of carved Pekin lacquer. *305 00*

418 CHINESE SACRIFICIAL VESSEL OR VASE, rhinoceros horn, elaborately carved, boating scene, foliage, cloud effects, etc., in bold relief. Height 5 inches, exclusive of carved teak-wood stand. *122 50*

419 VASE, of white jade stone, carved in relief with floral and vine designs, and inlaid with jewels, silver and gilt mountings, ornamented with cloisonné enamel, engraved and pierced work. Height and diameter 10 x 3½ inches. *510 00*

SALE TUESDAY AFTERNOON, MARCH 9,

BEGINNING AT 2.30 O'CLOCK.

AT THE AMERICAN ART GALLERIES.

OLD CHINESE PORCELAINS.

DECORATED IN COLORS.

420 JAR-SHAPED VASE, painted with Moorish designs in Indian red, slight borders of pale green, chrysanthemum crest, arabesque and other designs in white reserve. Height and diameter 7 x 4½ inches. — $27 50

421 WALL VASE, gourd design, coral red glaze, with enameled ornamentation of fruits, flowers, and insects, in natural colors. Height 7½ inches. — 27 50

422 VASE, flat beakter shape, figures of mandarin lady and child, landscape and mountain scenery, etc., painted in medallions in various colors, light green glaze surrounding, on rough surface, scroll handles. Seal mark of Keen-lung period, 1736–1795. Height and diameter 8 x 4 inches. — 40 00

423 PLATE, deep form, inner surface covered with yellow glaze, and ornamentation of flying birds, and plum trees in blossom, enameled floral designs on outer surface. Mark of Keen-lung period, 1736–1795. Diameter 9 inches. — 42 50

424 SMALL VASE, ovoid shape, with slightly flaring neck, engraved white glaze with ornamentation of sprays of flowers, seal mark of Keen-lung period, 1736–1795. Height and diameter 8½ x 3 inches, has carved stand. — 30 00

425 BOTTLE VASE, low, flat form, with tall slender neck, white glaze with quail painted in coral red, and bamboo trees and rock in blue enamel over the glaze. Height and diameter 9 x 4 inches, has carved teak-wood stand. — 45 00

426 PIH-TING, hexagonal shape, light green glaze, with symbols, inscriptions, and flowers, in bright enamels and gold, gold seal mark of Kea-King period, 1796–1821. Height 5 inches. *$30 00*

427 LARGE BEAKER, mottled red ground, over which is painted blossoms and butterflies in black, green, red, and other colors. Height and diameter 15 x 8 inches. *250 00*

428 VASE, pilgrim bottle shape, with scroll handles at neck, ornamentation of flowers and vines in blue beneath glaze, and coral red, yellow, green, and pink applied over glaze. Seal mark of Keen-lung period, 1735–1796. Height 7 inches. *60 00*

429 PLATE, semi-egg-shell texture, in medallions on inner surface are sprays of flowers and butterflies, painted in blue beneath glaze, and various colors of enamels over glaze, similar ornamentation on outer surface, the blue and copper red being beneath the glaze. Mark of the Yung-Ching period, 1723–1736. Diameter 8 inches. *65 00*

430 WALL VASE, gourd shape, with double lobe, between which is the representation of a ribbon as though tied around vase and forming handles, engraved sea-green glaze, with clouds in various enamels, 7 flying bats in coral red, and inscription in gold. Gold seal mark of Keen-lung period, 1736–1795. Height 7½ inches, diameter 5½ inches. *70 00*

431 VASE, semi-egg-shell texture, ovoid shape, spreading at neck and base, painting of floral and vine designs in blue beneath glaze, groundwork of yellow enamel, which leaves the ornamentation in reserve. Height and diameter 10 x 5 inches. *165 00*

432 BOTTLE VASE, ovoid shape, with low neck, covered with deep rose-color glaze, over which is an enameled ornamentation of vine and fruit in purple and two shades of green. Height and diameter 9 x 5 inches. *230 00*

433 JAR, semi-egg-shell texture, ovoid shape, with wide mouth, vine, flowers, and birds painted in luminous greens and other colors. Mark of Yung-ching period, 1723–1736. Height and diameter 5 x 4 inches, has carved teak-wood stand. *40 00*

434 TEA-CANISTER, straight flat shape, with small neck, side panels ornamented with peonies, magnolias, blossoms, etc., in pink, white, coral red, and other colors, edges decorated in imitation cloisonné enamel to match lid, which is of that workmanship on bronze. Signed with seals and Chinese characters. 6 x 7
$205 00 inches, exclusive of carved stand.

435 BOTTLE VASE, globular body, with tall slender neck, outer surface covered with coral red glaze, over which is an ornamentation of floral and vine designs in bright enamels. Seal mark of the Keen-lung period, 1736–1795. Height and diameter 12 x 7
205 00 inches.

436 LARGE VASE, ovoid shaped body with flaring neck, decorated with figure of priest, mandarin and children, pine tree, etc., painted in bright greens, red and other colors, all applied over
145 00 glaze. Height and diameter $15\frac{3}{4}$ x 8 inches, has carved stand.

437 VASE, globular body with slender neck spreading at top, decoration in coral red, of five-claw dragon, phœnix, sprigs of flowers and fruit, gilt band top and bottom. Seal mark of Taou-Kwang period, 1821–1851. Height $11\frac{1}{2}$ inches, diameter 6
185 00 inches, has carved stand.

438 BOTTLE VASE, canteen shape, yellow iridescent glaze with painting of a flowering plant in blue beneath glaze and in reserve.
102 50 7 x 6 inches, exclusive of carved teak-wood stand.

439 CYLINDRICAL VASE, hexagonal shape, with horizontal incised division lines, scolloped neck, light yellow glaze, on which is painted lotus plants in bloom, plum tree in blossom, chrysanthemum flowers, birds, etc., in low tones of violet, greens, black, etc. Height 10 inches, diameter 4 inches, has carved
170 00 stand.

440 TALL CYLINDRICAL VASE, covered with a pale blue glaze, with cloud effects in a darker shade, ornamentation of sprigs of flowers and blossoms in bright enamels. Seal mark of Keen-
150 00 lung period, 1736–1795. Height and diameter $15\frac{1}{2}$ x 7 inches.

441 BOTTLE VASE, low circular body with tall slender neck, around the body are four medallions in which are painted landscape views, ornaments and symbols, on neck and between medallions are arabesque and diaper designs in green, red and violet enamels, on the neck and at the base of same are 7 seal marks in violet and red, beneath body of vase on speckled green glaze are detached flowers in bright colors. Height 13 inches, diameter 9½ inches. *$190 00*

442 BEAKER, with bell shaped base and swelling center, profuse decoration of chrysanthemum flowers and vine designs in blue beneath glaze and green, red and yellow applied over glaze, bands and border of archaic and other designs in various colors and gold. Height and diameter, 14 x 7 inches. *150 00*

443 VASE, ovoid shape with slender neck, light yellow glaze with iridescent effects, four-claw dragon, the precious pearl and clouds painted in blue beneath glaze and in reserve, green handles, engraved silver cap to neck. Mark of Kea-tsing Period. 1522–1567. Height and diameter 10½ x 4½ inches. *235 00*

444 COVERED VASE, globular shape with cylindrical support and spreading base, outer and inner surface covered with imperial yellow glaze, decorated with ten five-claw dragons, precious pearls, clouds, etc., in bright enamels, coral or mandarin button surmounting cover. Height and diameter 11 x 6 inches, has carved stand of teak-wood. *210 00*

445 PILGRIM BOTTLE VASE, sea-green glaze, with bold five-claw dragon in copper red on each face, clouds and water in blue beneath glaze, handles at neck. Seal mark of Keen-lung period. Height 12 inches, diameter 10 inches. *175 00*

446 JAR-SHAPED VASE, decorated with colors of *famille Verte*, Chinese garden scene, female figures, pine tree, etc. Height and diameter 11 x 7 inches. *100 00*

447 CYLINDRICAL VASE, with feet and pierced body of globular shape, clouded celadon glaze with decorations of archaic and floral designs in blue and gold, handles at neck. Height and diameter 13 x 6 inches. *62 50*

448 VASE, of irregular shape, four panels decorated with landscape views, river scenery, etc., in colors, four with text, balance of outer surface and that of the inner, covered with a glaze in imitation of agate. Gold seal mark of Keen-lung period, 1736–1795. Height and diameter including carved stand, 8 x 7½
$277 50 inches.

449 LARGE PLATE, bold decoration of lotus plant and flowers and flying birds in bright green, red, yellow and violet. Mark of
62 50 the "Swastika" Cross of Buddha. Diameter 13 inches.

450 CYLINDRICAL VASE, tall shape with flattened sides, on each of which are Chinese landscape and mountain scenery, figures, mythological subjects, etc., painted in various colors of enamel, balance of vase covered with a dark blue glaze and ornamented with floral and vine designs in gold applied over glaze, gilt scroll handles at neck. Seal mark of Keen-lung period, 1736–
205 00 1795. Height and diameter 18 x 8 inches.

451 BOTTLE VASE, ovoid shaped body with tall slender neck slightly spreading, vase decorated with boldly drawn five-claw dragon and sacred pearl in light green, blue, and coral red, bands of archaic and other designs in green, blue and red enamels. Mark of the Ching-hwa period, 1465–1488. Height and diam-
165 00 eter 15½ x 8 inches, has carved stand.

652 VASE, ovoid shape with spreading neck and wide mouth, semi-egg-shell texture, on body painted in bright enamels are peony, chrysanthemum and other flowers, trees in blossoms and rocks, neck and base glazed with imperial yellow and ornamented with flowers, fruits, vines and symbols in brilliant enamels, inscriptions in gold. Seal mark of the Kea-king period, 1796–
220 00 1821. Height and diameter 12 x 7½ inches.

453 GOURD VASE, with two lobes, the upper one with tapering neck, covered with sea-green glaze and ornamented with floral designs, inscriptions, etc., in red, yellow, dark blue, white, pink and other enamels and gold. Height and diameter 12 x 7
205 00 inches, has carved teak-wood stand.

From the collection of Count Kleczkowski, France.

454 Jar and Cover, ovoid shape, glazed with deep rose-color, and ornamented with flowers, trees in blossom, butterflies, birds, symbols, and other designs in various colors of enamel applied in low relief over the glaze. Height and diameter 16 x 9 inches. *$425 00*

455 —— Another, similar. *340 00*

456 —— Another, same. *340 00*

457 Pair Beakers, glazed and decorated to match above jars. Height and diameter 14 x 7½ inches. *800 00*

The above five pieces from a Garniture.

458 Cylindrical Vase, with low, spreading neck, body decorated with minature painting of landscape, water view and mountain scenery, boating parties in boats of dragon design, mandarins and children on balcony viewing same, etc., a festive or ceremonial subject, neck and base of yellow-green ground, with floral and vine designs in various colors. Seal mark of the Kea-King period, 1796–1821. Height and diameter 11 x 6 inches, has carved teak-wood stand. *230 00*

459 Large Gourd Shaped Vase, double lobe, on which are painted in bright colors processions of Chinese children carrying banners and symbols and playing musical instruments; trees in blossom, garden scenes, rocks, etc. Seal mark. Height 22 inches, diameter 12 inches, has carved teak-wood stand. *760 00*

460 Manchou Vase, ovoid shape with graceful neck, gold ground with decorations of melon vine bearing the fruit, flowers, blossoms, and butterflies, all painted in enamels of the natural colors and applied over glaze, bands at neck and base of Grecian design in light and dark blue enamel. Mark of the Keen-lung period, 1736–1795. Height 16 inches, diameter 8 inches, has carved stand. *740 00*

From the collection of I Wang-ye, a Mandarin Prince.

461 Large Beaker, painting of Chinese interior and garden scenes, mandarin ladies, children playing, pine and willow trees, etc., in colors of *famille verte.* Ring mark of the Kang-he period, 1661–1722. Height and diameter 29 x 12 inches. *310 00*

462 VASE, ovoid shape with bulb neck, celadon ground with floral and vine designs, carved in relief and painted with blue and copper red beneath glaze. Height and diameter 11⅛ x 6½ inches, has stand.

$160 00

463 LARGE BOTTLE VASE, with tube handles at neck, profuse ornamentation of lotus plants and flowers in light blue, green, red, and pink, the blue being beneath glaze. Seal mark of the Keen-lung period, 1736–1795. Height 21⅛, diameter 15 inches.

510 00

464 LARGE BEAKER, known as "Black Hawthorn," jet black glaze with ornamentation of magnolia tree in bloom, peonies, chrysanthemum flowers, young bamboo, birds, rocks, etc., all painted in bright colors and left in reserve by the black glaze. Mark of the Ching-hwa period, 1465–1488. Height and diamter 27 x 12 inches, has carved stand.

1,550 00

From the Bing collection, Paris.

465 —— Another "Black Hawthorn" Beaker, larger than the above, similar glaze but different decoration, hawthorn blossoms, birds, rocks and grasses, painted in white, yellow, purple, and opaque green. Mark of the Ching-hwa period, 1465–1488. Height and diameter 30 x 12 inches.

1,600 00

From the collection of Count de Semallé, member of the French Legation at Pekin, 1873–1885.

466 LARGE OVOID SHAPED VASE, glazed and ornamented in imitation of bronze, archaic and Grecian designs carved and incised, and decorated with gold, carved head and ring handles. Gold seal mark. Height and diameter 20 x 15 inches, has carved teak-wood stand.

725 00

467 MANCHOU GARDEN SEAT, barrel shape with pierced medallions and raised ornaments, decoration of flowering plants, bird, rocks, etc., painted in natural colors over glaze. Height and diameter 19 x 16 inches.

300 00

468 LARGE BOTTLE VASE, globular body with tall slender neck, spreading at top, body of vase decorated with landscape and mountain scenery, groups of priests and mandarins, boating scene, etc., in various colors, neck and base of engraved rose-color glaze with floral designs, symbols, etc., in bright enamels. Height and diameter 26 x 16 inches.

1,325 00

469 LARGE VASE, ovoid shape body with tall spreading neck, in two white ground panels are painted groups of priests, mandarins and children, pine tree and other foliage, etc., scenes from Chinese history and mythology, ground of vase of deep rose-color glaze, incised and ornamented with flowers and vines in natural colors, Grecian and archaic designs at base and top of neck. Seal mark of Keen-lung period, 1736–1795. Height and diameter 27 x 16 inches. *$1,325 00*

470 VERY LARGE VASE, cylindrical shape body, with tall gracefully spreading neck and spreading base, around body of vase are twelve vertical panels glazed in white, green, pink, yellow, and other colors, and decorated with flowers, landscape scenes, emblems, ornaments, etc., in various colors, spaces between panels of dark blue with ornaments in gold applied over the glaze, running around neck and base are bands of rose, sea-green, chocolate, celadon and other colors, with decoration of flowers in blue beneath glaze and different enamels applied over the glaze, raised ornaments and crests and scroll handles. This Vase, an important specimen of the Keen-lung period, 1736–1795, illustrates the various styles of ornamentation peculiar to the period it represents. Height, including decorated porcelain stand, 38 inches, diameter 20 inches, has an additional stand of plush. *1,675 00*

COLLECTION OF BOWLS.

471 TEA BOWL AND COVER, Chinese porcelain, engraved pink glaze outside with enameled ornamentation of floral designs, inner surface covered with robin-egg blue glaze. Seal mark of the Keen-lung period, 1736–1795. *35 00*

472 RICE BOWL, Chinese porcelain, outer surface covered with dark blue mottled glaze, two four-claw dragons in yellow, red and green enamels, sacred pearls and flames in red and in reserve. Mark of the Keen-lung period, 1736–1795. *27 50*

473 TEA BOWL AND COVER, Chinese porcelain, semi-egg-shell texture, in eight round medallions on bowl and cover are painted in various colors, Mandarin figure, boating scenes, etc., intervening space covered with imperial yellow glaze and ornamented with fruit, vines, and symbols. Mark of the Kea-King period, 1796–1821. *57 50*

474 TEA BOWL, COVER AND SAUCER, Japanese porcelain, egg-shell texture, outer surface decorated with landscape, river view, flowers, etc., in dark blue enamel.

$20 00

475 RICE BOWL, Chinese porcelain semi-egg-shell texture, outer surface covered with coral red glaze and decorated with 30 butterflies, painted in various colors, applied over glaze. Mark of Kea-King period, 1796–1821, has teak-wood high stand.

65 00

476 LARGE BOWL, with scalloped edge, Chinese porcelain, outer surface decorated with floral designs, vines and symbolical designs in bright colors on white ground. Mark of the Kea-King period, 1796–1821.

35 00

477 TEA BOWL AND COVER, Chinese egg-shell porcelain, outer surface of bowl and cover decorated with four five-claw dragons and sacred pearls, in coral red and Nankin blue, the latter color being beneath glaze, inside of cover and bowl, in medallion a five-claw dragon in coral red. Mark of Yung-Ching period, 1723–1736.

62 50

478 RICE BOWL, Chinese porcelain, decorated inside with floral designs in blue beneath glaze, on outer surface four white ground medallions with delicately painted flowers, intervening space of lavender glaze, ornamented with floral and vine designs in various colors. Seal mark of the Kea-King period, 1796–1821.

35 00

479 BOWL AND COVER, Chinese porcelain, semi-egg-shell texture, outer surface of bowl and cover etched and painted in India ink, red and gold, figures, mythological beasts, etc. Seal mark of the Taou-Kwang period, 1821–1851.

30 00

480 BOWL, Chinese porcelain, egg-shell texture, inner surface decorated with phœnix and floral crests in bright enamels. Seal mark of the Keen-lung period, 1736–1795.

67 50

481 TEA BOWL AND COVER, Chinese porcelain, semi-egg-shell texture, outer surface of bowl and cover decorated with branches of flowers and blossoms, painted in red, greens, and other color, on white ground. Mark of the Kea-King period, 1796–1821.

32 50

482 LARGE BOWL, hexagonal shape, with incised horizontal divisions, inner and outer surface decorated with Chinese peach, and flying bats, in violet color. Seal mark of the Keen-lung period, 1736–1795, has carved teak-wood tall stand.

150 00

483 LARGE BOWL AND COVER, with gilt edges, Chinese porcelain, semi-egg-shell texture, outer surface of bowl and cover of celadon glaze, over which is a vine design and blossoms painted in greens, red and gold. Mark of the Kang-he period, 1661–1722. *$77 50*

CABINET OBJECTS

IN CHINESE PORCELAINS, GLAZES, EGG-SHELL, ETC.

484 SMALL VASE, Chinese porcelain, coral red glaze, has stand. *45 00*

485 SMALL COUPE, globular shape, Chinese egg-shell porcelain, decorated with two five-claw dragons, water and clouds in coral red on white ground. *40 00*

486 SAUCER, Chinese porcelain, imperial yellow glaze with incised ornamentation on front surface, five-claw dragons, clouds, etc. Mark of the Kang-he period, 1661–1722. *15 00*

487 WINE CUP, Chinese semi-egg-shell porcelain, outer surface of engraved rose-color glaze with enameled ornamentation of flowers and vines, inner surface of light green glaze. Seal mark of the Keen-lung period, 1736–1795. *12 50*

488 SMALL VASE, or snuff bottle, ovoid shape with low neck, Chinese porcelain, mirror black glaze. *30 00*

489 —— Another, bottle shape with tall slender neck, rose *souffle* glaze. *42 50*

490 —— Another, same shape as above, but smaller, turquoise blue glaze with minute crackle. *35 00*

491 PENCIL VASE, beaker shape, Chinese porcelain, outer surface of light green glaze, over which is an ornamentation of hawthorn blossoms and leaf designs in various enamels and gold, inner surface of yellow green enamel with lemon-peel surface. Height 3½ inches, has carved stand. *50 00*

492 GLOBULAR JAR, Chinese porcelain, outer surface covered with lavender glaze with crackle beneath, inside of white glaze and brown crackle beneath. Height and diameter 4 x 3½ inches, has carved stand. *55 00*

493 Bottle Vase, ovoid shape with slender neck, Chinese porcelain, yellow glaze, with four-claw dragon, dark green, red and blue, clouds in bright enamels. Height 8 inches.

$45 00

494 Perfume Burner, Chinese porcelain, globular shape on three feet, and with handles, turquoise blue glaze with incised dragons and clouds beneath. Height and diameter 4 x 4½ inches.

42 50

495 Jar shaped Vase, Chinese porcelain, outer surface covered with iridescent yellow green glaze, bold crackle beneath and extending through the porcelain. Height 4½ inches, diameter 3 inches.

235 00

496 Wine Cup, Chinese porcelain, semi-egg-shell texture, pure white glaze, on outer surface in colored enamels mandarin lady, and sprig of blossoms. Seal mark of the Yung-ching period, 1723–1736.

30 00

497 Gourd Vase, Chinese porcelain, double lobe shape, outer surface covered with coral red glaze. Height and diameter 5½ x 4 inches.

92 50

498 Small Bottle Vase, globular body with slender neck, Chinese porcelain, camellia green glaze, with minute crackle beneath. Height 4½ inches, has carved stand.

42 50

499 Beaker Vase, low form, Chinese porcelain of light texture, outer surface of yellow glaze, with incised ornamentation of five-claw dragons, clouds, etc., beneath. Height and diameter 3½ x 3½ inches.

40 00

500 Small Vase, or snuff bottle, cylindrical shape, with low neck, Chinese porcelain of soft paste and crackled, surface covered with a light pink glaze, over which are plum tree in blossom, numerous birds and flowers, painted in various colors, has carved stand.

37 50

501 Vase, jar shape, with head and ring ornaments in relief for handles, Chinese porcelain, outer and inner surface covered with dark lavender color glaze, beneath which is a bold crackle. Height and diameter 5½ x 4½ inches.

85 00

502 Bottle Vase, ovoid body with slender neck spreading at top, Chinese porcelain, mustard yellow crackle glaze, with iridescent lustre. Height and diameter 5½ x 3 inches.

72 50

503 SPRINKLER, Chinese porcelain, globular body with tapering neck, outer surface covered with lavender color glaze. Mark of Kang-he period, 1661–1722. Height $7\frac{3}{4}$ inches, has carved stand. $105 00

504 VASE, ovoid shape, with low spreading neck, Chinese porcelain, semi-egg-shell texture, outer surface covered with brown metallic glaze and ornamented with flowers, magnolia tree in bloom, etc., in various enamels, applied over glaze. Height and diameter $7\frac{3}{4}$ x $3\frac{1}{2}$ inches, has carved stand. 80 00

505 PERFUME JAR AND COVER, Chinese porcelain, decorated with flowers, vines and arabesques in red, blue, green, and other colors, the red and blue being beneath glaze. Height and diameter, exclusive of carved stand, $2\frac{1}{2}$ x 3 inches. 32 50

506 BOTTLE VASE, ovoid body with slender neck, Chinese porcelain, decorated beneath glaze with four-claw dragon and symbolical designs in Nankin blue and brown. Mark of the Ching-hwa period, 1465–1488. Height and diameter 8 x $8\frac{1}{8}$ inches. 62 50

507 PENCIL VASE, cylindrical shape, Chinese porcelain, decorated with garden and interior scenes, Mandarin figures, foliage, etc., in various colors. Height and diameter $4\frac{3}{4}$ x $3\frac{1}{2}$ inches. 35 00

508 SMALL COUPE, globular shape, Chinese porcelain, soft paste and egg-shell texture, decoration of peach tree bearing fruit in green, red and bronze enamels, has carved stand. 27 50

509 BOWL AND COVER, of Chinese vermilion lacquer, fluted design, in representation of chrysanthemum flower, black medallions inside with engraved text. Gold seal mark of the Keen-lung period, 1736–1795. 55 00

510 BOWL AND COVER, of Chinese porcelain, same size and form as the above, and glazed in imitation of same. Gold seal mark of the Keen-lung period, 1736–1795. 40 00

511 PAIR WINE CUPS, Pekin enamel on copper, outer surface of lapis blue enamel with painting of hawthorn blossoms and bamboo branches in red, green, yellow, and white, inner surface of robin's-egg blue enamel. 2 pieces. 20 00

512 BOTTLE VASE, Chinese porcelain, ovoid shape with slender spreading neck, heavy texture, brown metallic glaze. Height and diameter, $7\frac{3}{4}$ x 3 inches. 110 00

$180 00 513 SMALL BOWL, Chinese porcelain, inner and outer surface covered with *clair de lune* glaze with crackle beneath, has carved stand.

From the collection of Comte de Semallé, member of the French Legation at Pekin, 1873–1885.

100 00 514 VASE, Chinese porcelain, shape and design of chrysanthemum flower, stem and birds forming feet, *flambé*, celadon and brown glaze. Height and diameter 3 x 5 inches, has carved stand.

110 00 515 CYLINDRICAL VASE, with spreading base, Chinese stoneware, brown metallic glaze of great iridescence. Height 6¾ inches.

42 50 516 GOURD SHAPED VASE, Chinese porcelain, turquoise and violet glaze. Height and diameter 8 x 3½ inches.

155 00 517 OVOID JAR, Chinese porcelain, with pierced designs of flowers and vines filled in with the glaze, white semi-egg-shell texture. Height and diameter 6½ x 6 inches, has carved teakwood stand and cover.

185 00 518 SMALL BEAKER, with swelling center, Chinese porcelain, heavy texture, outer surface covered with *sang de bœuf* glaze, neck mounted in Oriental silver work. Height and diameter, exclusive of carved wood stand, 6¼ x 3 inches.

140 00 519 CYLINDRICAL TEAPOT, Chinese ivory white porcelain, two lizards in relief forming spout and handle. Height and diameter 6½ x 6 inches.

205 00 520 GOURD VASE, Chinese porcelain, semi-egg-shell texture, imperial yellow glaze with flying bats in coral red, and vine and floral designs in bright colors, gilt bands running around neck. Seal mark of the Keen-lung period, 1736–1795. Height and diameter 7½ x 4½ inches.

From the collection of Comte de Semalle, member of the French Legation at Pekin, 1873–1885.

160 00 521 VASE, ovoid bottle shape with 9 necks, Chinese pottery, *clair de lune* glaze. Height and diameter 5½ x 4 inches, has carved stand.

From the same collection as above.

185 00 522 BOWL ON STAND, Chinese porcelain, egg-shell texture, outer surface of rose *souffle* glaze, "Rose-back." Mark of the Taou-Kwang period, 1821–1851. Height and diameter 3½ x 4 inches.

From the collection of I Wang-ye, a Mandarin Prince.

523 VASE, amphora shape, Chinese porcelain, peach glaze with a verdigris green running over same, producing what is called "Frog-skin" effect. Mark of the Kang-he period, 1661-1722. Has gilt mounting at neck. Height 6¾ inches, diameter 2⅝ inches, has carved stand. *$590 00*

From the same collection as above.

524 BOTTLE VASE, Chinese porcelain, semi-egg-shell texture, pure white glaze, entire outer surface covered with carved designs of basket work, leaf patterns running up neck, and band of Grecian design. Height and diameter 8¼ x 5 inches, has carved teak stand. *135 00*

525 AMPHORA SHAPED VASE, Chinese porcelain, outer surface covered with glaze of the color of "Ashes of Roses." Height and diameter, exclusive of delicately made stand, 6½ x 2 inches. *1,200 00*

From the collection of I Wang-ye, a Mandarin Prince.

526 PAIR VASES, cylindrical shape with low necks, Chinese porcelain, mottled turquoise glaze with decoration of mountain scenery, Chinese figures, etc., painted in black, mounted in gilt bronze. By Houdabine of Paris. Height and diameter 12½ x 4½ inches. 2 pieces. *300 00*

From the collection of Count Kleczkowski of France.

527 CYLINDRICAL VASE, Chinese pottery, gray crackle glaze with splashes of metallic brown and green. Height and diameter 9 x 4 inches. *40 00*

528 OVOID VASE, with flat sides and low neck, Chinese porcelain, turquoise blue glaze, with ornamentation of symbols, clouds and other designs carved in low relief and gilt lizard handles at neck. Engraved seal mark of the Keen-lung period, 1736-1795. Height and diameter 9¼ x 5½ inches, has carved stand. *175 00*

529 OVOID VASE, Chinese porcelain, egg-shell texture, rose pink *soufflé* glaze of the "Rose-back" family. Height and diameter 8 x 3½ inches, which has carved stand. *575 00*

From the collection of Prince I Wang-ye, a Mandarin Prince.

530 VASE, ovoid shape with spreading neck, Chinese porcelain, outer and inner surface covered with brown metallic glaze, bold crackle beneath. Height and diameter, including carved ivory stand, 9½ x 4½ inches. *260 00*

From the collection of Count Kleczkowski of France.

531 **Pair Manchou Vases**, bottle shape, Chinese porcelain, semi-egg-shell texture, perfection of decoration, magnolia tree in blossom, peonies and other flowers, rich plumaged birds, etc., painted in natural colors, inscription and seals in black and red. Height and diameter 8½ x 4½ inches, have carved teak-wood
$830 00 stands of lotus design. 2 pieces.

From the collection of Count Kleczkowski of France.

532 **Pair Mandarin Lanterns**, Chinese porcelain, egg-shell texture, tall hexagonal shape with pierced band of Grecian design around the tops, panels painted in colors of *famille Verte*, Chinese historical and domestic scenes, interior views, mandarin figures, etc. Height and diameter 11½ x 7 inches, have carved wood and plush stands made by Messrs. Herter
1,750 00 Brothers. 2 pieces.

From the Bing collection, Paris.

533 **Vase**, ovoid body with tall neck, Chinese glaze of canary yellow color, ornamentation carved in relief, in various glazes in imitation of lapis lazuli, green jade and tortoise shell, designs of bamboo tree, flowers and flying bird. Height 9½ inches,
725 00 diameter 4½ inches, has carved teak-wood and plush stand.

From the collection of Count Kleczkowski of France.

534 **Vase**, of turquoise blue glaze, globular body with tall neck spreading at top. Engraved mark of Kea-King period,
200 00 1796–1821. Height and diameter 10½ x 6 inches.

535 **Bottle Vase**, globular body with tall slender neck, Chinese glaze of canary yellow color. Engraved mark of Kea-King
180 00 period, 1796–1821. Height 8¾ inches, diameter 4½ inches.

536 **Large Bottle Vase**, Chinese porcelain, egg-shell texture, pure white glaze, with ornamentation carved in low relief, on body of vase floral and vine designs, and at neck leaves running up-
115 00 ward. Height and diameter 12½ x 9 inches, has carved stand.

537 **Vase**, Chinese Pekin lacquer, ovoid shaped body with high neck spreading at top, entire outer surface ornamented with floral, vine, and other designs carved in relief, handle at neck, shape of sceptre of longevity. Height and diameter 11½ x 8 inches,
460 00 has carved teak-wood stand.

ANTIQUE CHINESE PORCELAINS.

MISCELLANEOUS SPECIMENS.

538 BOTTLE VASE, ovoid shape with low neck, Chinese porcelain, wavy red ground with four five-claw dragons engraved in low relief. Mark of Yung-ching period, 1721–1736. Height and diameter 14 x 10 inches. *$225 00*

539 VASE, similar shape to above, Chinese soft paste, pure white glaze with profuse ornamentation, symbols, fruit, flying bats and inscriptions carved in relief. Height and diameter 13 x 8 inches, has carved stand. *120 00*

540 LARGE BEAKER, with swelling center and wide mouth, Chinese porcelain, outer surface covered with *flambé* glaze, showing *sang de bœuf*, celadon, brown, purple and other colors, band of gold lacquer around neck. Mark of the Ching-Hwa period, 1465–1488. Height and diameter 15¼ x 7¾ inches, has carved teak-wood stand. *230 00*

541 BOTTLE VASE, globular shaped body with low wide neck, around body two ribs and four ornaments of heads and rings in relief and glazed with celadon, outer surface of vase covered with celadon glaze, beneath which is a crackle, overlaid with *flambé* glaze of *sang de bœuf* and violet. Height and diameter 11 x 9 inches. *135 00*

542 DISH, circular, deep form, Chinese porcelain, outer and inner surface covered with a mottled purple glaze. Diameter 11 inches. *3,750 00*

543 LARGE PLATE, Chinese porcelain, circular, deep form, with pierced border, front and reverse side covered with a deep rose color *soufflé* glaze. Seal mark of the Kea-King period, 1796–1821. Diameter 16 inches, has finely carved teak-wood stand. *95 00*

544 SMALL DISH, scalloped edge, Chinese porcelain of heavy texture, covered with *flambé* glaze, colors purple and gray. Impressed seal mark, has carved teak stand of lotus design. *62 50*

JAPANESE OBJECTS.

546 SMALL VASE, old Imari porcelain, jar on rock with flowers and
$7 50 plants in relief, decorated in colors.

547 JAR SHAPED VASE, Hirado or Shirato porcelain, pure white glaze and texture, decoration of bamboo branches in blue. Height
100 00 and diameter 7¼ x 6 inches.

548 BOX AND COVER, of bamboo, ornamented in relief with pearl,
17 50 ivory and metals, grape vine, grapes, and ants.

549 BOWL STAND, Japanese white metal, engraved ornamentation of
12 50 vine designs and Tycoon's crests.

550 CYLINDRICAL VASE, outer surface of Soochow or cinnabar lacquer, carved in bold relief, with figures, foliage, mountain
120 00 scenery, etc. Height and diameter 5 x 5¼ inches.

551 INCENSE BURNER, of Japanese bronze gilt, shape of temple drum on pedestal, chicken cock surmounting cover, engraved ornamentation of crests, birds, diaper patterns, flowers, etc. Height
47 50 9½ inches.

552 ORNAMENTAL PIECE, Dog Foo, of Shirato porcelain, pure white
37 50 texture. Height and diameter 9 x 11 inches.

553 INCENSE BURNER, with cover, modern Satsuma ware, square shape with scroll handles, supported by figures of three Japanese boys, cover surmounted by Dog Foo, decoration of figures of Japanese warriors, vase of flowers, etc., painted in colors, groundwork of crests, lattice designs, etc., in various enamels
17 50 and gold. Height and diameter 8½ x 6 inches.

554 PLAQUE, circular shape, black lacquer, ornamentation of branch of chestnut tree and burrs. Seal of artist in gold. Diameter
22 50 12 inches.

555 BOX AND COVER, of ivory, tall ovoid shape, outer surface ornamented with flowers, birds, and insects in gold lacquer, pearl,
100 00 coral and ivory. Height and diameter 5½ x 3½ inches.

556 TEA JAR, Japanese earthenware, outer surface of "Raindrops"
50 00 glaze. Height and diameter 4¾ x 4½ inches.

557 FIRE BOWL, Sedji ware, circular shape, on three feet, ornamentation of vine design carved in relief beneath celadon glaze, openwork cover of silver, design of chrysanthemum flowers, Mikado's private crest, etc. Height and diameter 5½ x 5½ inches. *$50 00*

558 BOWL STAND, black and avanturine lacquer, with ornamentation of flowers and vines in green, red and gold lacquer. *17 50*

559 PERFUME BURNER, Japanese white metal, globular shape with engraved designs of vines and flowers, pierced or openwork cover. Height and diameter 3½ x 3½ inches. *27 50*

560 TEA JAR, with cover, Satsuma ware, of creamy white texture, in two medallions are figures of Daimio lady and children, vase of flowers, etc., intervening space covered with diaper arabesques and other designs embossed in various colors and gold. Height and diameter 4 x 3½ inches. *30 00*

561 PERFUME BURNER, of Awata ware, in medallions are painted over one hundred minute figures of Japanese children playing games, etc., enamel fish beneath embossed net work, other portions ornamented with embossed designs. Height and diameter 4 x 3½ inches. *27 50*

562 PERFUME JAR AND COVER, modern Satsuma ware, ovoid shape, outer surface ornamented with figures of Japanese children at play, painted in colors and gold in various shaped panels, arabesques, diaper and floral designs embossed in gold and enamels, gilt Dog Foo surmounting cover. Height and diameter 5 x 3 inches. *40 00*

CABINET OBJECTS

IN JAPANESE SILVER, GOLD LACQUER, OLD SATSUMA AND ROCK CRYSTAL.

563 BOX AND COVER, oblong shape, Japanese old lacquer, outer and inner surface of avanturine lacquer, on outside ornamentation of cherry trees in blossom and pine tree in gold lacquer and in relief. Height and diameter 3¼ x 5 inches. *60 00*

564 PERFUME BOX, made of an egg-shell, outer surface ornamented with chrysanthemum flowers and grasses in gold lacquer, lining of gold lac. *25 00*

565 Box and Cover, of solid silver, square shape with feet at corners and scroll handles, profusely ornamented on the outer surface with hand-chased designs of chrysanthemum flowers, on cover sprig of same flowers in relief, modern Japanese specimen,
$220 00 signed by artist. 4¼ x 6½ inches.

566 Bottle Vase, globular shaped body of fluted design, with long neck, old Satsuma ware of exceedingly fine creamy white texture, on body of vase painted in green, red, dark blue and gold, three Japanese hats, around top of neck neat band in blue enamel, gold and crimson. Height and diameter 7¾ x 4½ inches, has stand of hard wood, which bears the crest of the
325 00 Prince of Kaga.

From the collection of the Prince of Kaga, presented by the Prince to a Japanese naval officer about 1820, from whose family it was obtained by Mr. R. Austin Robertson, of the American Art Association.

567 Crayfish, in Japanese bronze, exact reproduction, with mov-
150 00 able joints, etc., has plush stand.

568 Box, of gold lacquer, made in shape of Japanese hut, the cover forming roof, box has two compartments, outer surface is of pure gold lacquer and ornamented with mountain scenery, coolies cultivating rice, birds, foliage, huts, etc., in low relief; inside of lid in round medallion figure of Japanese children formed in a ring, inner surface of avanturine lacquer, an old
205 00 specimen. Height and width 5½ x 5½ inches.

569 Rock Crystal Ball and Silver Stand, ball of exceeding purity 4½ inches in diameter, silver stand of diamond shape on four slender legs with base. Cup or holder for ball, represents clouds through which is penetrating a gold dragon, stand engraved and ornamented in relief with the private or palace seal of the Mikado and other designs. Height and
1,725 00 diameter of stand 12 x 9 inches, gold seal of maker beneath.

570 Drum Shaped Box, of pure gold lacquer, cover surmounted with chicken cock of same material, the shell of drum decorated in imitation of the veins of the wood, on each end dragon crests in low relief, box lined with silver. Height and diameter
200 00 9 x 5½ inches.

571 PERFUME JAR, of solid gold, silver and Shibu-ichi, on side panels in relief in gold, silver and Shakudo, figure of Japanese with sack into which mice with coin in their mouths are running, the subject a Japanese fable; on ends etched designs of birds, vines, etc., borders of diaper patterns and arabesques inlaid, on bottom of jar seal of maker, and floral designs inlaid in gold and silver on Shibu-ichi. Height and diameter $4\frac{1}{2}$ x $2\frac{3}{4}$ inches. *$235 00*

572 SAUCER, Japanese egg-shell porcelain, decorated with colored enamels, pine tree, flowering plants, birds, etc., has carved teak-wood stand. *7 50*

573 PERFUME HOLDER, button shape, avanturine lacquer with bust of Buddhist priest in low relief. *7 50*

574 PERFUME BOX, of gold and avanturine lacquer, shape of butterfly. *25 00*

575 BOWL, old Satsuma ware, light brown crackled texture, outer surface covered with an ornamentation of chrysanthemum flowers, painted in red, dark blue, and light green enamels and gold, has metal rim. Height and diameter 3 x $4\frac{1}{2}$ inches. *75 00*

576 PERFUME BOX, of old avanturine lacquer, horse-shoe shape on three slender feet, lattice work ornamentation over which is cherry tree in blossom, in gold and silver lacquer. Height $2\frac{5}{8}$ inches, has three compartments. *80 00*

577 BUTTERFLY BOX, old gold and avanturine lacquer, lid delicately penciled. Height and diameter $1\frac{1}{2}$ x 4 inches. *70 00*

578 GOURD VASE, old Satsuma ware, creamy white crackled texture, double lobe ornamented with chrysanthemum flowers, vines, and the Mikado's private crests in red, green, dark blue and gold. Height and diameter $7\frac{1}{2}$ x 5 inches, has carved teak-wood stand. *280 00*

579 SQUARE BOX AND COVER, old avanturine lacquer, outer surface covered with butterflies, arabesques and other designs in gold and other lacquer in low relief. Height and diameter $3\frac{1}{2}$ x $3\frac{1}{2}$ inches. *55 00*

580 TOBACCO POUCH, made in design of a mask carved in ivory, netsuke of same material, a grotesque mask, and a group of ivory masks for slide, cash pouch of Japanese chintz attached. *85 00*

581 Bowl, old Satsuma ware, soft creamy white texture, on outer surface in three panels dogs Foo in gold, intervening space of crimson glaze, with ornamentation of flowers and vines in light blue, green and gold, Grecian border around top in same
$75 00 colors. Height and diameter $3\frac{3}{4}$ x 4 inches.

582 Miniature Cabinet, of irregular shape, black lacquer with gold
185 00 crest and vine decoration, silver mountings.

583 Perfume Box, old avanturine lacquer, lid ornamented with owl
25 00 on rock, flowers, etc.

584 Cup and Saucer, old Chinese porcelain, decorated with blue beneath glaze, cup has outside covering of pierced work in
42 50 white, border of saucer also pierced.

585 Cylindrical Vasè, of carved soapstone, in two panels, are Chinese landscape, mountain and water scenes in relief, dragon
90 00 handles. Height and diameter 9 x 6 inches.

586 Small Vase, Chinese glaze, red with yellow streaks and clouds,
92 50 ovoid shape. Height and diameter 6 x 4 inches.

587 Wine or Oil Vessel, old Persian bronze, *repoussé* and carved ornamentation of floral designs, animals, etc., silver lizard
65 00 forming handle.

588 Pair Flower Pots, Chinese porcelain, bamboo design, and celadon glaze, band running around with inscription in blue
70 00 beneath glaze. Height and diameter 8 x 10 inches. 2 pieces.

JAPANESE IVORY CARVINGS.

589 Group of Three Figures, the central one being a female deity, on the right a Mandarin in an imperial robe seated on a treasure chest, to the left a man servant in kneeling posture holding a turtle with tail of long hair, the Japanese symbol of longevity, each figure being carved from the solid piece and showing high order of workmanship, the group is sold with a stand of Japanese hard wood, carved and ornamented with gold lacquer, the several sizes of figures are 9 x 4, 6 x 4 and 4 x $4\frac{1}{2}$
1,100 00 inches.

590 SACRED ELEPHANT, surrounded by group of five children playing on musical instruments, all ornamented with gold lacquer, and inlaid with mother of pearl, coral, malachite and various metals. Height 6 inches, width 4½ inches. *$360 00*

591 GROUP OF THREE FIGURES, Mandarin lady, child, and priest, the latter kneeling and performing ceremonies over a skull in the foreground. A Japanese historical subject, mounted on black lacquer stand, ornamented with gold, outside measurement of all 7 x 7 x 4 inches. *100 00*

592 —— ANOTHER GROUP, companion to the above, figures of Japanese children making offering of fruit to female deity, outside measure of stand and figures 7 x 7 x 4 inches. *130 00*

593 GROUP OF TWO FIGURES, Japanese wood-cutter with load of fagots on his back, child presenting him with a peach. Height 7 inches, width 3½ inches. *105 00*

594 MINIATURE SHINTO SHRINE, with silver and gold figure of the happy rice merchant. Japanese Symbol of Prosperity. Height and diameter 5 x 2½ inches. *77 50*

595 GROUP OF MONKEYS. Height and width 4 x 4 inches. *80 00*

596 COVERED VASE, cylindrical shape, being section of a tusk. On vase is carved in relief a Japanese mythological subject, figure of priests burning incense, through the clouds of smoke arising is seen a golden dragon, on other portions of vase pine tree, rocks, etc., surmounting cover, figure of Buddhist priest with scroll and incense burner, mounting of carved wood. Height and diameter of all 9 x 4 inches. *102 50*

597 GROUP, five Japanese warriors in armor and armed with spears, lances, swords, and battle axe. Height and diameter 5¼ x 4 inches. *180 00*

598 VASE, made from section of tusk, ornamented in relief with gold lacquer, pearl and ivory, figure of Daimio lady, plants, flowers and insects, mounted in carved wood. Height and diameter, 8 x 4 inches. *125 00*

599 LARGE GROUP of five figures, Japanese mythological subject, robbers attempting to steal a golden shrine or temple piece frightened by goblins. Height and diameter 6 x 4½ inches. *82 50*

600 GROUP, three figures, the long-legged and long-armed fishermen
$65 00 with devil fish. Height 4 inches.

601 SMALL GROUP, three skeletons quarreling, "the fight of death."
50 00 Height 3 inches.

17 50 602 —— Another, Japanese playing with monkey. Height 2 inches.

42 50 603 —— Another, witch and temple bell. Height 2 inches.

15 00 604 —— Another, witch fighting a demon.

15 00 605 —— Another, two puppies.

606 —— Another, larger, equestrian figure crossing bridge, Japanese presenting an offering, serpent, etc., a Japanese historical sub-
42 50 ject. Height 3 inches.

12 50 607 —— Another, equestrian figure.

608 LARGE CARVING, Japanese with sack on his back made of a large lotus leaf and loaded with live toads of various sizes. Height
105 00 5 inches.

609 ORNAMENT OR VASE STAND, carved in relief and with pierced
25 00 designs.

22 50 610 SMALL CARVING, small monkey carrying large peach.

611 SMALL VASE, or ornament, ornamented in relief with pearl lac-
15 00 quer, etc.

612 SMALL CARVING, designs of lotus plant and gourd vines intertwined, inside a gourd shaped ornament, which when opened shows intricately carved landscape views, figures, etc. Height
95 00 and diameter $2\frac{1}{2}$ x $1\frac{1}{2}$ inches.

22 50 613 NETSUKE, two quail on an old bamboo hat.

15 00 614 —— Another, puppy playing with shell.

10 00 615 —— Another, mask, face of Japanese girl.

12 50 616 —— Another, group of masks and heads.

17 50 617 —— Another, priest punishing demon.

22 50 618 —— Another, cat stung by a dragon-fly.

12 50 619 —— Another, group of horses.

12 50 620 —— Another, group of masks.

15 00 621 —— Another, demons being stoned.

622 —— Another, Japanese boy with mask. *$10 00*

623 —— Another, Japanese children teasing a mouse. *27 50*

624 —— Another, sacred elephant, inlaid ornamentation of pearl, coral, and metals. *20 00*

625 —— Another, mask. *12 50*

626 —— Another, dog Foo. *12 50*

627 —— Another, chicken cock and hen. *17 50*

628 —— Another, two demons quarreling. *15 00*

629 —— Another, Japanese with gourd from which is issuing a horse, mythological subject. *12 50*

630 —— Another, two monkeys. *17 50*

631 —— Another, quail on rice head. *37 50*

632 —— Another, two masks, grotesque. *20 00*

633 —— Another, grotesque figure with movable head. *20 00*

CARVINGS IN WOOD.

634 Netsuke Mask, carved in wood, face of young Japanese girl. *7 50*

635 —— Another, two masks, carved in wood. *7 50*

636 Small Group, two turtles. *12 50*

637 Large Group, turtle of longevity and two small turtles. *30 00*

638 Incense Burner, tall form, incense burner of globular shape supported by three tall slender legs, around each is a dragon encircling, and between them a ball of rock crystal, in bold relief on cover, figure of dog Foo with ball in his mouth, the whole mounted on a pedestal in which is inlaid a ring of white jade stone, the ornamentation besides being carved is of inlaid work in ivory, coral, and gold lacquer. Height 18 inches, diameter 5 inches. *235 00*

639 Ornamental Piece, Chinese figure reclining, jar and stump of tree forming vase, all mounted on stand. Height and diameter 9 x 7 inches. *15 00*

A COLLECTION OF SNUFF BOTTLES.

640 COLLECTION OF ORIENTAL SNUFF BOTTLES—Two hundred and twenty-one specimens in carved jade stone, agate, rock crystal, lapis-lazuli, carved lacquer, cloisonné enamel, Chinese glazes, porcelains, metal work, etc., etc.; all are of rare quality and many of unique shape. The collection will be sold as a whole, including two exceedingly fine rosewood cabinets, with carved and applied ornamentation, made to order from special designs by Messrs. Herter Brothers.

$4,700 00

The above includes a collection of Snuff Bottles formerly the property of Comte de Semalle, member of the French Legation at Pekin, 1873–1885, and as now formed the collection is acknowledged by connoisseurs to be the most complete and finest in the country.

ART IN STERLING SILVER

SALE WEDNESDAY AFTERNOON, MAR. 10,

AT 2.30 O'CLOCK.

AT THE AMERICAN ART GALLERIES.

STERLING SILVER WARE.

WITH FEW EXCEPTIONS MADE TO ORDER BY MESSRS. TIFFANY & CO.

641 INK STAND, design of a weight. *$17 50*

642 DESK TABLET, with pencil and eraser attached. *22 50*

643 SPOON, Oriental design, gold lined, hand chased and applied ornamentation on handle. *12 50*

644 —— Another, smaller, similar pattern. *7 50*

645 PAIR BOTTLE STANDS, Oriental design, oxidized finish. *25 00*

646 BUREAU SET, puff-box, and pair of cologne bottles, Oriental design, hand chased, and relief ornaments, tall slender shape. *75 00*

647 HANGING VASE, Oriental design, hammered cylindrical shape, with gourd vine, gourds, and insects in relief. *45 00*

648 BOWL, hammered design and oxidized, gold lined. *32 50*

649 OLIVE TRAY, oblong shape, Oriental design, vine and insects in relief. *25 00*

650 HAND MIRROR, mountings of hammered silver, *repoussé* and chased ornamentation. *37 50*

651 SET INDIVIDUAL SALTS AND SPOONS, shell designs, gold lined, have fabric case. 24 pieces. *120 00*

652 INDIVIDUAL PEPPERS, bull-dogs and Pugs, oxidized finish. 4 pieces. *40 00*

653 TETE-A-TETE SET, Oriental design, "Niello" and copper inlaid, comprises teapot, sugar bowl, creamer and bowl. *120 00*

654 COMPOTE, peacock design, *repoussé* and hand-chased ornamen-
$660 00 tation. 4 pieces.

655 PAIR CANDLESTICKS, Oriental design, tall form, hammered finish, with ornamentation of the Mikado's crest in relief in copper
55 00 and gold. 2 pieces.

10 00 656 MATCH STAND, to match above.

657 OVAL TRAY, on feet, bamboo border, hand chased, ornamenta-
50 00 tion of chrysanthemum flowers, blossoms, bird, etc.

658 WINE CARRIAGE, gold lined, *repoussé* ornamentation, ram's head
140 00 handle.

659 SET, teapot, sugar-bowl, creamer and bowl, Oriental design,
160 00 *repoussé* ornamentation of ferns and flowers.

75 00 660 CHOCOLATE POT, to match above set.

80 00 661 BLACK COFFEE POT, to match above.

662 VASE, hammered pattern, with Japanese designs of fish, crab,
30 00 grasses, etc., in applied metals, gold lined.

663 CREAM PITCHER, Oriental design, relief ornaments of grasses,
35 00 birds, etc.

664 COLOGNE BOTTLE, Oriental design, gourds, vine and snail in
40 00 relief, in various metals.

665 BRUSH TRAY, Japanese hammered design, etched and relief,
20 00 ornamentation, fish, water-plants, etc.

666 INDIVIDUAL SET, salt, pepper and mustard, on tray, *repoussé*
57 50 and chased ornamentation.

667 INDIVIDUAL PEPPERS, Oriental design, oxidized finish, fish and
40 00 insects in applied metals. 4 pieces.

668 ANTIQUE PLAQUE, oval shape, *repoussé* ornamentation, "Music
100 00 and Poetry."

669 INDIVIDUAL SALT STANDS AND SPOONS, Japanese shell pattern,
60 00 gold lined, have fabric cases. 12 pieces.

670 LIQUEUR FLAGONS, Oriental design, chased, and *repoussé* orna-
200 00 mentation, bands of "Moku-me." 4 pieces.

155 00 671 CLARET TANKARD, very fine *repoussé* chased figures and vines.

672 ROUND TRAY, on feet, *repoussé* ornamentation, gold gilt, diam-
62 50 ater 12 inches.

673 PAIR WINE COOLERS, tub shaped, with ring handles. 2 pieces. *$160 00*

674 VASE, Oriental design, ornamented in relief with various metals. *115 00*

675 PAIR CANDLESTICKS, tall form, English pattern. 2 pieces. *100 00*

676 ENGLISH QUEEN'S COIN TANKARD, bears the inscription, "This Tankard, weighing oz. 33-10, was made to receive 43 coins of England's Queen's." *675 00*

677 BUREAU SET, Oriental design, puff box and two cologne bottles, hammered surface, with flowering plants, insects, etc., in applied metals. *112 50*

678 TOILET CUP, Japanese design, gold lined, relief ornamentation of gourds, vines and insects. *20 00*

679 TEA JAR, made in imitation of Japanese metal work, known as "Moku-me," or "Veins of the wood," has carved ivory group surmounting cover. *77 50*

680 PAIR PUFF BOXES, Oriental design, hammered surface with relief ornamentation of insects, flowers, etc., in various metals. 2 pieces. *50 00*

681 VASE, hammered design. *22 50*

682 ANTIQUE KETTLE, *repoussé* chased ornamentation, with stand and lamp. *155 00*

683 TANKARD, to match above. *62 50*

684 SALAD DISH, oval shape, satin finish, with relief ornaments and gold gilt lined. *137 50*

685 PAIR OVAL VEGETABLE DISHES, with covers, satin finish, flat chased and parcel-gilt ornamentation. 2 pieces. *140 00*

686 OVAL ENTRÉE DISH, to match above. *100 00*

687 PAIR ROUND VEGETABLE DISHES, with covers, to match the above. 2 pieces. *150 00*

688 PAIR GRAVY BOATS, to match the above. 2 pieces *80 00*

689 CLARET JUG, shape of duck, with crystal glass body and handle. *87 50*

690 LIQUEUR FLAGON, Oriental design, gourd shape, hammered surface, with relief ornamentation of vines and insects in various metals and etched. *62 50*

691 VASE, tall cylindrical shape, Japanese design, *repoussé*, inlaid and applied ornamentation, bears the palace or private crest of the Mikado. Height and diameter 11½ x 4⅓ inches. *$100 00*

105 00 692 SQUARE TRAY, on feet, *repoussé* chased border, 12 x 12 inches.

693 BLACK COFFEE POT, Oriental design, chrysanthemum and other flowers in very best style of *repoussé* chasing, under cut. *290 00*

694 CREAMER AND SUGAR BOWL, to match the above, gold lined. 2 pieces. *285 00*

695 ENTRÉE OR TERRAPIN DISH, Oriental design, hammered and water finished, with applied ornaments of leaves, insects, etc. *175 00*

696 CLARET JUG, Oriental design, hammered finish, with applied ornamentation of grape vine in bearing. *115 00*

697 ANTIQUE PLAQUE, circular form, with scalloped edge, *répousse* ornamentation, biblical subject in centre: "Noah entering the Ark." Diameter 15⅓ inches. *120 00*

698 INDIVIDUAL BUTTER PLATES, gold finished, have case. 18 pieces. *135 00*

37 50 699 INDIVIDUAL PEPPERS, hand chased ornamentation. 3 pieces.

700 CENTRE PIECE, gold lined, figures and shields in relief, very heavy. 24 x 15 x 8 inches. *247 00*

27 50 701 SPICE MILL, chased and applied ornamentation.

702 EASEL MIRROR, mounted in *repoussé* silver and other metals, hammered finish and Japanese designs in relief. *90 00*

703 OLD ENGLISH COASTERS, grape-vine pattern borders, engraved royal crest. Made by Hunt & Roskell, London. 4 pieces. *410 00*

132 50 704 CLARET JUG, shape of walrus, crystal glass body.

705 WINE COOLER, Grecian pattern, *repoussé* chased ornamentation, straight shape on four feet, with side handles. *187 50*

706 ANTIQUE PLAQUE, circular shape, *repoussé* ornamentation, of battle scene. Diameter 16½ inches. *95 00*

707 LARGE VASE, tall cylindrical shape, Oriental design, hammered finish, *repoussé* ornamentation of flowering plant, gold gilt. Height and diameter 13½ x 5½ inches. *140 00*

708 TANKARD, body made of a section of an ivory tusk, mountings of Japanese designs hand chased, boldly modelled Dragon forming handle, bottom of heavy crystal glass. *300 00*

709 TANKARD, of Indian workmanship, ornamented with hunting scenes in bold *repoussé*. *$120 00*

710 TEA CANISTER, illustrating the Japanese difficult workmanship in metals of "Moku-me" or "veins of the wood," ivory Ki-lin surmounting cover, gold lined. *62 50*

711 CENTRE DISH, for flowers or fruit, very elaborate chrysanthemum pattern, *repoussé* chased, ball feet, gold gilt lined. Length 26 inches, width 16 inches, height 7 inches. *720 00*

712 LARGE PLATEAU, for above, bevelled mirror with chrysanthemum pattern mountings in *repoussé* chased. Length and width 26½ x 18 inches. *365 00*

713 EPERGNE WITH DISH, the dish alone can be used as a fish dish, has chrysanthemum pattern border, stand of original design by Tiffany & Co. Height and width of all, 12¾ x 30 inches. *370 00*

714 ROAST BEEF DISH, with well, heavy chrysanthemum pattern border and feet. 24 x 17 inches. *190 00*

715 MEAT DISH, to match. 22 x 15½ inches. *155 00*

716 —— Another. 20 x 14 inches. *145 00*

717 —— Another. 18 x 13 inches. *130 00*

718 —— Another. 16 x 11½ inches. *135 00*

719 PAIR ROUND DISHES, to match. Diameter, 13 inches. 2 pieces. *290 00*

720 ENTRÉE DISHES, to match, oval shape with handles. 16½ x 9. 2 pieces. *200 00*

721 COMPOTE DISHES, to match above. 4 pieces. *360 00*

722 SWEET-MEAT TRAYS, to match. 4 pieces. *160 00*

723 SALT-STANDS, to match. 4 pieces. *110 00*

724 ANTIQUE PLAQUE, oval shape, *repoussé* ornamentation, classical subject. 15½ x 11½ inches. *105 00*

725 TEA SERVICE, Oriental designs in the very best style of *repoussé* chased under cut, ornamentation of chrysanthemum, lotus, and other flowers, pierced borders. Comprises tea-pot, black coffee-pot, covered sugar bowl, creamer, and bowl. *2 800 00*

726 HOT WATER KETTLE, to match the above. *600 00*

727 CHOCOLATE CUPS AND SAUCERS, Japanese design, hammered and water finish, ornamentation of vine and insects in applied
$120 00 metals. 6 pieces.

728 FINGER BOWLS, best style of *repoussé* chased ornamentation,
990 00 pierced borders, gold finished. 18 pieces.

990 00 729 PLATES, to match above. 18 pieces.

730 FRAME, for dish as centre piece, Egyptian design of ornamenta-
90 00 tion. Diameter 10 inches.

731 COMPOTE DISHES, *repoussé* chased ornamentation, of chrysanthemum flowers, pierced medallions on standards, gold lined.
320 00 4 pieces.

732 ELABORATE CENTRE PIECE, with large bowl and six branches, and small dishes which are removable, made from original designs, *repoussé* and chased ornamentation, figures in bold relief, extreme outside measurement, 48 x 21 inches, by 17 inches
825 00 high.

733 EWER AND BASIN, Oriental design, *repoussé* chased ornamenta-
210 00 tion of birds, branches, etc.

145 00 734 JAR, with cover and top handle, to match above.

735 PAIR CANDELABRA, for 12 lights each, old English *repoussé* pat-
820 00 tern. Height 28 inches. 2 pieces.

736 PAIR CANDELABRA, for 9 lights each, similar pattern as above, but different arrangement of branches. Height 21 inches.
345 00 2 pieces.

737 SMALL TRAY, round shape on ball feet, Japanese pattern, mixture of various metals with the silver, ornamentation of two flying birds in gold, and silver moon beneath cloud effect.
72 50 Height 9 inches.

738 TEASPOONS, Oriental pattern, hammered handles with applied
33 00 ornaments. 6 pieces.

739 DESSERT SPOONS, Oriental pattern, each spoon being of dif-
168 00 ferent design, gold gilt bowls. 24 pieces.

740 DESSERT KNIVES, chased and Parcel-Gilt ornamentation.
180 00 24 pieces.

87 50 741 ANTIQUE SPOON, bold *repoussé* and gold gilt ornamentation.

742 RUSSIAN AFTER-DINNER COFFEE SPOONS, from the royal factory, St. Petersburg, Etruscan and enamelled jeweled ornamentation, gold finish, have case. 12 pieces. *$330 00*

743 SUGAR TONGS, to match above, design of stork, from same factory. *62 50*

744 AFTER-DINNER COFFEE SPOONS, same make and pattern as above. 12 pieces. *210 00*

745 AFTER-DINNER COFFEE SPOONS, "Moku-me" handles, gourd shape gold gilt bowls. 18 pieces. *144 00*

746 GAME KNIVES, steel blades of scimeter shape, handles of silver in the best style of *repoussé* chased under cut. 12 pieces. *240 00*

747 GAME FORKS, to match the above. 12 pieces. *240 00*

748 SCONCES, or wall candlesticks, bold *repoussé* pattern. 4 pieces. *180 00*

749 AFTER-DINNER COFFEE CUPS AND SAUCERS, "Moku-me" or "Veins of the wood" design. 18 pieces. *450 00*

750 LIQUEUR CUPS, Oriental designs, match liqueur flagons, No. 670. 18 pieces. *180 00*

751 PAIR ELABORATE CANDELABRA, for 6 lights each, ornamentation of scenes illustrating the life of the North American Indian, oxidized finish. Height 32 inches, spreading 17 inches. 2 pieces. *3,500 00*

The above made to order by Messrs. Tiffany & Co. from designs, carefully studied from Catlin's North American Indian Portfolio, figures modelled by Augustus St. Gaudens.

752 TABLE KNIVES, Rodgers & Sons' blades, handles in *repoussé* chased silver, Olympian pattern. 30 pieces. *315 00*

753 —— Same. 30 pieces. *270 00*

754 TABLE FORKS, to match, very heavy and bold ornamentation. 30 pieces. *330 00*

755 —— Same. 30 pieces. *330 00*

756 TABLE SPOONS, to match. 24 pieces. *180 00*

757 DESSERT KNIVES, to match above, Rodgers & Sons' blades. 30 pieces. *195 00*

758 —— Same. 30 pieces. *180 00*

759 DESSERT FORKS, to match. 30 pieces. *135 00*

Price	No.	Description	Pieces
$120 00	760	DESSERT FORKS, to match.	30 pieces.
96 00	761	DESSERT SPOONS, to match.	24 pieces.
144 00	762	TEASPOONS, to match.	48 pieces.
75 00	763	SERVING SPOONS, to match.	6 pieces.
52 00	764	GRAVY SPOONS, to match.	2 pieces.
24 00	765	SOUP LADLE, to match.	
20 00	766	OYSTER LADLE, to match.	
20 00	767	GRAVY LADLES, to match.	2 pieces.
30 00	768	ASPARAGUS TONGS, to match.	
72 00	769	FISH KNIVES, to match.	18 pieces.
72 00	770	FISH FORKS, to match.	18 pieces.
96 00	771	OYSTER FORKS, to match.	24 pieces.
99 00	772	NUT PICKS, to match.	18 pieces.
108 00	773	ICE CREAM FORKS, to match, gold finish.	24 pieces.
40 00	774	ICE CREAM SERVING KNIVES, to match.	2 pieces.
12 50	775	ICE TONGS, to match.	
25 00	776	SALAD SPOON AND FORK, to match.	2 pieces.
35 00	777	FISH SERVING KNIVES, to match.	2 pieces.
25 00	778	FISH SERVING FORKS, to match.	2 pieces.
99 00	779	FRUIT KNIVES, to match, gold finish blades.	18 pieces.
14 00	780	WAFFLE SERVER, to match.	
35 00	781	SALAD FORK AND SPOON, to match.	2 pieces.
10 00	782	SUGAR TONGS, to match.	
27 00	783	INDIVIDUAL SUGAR TONGS, to match	6 pieces.
6 00	784	SALT SPOONS, to match.	4 pieces.

785 ANTIQUE PLAQUE, round deep form, *repoussé* chased ornamentation in the best style. Diameter 16 inches. *100 00*

786 LARGE WINE COOLER, Oriental design, oxidize finish and gold gilt lined, bold *repoussé* ornamentation of birds, leaves, bamboo branches, etc., oblong shape with scalloped edge. Height and width 8¾ x 23 inches. *200 00*

787 PAIR CANDELABRA, for 9 lights each. Height 30 inches, branches spreading 18 inches. 2 pieces. *$770 00*

788 PAIR VERY ELABORATE CANDELABRA of Roman design, for 20 lights each, with tall pedestals, bold chased ornamentation in the very best style. Extreme outside measurement of candelabra and pedestal 68 x 23 inches, can be used with or without pedestals. 2 pieces. *8,100 00*

The above masterpieces of the silversmith's art were made to order from original designs by Messrs. Tiffany & Company, and are the most important specimens of their class in this country.

789 LARGE GROUP, "The Buffalo Hunt," by R. Monti, 1873, has bronze and black marble base. Extreme measurement of all 23 x 25 x 16 inches. *800 00*

790 CARVED EBONIZED PEDESTAL for the above, made by Messrs. Herter Brothers. *55 00*

791 LAMP, of sterling silver and other metals, made from original design by the Gorham Company. Cornucopia supported by a griffin, illuminated glass globe. *240 00*

792 LARGE PLAQUE, sterling silver, "Niello" and copper inlaid, subject: "Lequel Des Deux, Escouteray—Je." Diameter 20 inches. *300 00*

793 PLAQUE, *repoussé* silver medallion, "Night," border of "Niello" and copper inlaid work. Diameter 13½ inches. *175 00*

794 —— Another, with scalloped edge, *repoussé* silver medallion, "Hen and chickens," border of various metals with applied ornaments. Diameter 10½ inches. *150 00*

795 —— Another, oval shape, *repoussé* and oxidized silver medallion, "A North American Indian," "Niello" and copper border with applied ornaments. 15 x 19¾ inches. *170 00*

EUROPEAN CERAMICS

CRYSTALS AND ENAMELS

SALE THURSDAY AFTERNOON, MARCH 11,

BEGINNING AT 2.30 O'CLOCK.

AT THE AMERICAN ART GALLERIES.

EUROPEAN CERAMICS.

ROYAL WORCESTER.

796 PAIR SMALL VASES, shape of hand grenade, yellow glaze with sprigs of flowers painted in colors, gold gilt feet, handles and neck. 2 pieces. *$10 00*

797 VASE, bamboo design, ivory white glaze. Height 8 inches. *4 00*

798 PAIR STATUETTES, decorated in gold and colors. Height 6 inches. 2 pieces. *22 00*

799 SMALL VASE, design of bag tied with cord and tassel, ivory white glaze with applied ornamentation in gold. *7 00*

800 PAIR SMALL BOTTLES, Etruscan design, imperial yellow glaze, with leaves and blossoms in crimson and embossed gold. 2 pieces. *34 00*

801 VASE, with cover, antique shape, pierced and other ornamentation in gold matte, platina and enamels. Height 8½ inches. *52 50*

802 VASE, Japanese design, with monkey in bold relief, ivory white finish with relief ornamentation of storks in gold matte and colors. Height 7½ inches. *25 00*

803 EWER, Persian design, decoration of flowers, etc., in enamels and gold matte, handle spout and stopper of chocolate glaze decorated with gold. Height 9½ inches. *55 00*

804 PAIR SMALL VASES, shape of hand grenade, canary yellow glaze with ornamentation of Japanese crests, fan and other designs in bright colors and gold. 2 pieces. *30 00*

805 CUP AND SAUCER, egg-shell texture and ivory finish, ornamented
$37 50 with jeweled and pierced designs.

806 SMALL VASE, design of bag .tied with cord and tassels, ivory
9 00 finish with rich plumaged bird, flowers, etc., painted in colors.

807 OVOID VASE, Japanese design, ornamentation of flying stork, butterflies, cherry branch and blossoms, etc., in embossed gold and
17 50 platina. Height 9½ inches.

808 PAIR STATUETTES, 'Fisher Boy' and "Young Huntsman,"
25 00 decorated in colors. 2 pieces.

809 PAIR VASES, flat beaker shape, with handles at necks, Japanese design, ivory finish, semi-egg-shell texture, decorated with figures of monkeys, frogs, etc., in applied gold and colors.
85 00 Height 10 inches. 2 pieces.

810 JAR AND COVER, Persian design, ornamented with pierced and
47 50 incised designs in turquoise and crimson enamels and gold.

811 PAIR PITCHER VASES, Etruscan design, ornamentation of various birds and flowers painted in delicate colors, relieved by
150 00 gold. Height 11 inches. 2 pieces.

812 TEA POT, tall ovoid shape, with pierced band at neck, decorated with flowers, vines and other designs in gold matte
80 00 and enamels.

813 CHALICE SHAPE VASE, pierced and jeweled ornamentation,
67 50 ivory texture. Height 10 inches.

814 PAIR CYLINDRICAL VASES, Egyptian design, relief and painted
65 00 ornamentation in gold matte and enamels. 2 pieces.

815 LAMP SHADE, for night lamp, shape of cat, turquoise blue glaze,
27 50 with stand in imitation of bronze.

816 PAIR VASES, Japanese design, made in imitation of carved ivory tusks, ornamented in relief with serpents, frogs, pine
95 00 trees, etc. Height 8 inches. 2 pieces.

817 PAIR BOTTLE VASES, globular body with tall, slender necks, ornamented with pierced and incised design, and decorated with enamels and gold matte. Height and diameter 11 x 6 inches.
165 00 2 pieces.

818 ORNAMENTAL PIECE, Japanese Dog Foo, opalescent green and
42 50 gold glaze. 11 x 8 inches.

819 PAIR SMALL VASES, of antique shape. Serpent handles extending over and into mouth of vase, decorated with gold and silver. 2 pieces. $60 00

820 LARGE CENTRE PIECE, for flowers, antique shape with four handles, decoration of flowers, vines, dragons and other designs in various colors and gold. Height and diameter 6 x 12 inches. 62 50

821 PAIR BOTTLE VASES, globular shape body, with slender necks spreading at top. Around body of vase painting of peacock feathers, at neck gilt handles, and incised and gold ornamentation. Height and diameter 10½ x 6 inches. 2 pieces. 110 00

822 CENTRE VASE, reclining Dromedary, modeled by Hadley, and decorated in colors. 30 00

823 PAIR VASES, Japanese design, straight shape with bamboo corners and base. Ornamentation of flowers, grasses, insects, etc., in pierced work and gold matte and platina. Height and diameter 11 x 6 inches. 2 pieces. 285 00

824 PILGRIM BOTTLE, dark green glaze, with floral and other ornamentation in gold, silver, and various colors, gold gilt handles and stand. Height 8 inches. 37 50

825 PAIR BOTTLES, semi-egg-shell texture and ivory finish, reticulated bodies and jeweled ornamentation. Height 9 inches. 2 pieces. 42 00

826 CYLINDRICAL VASE, Japanese design, pierced pattern of pine trees in ivory finish and gold. Monkey, owl, deer, and insect in relief in imitation of bronze. Height and diameter 5¾ x 4 inches. 40 00

827 PAIR LARGE BOTTLE VASES, globular body with tall slender necks, with pierced bands at top. King's blue glaze with very rich jeweled ornamentation, applied over glaze. Height and diameter 15½ x 7½ inches. 2 pieces. 460 00

828 LOW VASE, Persian design, jeweled and pierced ornamentation. Height and diameter 6 x 6 inches. 72 50

829 EWER, Japanese bottle shape, with boldly modeled lizard forming handle, decoration of floral designs in enamels and gold, incised ornaments. Height 12 inches. 60 00

830 Vase, ovoid shape, three serpents in relief at neck, ornamentation of branch of blossoms, flying bird, etc., in gold matte.
$30 00 Height and diameter 6 x 5 inches.

831 Pair Vases, tall cylindrical shape, ornamented in relief with intricately modeled design of wild flowers, thistles, vines, etc., and glazed with natural colors; other portion of vases of incised patterns. Height and diameter 14½ x 9 inches.
520 00 2 pieces.

832 Pitcher Vase, Grecian shape, decoration painted in low tones.
150 00 Jeweled and incised ornaments. Height 15 inches.

833 Pair Vases, low bottle shape, with short necks and handles, ornamention of frog fishing, foliage, etc., in gold matte and
85 00 enamels. Height and diameter 7 x 7 inches. 2 pieces.

834 Vase, Persian design, on base formed by four swans. Ornamentation of pierced and relief work, decorated in colored enamels
125 00 and gold matte. Height and diameter 11½ x 4 inches.

835 Pair Bottle Vases, with pierced stoppers and gilt handles, imperial yellow glaze, with ornamentation of floral and vine designs in colors and gold applied over the glaze. Height
185 00 and diameter 14½ x 7 inches. 2 pieces.

836 Large Vase, bamboo design with decoration of birds, monkey, etc., painted in colors, bamboo branches carved in relief and
125 00 gold gilt. Height and diameter 12½ x 8 inches.

837 Pair Large Vases, beaker shape with swelling bodies, and mounted on pedestals, body of vases glazed in chocolate color, necks of sea green glaze relief, incised and painted ornamentation of floral designs, etc. Height and diameter 18½
440 00 x 10 inches. 2 pieces.

838 Large Pitcher, with dragon handle, lavender and cream
omitted color glaze, very rich jeweled and gold matte ornamentation
from of floral and vine designs. Height and diameter 15 x 9
sale. inches.

839 Pair Bottle Vases, globular bodies with tall cylindrical necks, ivory finish and Japanese style of decoration, in relief work, enamels and gold matte. Height and diameter 11 x 7 inches.
115 00 2 pieces.

840 LARGE BOTTLE VASE, of Persian design, ornamented with Japanese and other subjects in gold matte, platina, etc. in low relief, handles and band around neck of pierced work. Height and diameter 24 x 11 inches. *$555 00*

841 PAIR FIGURES, Japanese nobleman and lady, carefully modeled and decorated with gold and various delicate colors. Height 16 inches. 2 pieces. *140 00*

842 PITCHER VASE, Egyptian design, ornamented with carefully modeled relief work, and pierced designs, and decorated with gold and colors. Height and diameter 16½ x 8 inches. *460 00*

843 BOTTLE VASE, with stopper, Persian design, ornamented with birds, flowers, arabesques and other patterns in embossed gold, silver and turquoise enamel. Height and diameter 15½ x 8 inches. *140 00*

844 PAIR LARGE VASES, with covers, ovoid shape bodies, with spreading necks and bases, in four salmon color panels are jeweled and painted designs of crests, etc., other portions of vases ornamented with incised and relief designs in crimson and gold, handles of pierced work. Height and diameter 25 x 11 inches. 2 pieces. *omitted from sale.*

845 EWER, of Moresque design, ornamentation of pierced, embossed and painted designs, in gold, silver and turquoise, crimson and white enamels. Height 15 inches. *320 00*

846 PAIR BOTTLE VASES, semi-egg-shell texture, ivory finish, necks and upper part of bodies of pierced designs, bodies decorated with flowers and vines in bright colors on gold ground. Height and diameter 11 x 6 inches. 2 pieces. *180 00*

847 LARGE VASE, Persian design, graceful bottle shape on pedestal, vase decorated in imitation of Damaskeen work, relief and pierced handles and ornaments, pedestal of pierced and relief designs, and decorated with gold over chocolate and green glaze. Height and diameter 27 x 10 inches. *525 00*

848 PAIR BOTTLE VASES, globular bodies with tall slender necks, ornamentation of floral crest and other designs in matte, silver and enamel, pierced band around top of necks. Height and diameter 16 x 8 inches. *620 00*

omitted from sale. 849 VASE, Persian bottle shape, canary yellow glaze with an ornamentation of floral and other designs in gold and dark blue, scroll handles of pierced pattern. Height and diameter 19 x 9½ inches.

850 BOTTLE VASE, ovoid body with tall, slender neck, on spreading base, ornamentation of intricate pierced designs and relief work, decorated with gold matte, platina, and green and crimson enamels, ivory finish. Height and diameter 22½ x 8 inches. *$810 00*

851 PAIR SMALL BOTTLES, Hispano-Moresque design, ornamentation in jewels and gold matte over brown and turquoise glaze. Height 10 inches. 2 pieces. *125 00*

852 PAIR EWERS, Egyptian pattern, tall form, ornamentation of birds, flowers, arabesques and other designs in gold matte, platina and enamels. Height 13 inches. 2 pieces. *120 00*

853 OVOID VASE, on gilt feet, surface of vase reticulated and glazed with turquoise glaze, coral pink band top and bottom, floral designs painted in three small panels, semi-egg-shell texture. Height and diameter 7½ x 4¾ inches. *260 00*

854 COFFEE POT, Persian design, ornamented with pierced and relief work and decorated with gold matte, platina, and delicate colors. Height and diameter 13½ x 6 inches. *180 00*

855 PAIR BOTTLE VASES, Hispano-Moresque design, pierced medallions and handles, decoration in gold, enamels and penciled work. Height and diameter 14½ x 7 inches. 2 pieces. *500 00*

856 PAIR CANDLESTICKS, for two lights each, lotus design, with flowers, leaves, etc., in relief, and painted with natural colors relieved by gold. Height 10½ inches. 2 pieces. *100 00*

857 PAIR BOTTLE-SHAPE VASES, ovoid bodies with tall, slender necks spreading at top, ornamented with gold and platina, and jeweled, ivory finish and light texture, pierced band around top of necks. Height and diameter 15 x 6½ inches. 2 pieces. *300 00*

858 PAIR SMALL VASES, Canteen shape, egg-shell texture with pierced panels and jeweled ornamentation, coral pink and turquoise blue glaze. Height 6½ inches. 2 pieces. *130 00*

859 PAIR COVERED JARS, tall hexagonal shape, ivory finish with gold *soufflé* glaze. Carefully modeled relief ornamentation of flowers, insects, etc., painted in natural colors. Height and diameter 16 x 8 inches. 2 pieces. *$220 00*

860 PAIR TALL BOTTLES, with pedestals, Egyptian design, ivory finish, with reticulated panels and handles, decorated with penciled gold platina and jewels. Height and diameter 22 x 6¼ inches. 2 pieces. *510 00*

861 LARGE JAR, with cover, Hispano-Moresque design, copied from an antique glass vase in the Alhambra, three panels decorated with floral designs in gold and platina, other portion of jar, the handles and cover, of pierced or open work, and decorated with gold. Height and diameter 19 x 10½ inches. *420 00*

862 PAIR VASES, cylindrical shape on pedestals, ivory finish, ornamented with floral designs in bold relief and decorated with gold, platina and enamels. Band at neck of Grecian patterns incised. Height and diameter 16 x 7 inches. 2 pieces. *250 00*

863 LARGE VASE, tall hexagonal shape of twisted design, feet and three handles of boldly modeled dragons, three panels of open-work designs, others of ivory finish, ornamented with fish, grasses, etc., in gold and platina, jeweled and relief ornaments top and bottom and on cover. Height and diameter 23 x 9 inches. *600 00*

SÈVRES PORCELAIN.

864 VASE, Amphora shape, with cover, fawn color glaze with ornamentation in white *pâte sur pâte*, subject music, handles and base of gold gilt bronze. Height and diameter 15½ x 6 inches. Factory mark of 1870. *165 00*

865 VASE, ovoid body with tall neck slightly spreading, dark green glaze, with ornamentation of female figure and cupids in gold and colors in low relief, subject of decoration "Summer." Height and diameter 13¾ x 6 inches. Factory mark of 1876. *200 00*

866 LARGE VASE, Etruscan design, around body of vase painting of Roman women weaving, landscape view, etc., by Leonard Schilt. Base and neck of lapis blue, decorated with gold applied over the glaze. Height and diameter 17½ x 10 inches. Factory mark of 1859. *670 00*

867 VERY LARGE VASE, *pâte tendre*, tall, graceful ovoid shape with spreading neck and base, body of vase decorated with figures and flowers in delicate colors, subject "Summer," by d'Apoil. Base, neck and cover of vase of King's blue with applied ornamentation in gold and silver, mountings of gold gilt bronze.
$3,600 00 Height and diameter 51 x 16 inches.

868 PEDESTAL for the above, carved cherry, ebonized gold gilt ornaments to match mountings of vase, made to order by Messrs
425 00 Herter & Brother.

869 PAIR VERY LARGE VASES, of graceful ovoid form, spreading at base and neck, in panels are painted figures, flowers, foliage, etc., "the Seasons," by C. Labarre, other portions of vases of King's blue glaze, decorated with vine and floral designs in gold applied over the glaze. Mountings of gold gilt bronze.
1350 00 Height and diameter 40 x 14 inches. 2 pieces.

870 PAIR PEDESTALS for the above, made to order by Messrs. Herter
105 00 & Brother. 2 pieces.

870A AMPHORA-SHAPE VASE, maroon glaze, with *pâte sur pâte* ornamentation of figure of mice, etc., in two medallions, by Giely, black and gold decoration on neck, gold gilt bronze base.
255 00 Height and diameter 17 x 6 inches.

DRESDEN PORCELAIN.

26 00 871 SCENT HOLDER, female arm and hand with bunch of grapes.

872 PAIR SMALL FIGURES, male and female with pet cat and pet
55 00 monkey. 2 pieces.

873 SET OF THREE GROUPS, "Arts and Science," size of each group
135 00 7½ x 7 inches. 3 pieces.

874 SET OF FOUR STATUETTES, the four seasons—spring, summer,
120 00 autumn and winter. Height of each 8¾ inches. 4 pieces.

875 GROUP, three cupids, "History." Height and diameter 8 x 7
30 00 inches.

876 GROUP, four figures, "Affection." Height and diameter 9 x 7½
35 00 inches.

45 00 877 GROUP, two owls and serpent, 9½ x 9 inches.

878 GROUP, quail and young, 10½ x 10½ inches. $52 50

879 STATUETTE, lady in street costume, lace work ornamentation. Height 8 inches. 25 00

880 FIGURE, female asleep in chair, decorated in colors, lace work ornamentation. Height and diameter 8 x 5 inches. 40 00

881 GROUP, boy musicians, five figures. Height and diameter 6 x 4 inches. 42 50

882 GROUP, Cupids, 5 x 6½ inches. 27 50

MINTON FAIENCE.

883 PAIR SMALL VASES, cylindrical shape, dark blue glaze, with cupids and flowers in white *pâte sur pâte*, cloud effects in black and gold. 2 pieces. 50 00

884 PAIR PILGRIM VASES, chocolate glaze, with ornamentation of cupids, toad-stools and foliage in *pâte sur pâte*, by Solon, gold decorated feet and necks. 2 pieces. 140 00

885 BOTTLE VASE, with flattened sides and cylindrical necks, blue glaze, with branches of leaves and blossoms in *pâte sur pâte* relief and gold decoration on King's blue glaze at neck. Height 7½ inches. 42 50

886 PAIR CYLINDRICAL VASES, with slightly spreading necks, gilt ring handles in relief on sides, blue glaze, with floral designs in white *pâte sur pâte*. Height and diameter 9¼ x 5 inches. 2 pieces. 155 00

887 PAIR BOTTLE VASES, with flattened sides and tall, spreading necks, creamy white glaze with decoration of head of country boy and girl, fruits, flowers, etc., painted in colors by H. W. Foster. Height 10¼ inches. 2 pieces. 105 00

888 AMPHORA VASE, maroon glaze, with *pâte sur pâte* ornamentation of figures of mice, etc., in two medallions, by Giely, black and gold decoration on neck, gold gilt bronze base. Height and diameter 17 x 6 inches. *omitted from sale.*

889 PAIR PILGRIM BOTTLES, with open work pedestals and covers, bases of olive glaze, with *pâte sur pâte* ornamentation in white, by L. Solon. Height and diameter 14½ x 8 inches. 2 pieces. 1,400 00

890 CENTRE PIEÇE, boat shape, with open work cover, in one medallion miniature painting of subject after Tenier, in another "Music," other decorations of floral designs, vines, etc., in turquoise blue, gold and delicate colors. Height and diameter 17½ x 13 inches.

$410 00

891 PAIR LARGE VASES, of Etruscan shape, *pâte sur pâte* ornamentation by L. Solon, female figures, cupids, etc., subject "Love's Sacrifice." Height and diameter 16 x 9 inches. 2 pieces.

2,250 00

892 PAIR VASES, with covers, ovoid bottle shape on pedestals. *Rose du Barré* glaze, with relief and penciled decoration in gold. Pastural scenes and flowers painted in medallions. Height and diameter 14¾ x 6 inches.

420 00

893 LARGE VASE, Etruscan design, turquoise blue glaze, with *pâte sur pâte* ornamentation in white, by L. Solon, 1871, subject "The flight of Cupids." Height and diameter 15⅛ x 9 inches.

1,200 00

894 PAIR COVERED JARS, with handles, turquoise blue glaze, with ornamentation in penciled gold, in two medallions, paintings of convivial scenes after Tenier, at necks and on covers open work and relief ornamentation. Height and diameter 14½ x 8⅛ inches. 2 pieces.

440 00

895 PAIR VASES, Egyptian design, around bodies of vases in white *pâte sur pâte* ornamentation, subject, "Life and Death of Cupids," by L. Solon, on other portion of vases arabesques, vines and other designs in *pâte sur pâte*, gold and enamels. Height and diameter 17 x 8 inches. 2 pieces.

1,500 00

896 PAIR LARGE VASES, Etruscan design, around bodies of vase on olive green glaze, white *pâte sur pâte* ornamentation of Cupids, etc., by L. Solon, other decoration in gold and subdued colors. Height and diameter 19½ x 11 inches. 2 pieces.

1,800 00

897 ——, Another pair, similar design, ornamentation in white *pâte sur pâte* on chocolate glaze, subject "The Twelve Months," incised and penciled decoration in gold on dark green and lavender color glaze. Height and diameter 16 x 9¼ inches. 2 pieces.

5,200 00

898 PAIR VASES, same shape as above, but larger, olive green glaze, with ornamentation in white *pâte sur pâte* by L. Solon, subject "The Building and Collapse of Cupid's Temple," necks, handles and bases decorated in subdued colors and gold. Height and diameter 16 x 9¼ inches. 2 pieces. *$1,500 00*

899 PAIR TALL VASES, on pedestals, ovoid shape, with handles extending over and into necks, blue glaze with *pâte sur pâte* ornamentation in white by L. Solon, subject, "The Imprisonment and Escape of Cupids." Height and diameter 22 x 8¼ inches. 2 pieces. *750 00*

900 PAIR LARGE CYLINDRICAL VASES, on pedestals, ornamentation of moorish designs in *pâte sur pâte* in low tone of colors relieved by gold, artist C. Toft, ring and elephant head handles in gold gilt. Height and diameter 22 x 9 inches. 2 pieces. *320 00*

901 VERY LARGE VASE, amphora shape, supported by four silver gilt Cupids, vase of celadon glaze with band of lapis blue running around center on which are Cupids and floral designs in white *pâte sur pâte*, on other portions, festoons of flowers, vines and relief patterns in *pâte sur pâte*, gold, platina, and enamels, a very important example by L. Solon. Height and diameter 38 x 17½ inches. *2,900 00*

902 PEDESTAL, for above, made of cherry finely carved and ebonized, mosiac marble revolving top, made by order of Messrs. Herter Brothers. *100 00*

903 PAIR VERY LARGE VASES, Etruscan design, dark olive green glaze with *pâte sur pâte* ornamentation in white, by L. Solon, "on one vase group of female figures, nymphs with Cupids being put through the drill, forming step, etc., on reverse side Cupids in order of battle, other armed groups in the distance. Companion Vase shows the improvement and aptitude of the scholars, so that they outrun their teachers; on reverse, Cupids in a shower of arrows," other decoration of relief, floral and other designs in gold, silver, and neutral colors. Height and diameter 28 x 15½ inches. 2 pieces. *8,100 00*

The above are masterpieces of the celebrated artist L. Solon.

904 PAIR PEDESTALS, for the above, of carved onyx with gold gilt mountings. 2 pieces. *500 00*

ROYAL VIENNA PORCELAIN.

905 TEA CANISTER, gold ground with figures painted on sides, jeweled borders and penciled ends. $55 00

906 PAIR COVERED URNS, with pedestals, in four panels are miniature paintings of the following subjects, "Lady Ashton and her daughter," "Diana and Endymion," "Orpheus in Hades" and "The Duchess of Devonshire and the Viscountess Duncannon," by Hiedner, other portion of vases, pedestal, and covers decorated with penciled gold and colored enamels, over crimson and pink glaze, gold gilt handles. Height and diameter 14½ x 9 inches. 2 pieces. 680 00

907 SQUARE TRAY, Subject of decoration "Diana" by Burgman, rose pink border with vines and arabesques in gold. Height and diameter 10½ x 10½ inches. 100 00

908 PAIR ANTIQUE VASES, with pedestals, urn shapes, around body of vases painting of "The Wedding Feast," and "The Sacrifice," on four sides of pedestals "Gymnastic Games," "The Hunt," "The Vintage," etc., floral vine and other designs in gold matte on crimson glaze. Height and diameter 15 x 10 inches. 2 pieces. 760 00

609 OVAL DISH, in centre medallion painting by J. Zasche, border of gold ornaments on dark blue glaze. Height and diameter 14½ x 10 inches. 105 00

910 PAIR VERY LARGE VASES, graceful ovoid shape with covers and pedestals, in four oval shape medallions, are painted by Richter of Vienna, the following subjects, "Bacchus and Ariadne," "Venus and Vulcan at the Smithy," "Offering of Iphegenia Bacchus, Ceres, and Cybele" other portions of vase and covers of crimson glaze, decorated with vine designs, floral bands, etc., in gold and delicate colors, handles and mountings of covers and bases, of gold gilt bronze finely wrought. Height and diameter 37 x 15½ inches. 2 pieces. 4,600 00

911 PAIR OF PEDESTALS, for the above upholstered in crimson plush. 2 pieces. 50 00

EUROPEAN PORCELAIN AND FAIENCE.

MISCELLANEOUS.

912 PAIR SMALL JUGS, Chinese figure, by Copeland. 2 pieces. *$32 00*

913 PAIR GROUPS, peasant women and children. Berlin porcelain. 2 pieces. *32 00*

914 GROUPS, Pastoral subject, Chelsea. Height and diameter 9½ x 9½ inches. *26 00*

915 VERY SMALL VASE, Doulton ware, etched and relief ornamentation. *5 00*

916 PAIR OVOID VASES, with handles, canary yellow glaze with Japanese designs in gold "Crown Derby." Height and diameter 5½ x 4 inches. 2 pieces. *50 00*

917 VASES, tall ovoid form with spreading base, silver ground, with painting of butterflies, flowers, etc., in natural colors, French porcelain. Height and diameter 10 x 3½ inches. 2 pieces. *24 00*

918 TEA JAR, French porcelain, ornamentation of Japanese design, rich plumaged birds, etc., in imitation of cloisonné enamel. *27 00*

919 PAIR AMPHORA VASES, with spreading bases, sea green glaze, with cameo medallions and gold ornamentation. Height and diameter 17 x 7½ inches, French porcelain. 2 pieces. *80 00*

920 VASE, shape of stump of tree, peacock in relief, all decorated in colors. Height and diameter 11½ x 7½ inches. *30 00*

921 PAIR SMALL VASES, canteen shape, French porcelain, "raindrop" glaze on sides, with floral designs in *pâte sur pâte*. 2 pieces. *110 00*

922 SMALL OVOID VASE, with handles, turquoise blue glaze, with Japanese designs in gold, "Crown Derby." *26 00*

923 BOTTLE VASE, globular body with slender neck, Bennett faience, floral designs on mottled olive ground. Height and diameter 9 x 5½ inches. *20 00*

924 PAIR LARGE VASES, French porcelain, cylindrical shape on feet, gilt ring handles, silver ground, with decoration of rich plumaged birds, flowers, plants, etc., in bright colors, applied over-glaze. Height and diameter 15 x 7 inches.

$110 00 2 pieces

From Paris Exposition, 1878.

925 PAIR VASES, Copeland faience, Egyptian design, with relief and painted ornamentation, scroll handles. Height and diameter
220 00 15 x 8½ inches. 2 pieces.

926 PAIR SMALL PILGRIM BOTTLES, Moorish figures and floral designs, painted in side medallions, French porcelain.
55 00 2 pieces.

927 LARGE VASE, French porcelain, ovoid shape with spreading neck, turquoise glaze, with floral designs painted in natural colors, by Hürten, gilt lizard handles. Height and diameter
62 50 20½ x 11 inches.

928 PAIR LARGE VASES, royal Berlin, Etruscan shape, on pedestals decoration of figures of Cherubs, cloud effects, water, etc., in neutral colors. Height and diameter 24 x 10 inches. Marked
270 00 K. P. M. 2 pieces.

929 PILGRIM BOTTLE, Longwy faience, Hispano-Moresque design,
47 50 ornamented with enamels and gold. Height 11 inches.

930 PAIR SMALL JARS, with cover, "Crown Derby," canary yellow
42 00 glaze, with applied gold ornamentation. 2 pieces.

931 FLOWER TRAY AND HOLDER, of majolica, design of gloved hand holding lace handkerchief and fan, open work and painted
42 50 decoration.

932 PAIR MANTEL JARS, with covers, French porcelain, tall, ovoid shape on spreading base, silver ground, with painting of rich plumaged birds, flowers, cactus plant, etc., gold gilt bands
100 00 penciled. Height and diameter 16½ x 6½ inches. 2 pieces

933 LARGE VASE, by Deck of Paris, globular body with bold flaring neck, decoration of Persian designs in dark green and turquoise blue, lion's head in relief for handles. Height and diam-
190 00 eter 15 x 12 inches.

934 PAIR VASES, French porcelain, straight ovoid shape, on two sides are painted in colors birds, flowers, grasses, etc., on incised gold ground, other portion of vase butterflies, birds and blossoms in relief, and painted in bright colors on dark green ground. Height and diameter 17 x 5½ inches. 2 pieces. *$125 00*

935 FLOWER BOAT, French faience, cream color glaze, decoration of sprigs of flowers in colors and gold, silver and gold gilt bronze mounting. *35 00*

936 SMALL JAR, with cover, "Crown Derby," canary yellow glaze, with ornamentation of floral and other designs in dark blue and gold. *25 00*

937 PAIR OVOID VASES, with wide mouths, French porcelain, ornamented with rich plumaged birds, flowers, etc., painted in natural colors on silver ground, penciled gold bands. Height and diameter 12½ x 6 inches. 2 pieces. *35 00*

938 PAIR VASES, "Copeland," octagonal shape with spreading necks, decoration of flowers, ornaments and other designs in various enamels, gold gilt and jeweled butterflies in relief at neck for handles. Height and diameter 15 x 8 inches. 2 pieces. *180 00*

939 CENTRE PIECE, modern "Capo di Monti," swan shape, with figures of Neptune, mermaids, etc., in relief, and decorated in colors. 17½ x 14½ inches. *80 00*

940 PAIR VASES, straight ovoid shape, with handles and on feet, celadon glaze, with floral designs, butterflies, etc., carved in relief, and painted in natural colors. Height and diameter 14½ x 6 inches. 2 pieces. *80 00*

941 LARGE VASE, by Copeland, cylindrical shape, profusely decorated with pastoral and other subjects, by L. Besche, 1872. Height and diameter 20½ x 10½ inches. *220 00*

942 JARDINIÈRE, French porcelain, Chinese design, ornamentation of birds, blossoms, etc., on crimson ground, in imitation of cloisonné enamel, open work panels, three peacocks forming support, which together with base and mountings are of gold and silver gilt bronze, finely wrought. Height and diameter 15 x 13½ inches. *200 00*

943 PAIR COVERED JARS, "Capo di Monti," relief ornamentation of Bacchanalian subjects, painted in various gay colors. Height and diameter 16½ x 10½ inches. 2 pieces. *350 00*

944 Pair Vases, French porcelain, Chinese design, straight ovoid shape with spreading base and necks, decorated with flowers, arabesques, etc., in bright colors in imitation of cloisonné enamel, band running around body of vase in imitation of bronze, ring handles. Height and diameter 19 x 7 inches. 2 pieces.
$160 00

945 Pair Diamond Shape Vases, Japanese design, French porcelain, with pierced panels, and ornamented with flowers, birds, blossoms, etc., in bright colors on turquoise ground, in imitation of inlaid work, mountings and stands of gold and silver gilt bronze. Height and diameter 13 x 8 inches. 2 pieces.
140 00

946 Large Pitcher Vase, "Davenport," richly ornamented with jeweled and penciled decoration, Persian designs, flying dragon in bold relief forming handle, gold gilt and jeweled. Height and diameter 15 x 9 inches.
335 00

947 Vase, "Crown Derby," Persian bottle shape, canary yellow glaze, ornamented with floral and other designs in gold and dark blue, scroll handles of pierced designs. Height and diameter 19 x 9½ inches.
175 00

948 Pair Large Vases, with covers, "Crown Derby," ovoid shape, bodies with spreading necks and bases, in four salmon color panels, are jeweled, and painted designs of crests, etc., the other portions of vases ornamented with incised and relief patterns in crimson and gold, handles of pierced work. Height and diameter 25 x 11 inches. 2 pieces.
600 00

SPECIMENS OF AUSTRIAN CARVED CRYSTALS AND ENAMELS.

REPRODUCTIONS OF IMPORTANT EXAMPLES IN EUROPEAN MUSEUMS AND NOTED PRIVATE COLLECTIONS.

949 Small Coupé, oblong shape, enameled inside, and outside with pastoral scenes, etc., bronze and jeweled handles.
115 00

950 Pair Candlesticks, tall form, mythological subjects in medallions, carved bronze mountings. 2 pieces.
105 00

951 Covered Jar, ornamented with mythological subjects in medallions, gilt bronze handles and figures surmounting cover. Height and diameter 5½ x 4½ inches.
115 00

952 TAZZA, OR JEWEL STAND, carved crystal and enamel, support in form of stork wrought in bronze, enameled and jeweled. Height and diameter 7½ x 8 inches. *$300 00*

953 LARGE ORNAMENTAL PIECE, Nautilus shell on high support, figure of Neptune on sea-horse surmounting shell, and figure of mermaid supporting same, both of wrought bronze, ornamentation of mythological and other subjects in enamels, and jeweled. Height and diameter 20 x 9 inches. *600 00*

954 JEWEL STAND, carved crystal and enamel, wrought bronze and enameled figures for support. Height and diameter 5½ x 4½ inches. *150 00*

955 PAIR CANDLESTICKS, high form, enameled and ornamented in relief, with wrought bronze and gilt figures, and other designs. Height 7½ inches. 2 pieces. *105 00*

956 JEWEL STAND, carved crystal swan, with enameled and jeweled mountings, and ornamentation. Height 6 inches. *280 00*

957 TAZZA, oval shape, outer and inner surface of enamel, support of dolphin designs wrought in bronze and gilt, base also enameled, on outer surface Roman landscape, on inner surface mythological subjects. Height and diameter 4¾ x 8¼ inches. *190 00*

958 JEWEL STAND, shell design of carved crystal, with wrought bronze mountings of open work patterns, enameled and jeweled ornamentation. Height and diameter 10 x 8 inches. *800 00*

959 TREASURE SHIP, of carved crystal, with mountings and ornamentation in enamels and jewels, figure of Neptune for support, wrought in bronze and enameled, base of carved crystal with enameled and jeweled ornaments, top lifts off and shows figure in hold of vessel guarding treasure. Height and diameter 16 x 9½ inches, has morocco, plush-lined case. *1,000 00*

WEBB CAMEO GLASS

PORCELAIN PLAQUES

LARGE COLLECTION OF PLATES

BRONZES, SCULPTURE

AND

MISCELLANEOUS OBJECTS

SALE FRIDAY AFTERNOON, MARCH 12.

BEGINNING AT 2.30 O'CLOCK.

AT THE AMERICAN ART GALLERIES.

WEBB CAMEO GLASS.

960 Small Bottle, gourd shape, turquoise blue with ferns and chrysanthemum flowers in relief in white. *$13 00*

961 —— Another, similar shape as above, amber color with lilies and butterflies in white. *17 00*

962 Pilgrim Bottle, rose pink color with Cupids, floral and other designs in white. Height and diameter 6½ x 5¼ inches. *170 00*

963 Covered Jar, globular form on four feet, amber color with Cupids, vines and medallions in white. Height and diameter 7¾ x 6 inches. *200 00*

964 Vase, ovoid shape with spreading neck, rose pink, with flowers and ferns in white. Height and diameter 7¾ x 4½ inches. *160 00*

965 Globular Vase, on four feet, turquoise blue color, with flowers and leaves in white. Height and diameter 6 x 6 inches. *130 00*

966 Bottle Vase, turquoise blue body with floral designs in two layers of glass, green and white, deep cut. Height and diameter 9 x 5 inches. *155 00*

967 Ovoid Vase, with graceful spreading neck, rose pink body with chrysanthemum flowers, grasses and birds in white. Height and diameter 12 x 7 inches. *285 00*

968 Bottle Vase, with tall slender neck, light amber color, with birds, flowers and fruit in white. Height and diameter 18⅛ x 7 inches. *305 00*

969 Small Plate, ruby color, fruits and blossoms in creamy white. Diameter 7½ inches *125 00*

$210 00 — 970 Small Jar, globular shape, rose pink with amber clouding, moss rose, chrysanthemum and other flowers in white. Height and diameter 5½ x 5½ inches.

360 00 — 971 Reading Lamp, tall ovoid shape on spreading base, amber body with figure of "night," clouds, etc. in white, globe of amber color with floral designs in white, silver plated fittings.

140 00 — 972 Bottle Vase, Chinese design, rose pink color, floral, crest and other designs in white. Height and diameter 10 x 6 inches.

180 00 — 973 Beaker Vase, light amber color, with floral designs in white. Height and diameter 15 x 6½ inches.

405 00 — 974 Large Bottle Vase, ovoid shape body with tall slender neck, heavy texture, blue ground with floral and other designs in two layers of glass, white and pink, copy of an antique Chinese vase. Height and diameter 20 x 9¾ inches.

110 00 — 975 Small Jar, low bottle shape, blue ground with morning glory vine in bloom extending around jar, in white. Height and diameter 3¾ x 5½ inches.

400 00 — 976 Large Vase, Chinese design, white jade ground with floral and vine designs in ruby color, texture in imitation of jade. Height and diameter 10¾ x 8½ inches.

165 00 — 977 Pair Cologne Bottles, turquoise blue, with ornamentation of floral designs in white. 2 pieces.

690 00 — 978 Jardiniere, globular shape with wide mouth, ivory black ground with floral designs in white. Height and diameter 6 x 11 inches.

1,575 00 — 979 Finger Bowls, with plates to match, turquoise blue, ornamented with floral and other designs in white. 12 pieces.

The only set in this country, made to order from original designs.

5,900 00 — 980 Covered Vase, known as "The Dennis Vase," of lapis blue color with ornamentation in white, subject "Pegasus." Height and diametor 23 x 13 inches.

The above vase reputed to be the finest and most important example of cameo glass in existence, was first exhibited in an unfinished state at the Exposition Universelle, Paris, 1878, was completed in 1882, and sent direct to Messrs. Tiffany & Co. from whom the late Mrs. M J. Morgan procured it. Five years were consumed in its production.

570 00 — 981 Pedestal, for the above, finely wrought bronze with gold gilt finish, made to order from special designs.

982 PAIR VASES, ovoid shape, with wide mouths, amber color, with ornamentation of grapes, berries, plums, and other fruits and branches in darker shade of amber, gold gilt. Height and diameter 10 x 6½ inches. 2 pieces. $600 00

983 PAIR OVOID VASES, canary yellow color, with branches of cherries and peaches in natural colors, and gold and silver gilt. Height and diameter 9½ x 5½ inches. 2 pieces. 380 00

---

984 WEBB GLASS PUNCH BOWL, low circular form on feet, painted and embossed gold decoration, relief designs, very heavy texture. Height and diameter, 5¼ x 14 inches. 200 00

985 PAIR BOTTLE VASES, by Webb, ruby color, ornamented with floral and other designs in applied gold and platina. Height and diameter 9¼ x 4¾ inches. 2 pieces. 120 00

986 PAIR GLASS VASES, by Baccarat, heavy, clear texture, intaglio ornamentation of birds, flowers, etc., decorated in gold matte and colors. Height and diameter 10¾ x 6 inches. 2 pieces. 120 00

987 PAIR SMALL VASES, Baccarat glass, heavy texture, decorated with Japanese designs in gold and colors. Height and diameter 7¾ x 3¼ inches. 2 pieces. 60 00

988 VASE, goblet shape, Bohemian glass, white, with overlaying of deep blue, intaglio ornamentation of deer, foliage, etc., old specimen. 37 50

989 VASE, similar to above, intaglio ornamentation of grape-vine, cameo medallion of horse in blue. 22 50

990 FRENCH GLASS VASE, Persian design, enameled ornamentation in bright colors and gold. Height and diameter 9¼ x 6½ inches. 75 00

991 VENETIAN GLASS VASE, ovoid body with slender neck and base, flying dragons for handles, serpent in relief coiling around neck. Height and diameter 15½ x 9½ inches. 32 50

992 BOAT-SHAPE ORNAMENT, Venetian glass, amber color, ornamented in relief with medallions and other designs. Height and diameter 16½ x 11 inches. 50 00

993 COVERED BOX, shape of turtle, Baccarat glass, iridescent texture. 750 00

994 PUNCH GLASSES, by Webb, embossed ornamentation in gold
$312 00 and enamels. 12 pieces.

994A INTAGLIO GLASS PLAQUE, subject of ornamentation, "Sea
162 50 Nymph Racing with Cupid." Diameter 13 inches.

CAMEO FLINT GLASS SERVICE.

MADE TO ORDER BY WEBB OF LONDON, FROM ORIGINAL DESIGNS FURNISHED BY MESSRS. TIFFANY & CO., BEING THE ONLY SERVICE OF THIS DESCRIPTION IN EXISTENCE.

Will be sold as follows:

995 OVAL DISHES. 8 pieces.

996 ROUND DISHES. 2 pieces.

997 QUART DECANTERS. 4 pieces.

998 CLARET DECANTERS. 4 pieces.

999 LIQUEUR DECANTERS. 4 pieces.

1000 PINT DECANTERS. 4 pieces.

1001 SHERRIES. 18 pieces.

1002 CLARETS. 18 pieces.

1003 GOBLETS. 18 pieces.

1004 LIQUEURS. 18 pieces.

1005 PORT GLASSES. 18 pieces.

1006 CHAMPAGNES. 18 pieces.

1007 LEMONADE GLASSES. 18 pieces.

1008 TUMBLERS. 18 pieces.

1009 FINGER BOWLS. 18 pieces.

1010 ICE-CREAM PLATES. 18 pieces.

1011 SWEET-MEAT TRAYS, WITH HANDLES. 18 pieces.

LIMOGES AND OTHER ENAMELS.

1012 PLATE, by E. Sieffert, *Marionettes Gros-René*. Diameter 8½ inches. *$120 00*

1013 JEWEL CASKET, carved wood, ebonized, with enameled panels, and gilt bronze mountings and ornaments, satin lined. *60 00*

1014 PLATE, "Sea Nymph." Diameter 9 inches. *67 50*

1015 BONBONNIÈRE, round form, Venus, chariot and Cupids in medallion on cover, other surface of dark blue enamel, with vine designs in white and gold, bronze gilt mountings, and satin lined. Height and diameter 3½ x 8 inches. *130 00*

1016 PAIR PLATES, "Henry II. of France" and "Catherine dé Medicis." Diameter 9 inches. Frame in plush. 2 pieces. *145 00*

1017 BONBONNIÈRE, round form, ornamented in white and gold enamel on black ground, gold gilt bronze mountings, and satin lined. Height and diameter 3½ x 7 inches. *102 50*

1018 OVÀL PLAQUE, "Toilet of Venus," by Paul Soyer, 1875, ebonized and gilt frame. *125 00*

1019 PAIR PLATES, head of "Henry II. of France" and "Catherine dé Medicis." Diameter 9 inches. Framed in ebonized, gilt, and plush frames. 2 pieces. *165 00*

DECORATED PLAQUES.

MOUNTED IN PLUSH AND GILT FRAMES.

1020 OVAL PLAQUE, Berlin porcelain, Dresden decoration. "Ideal Head," carved and gilt frame. *102 50*

1021 ROUND PLAQUE, royal Vienna, subject of decoration "Rembrandt and his Wife," rich penciled gold border. Diameter exclusive of plush frame, 10 inches. *82 50*

1022 OVAL PLAQUE, royal Vienna, subject of decoration, "Alexander the Great cuts the Gordian Knot," maroon ground, border with embossed gold ornamentation. 11 x 8½ inches, has plush frame. *75 00*

1023 Large Plaque, round form, French porcelain, silver ground, with rich plumaged birds, butterflies, flowering plants, etc., painted by N. Vivien. Diameter 14 inches, mounted in plush frame.
$47 50

1024 —— Another, companion to above, decorated by the same artist.
47 50

1025 French Faience Plaque, olive glaze with *pâte sur pâte* decoration by G. T., "Cupids." Diameter 11 inches, ebonized gilt and plush frame.
100 00

1026 Large Plaque, "Crown Derby," decorated with classical subjects. Diameter 17 inches, has plush frame.
70 00

70 00 1027 —— Another, companion to the above.

1028 French Porcelain Plaque, Ideal Head by G. Siever, 1879, gold ground. Diameter 18 inches, mounted in plush.
75 00

1029 Pair Minton Plaques, round form, fish, shells, and marine plants, painted on dark green ground, by Mussillé. Diameter 17 inches, mounted in plush. 2 pieces.
150 00

1030 Royal Vienna Plaque, oval form, subject of decoration, "Meleager and Atalanta," by Herber. 16 x 13 inches, has plush frame.
180 00

1031 Pair Oblong Plaques, French porcelain, King's blue glaze with decoration of figure of "Asia and Africa," mounted in ebonized and gilt frames with plush mats. 2 pieces.
80 00

1032 Square Plaque, "Dresden," decorated by F. Till. 10 x 7½ inches, has plush frame.
62 50

1033 Oval Plaque, Dresden, "Girl of Constantinople," mounted in plush easel frame. 10½ x 8½ inches.
27 50

1034 Round Plaque, Royal Vienna, decorated by Vogster, "Juno and Aeolus," dark blue border with rich ornamentation in applied gold. Diameter 12 inches, has deep plush frame.
135 00

1035 Pair Faience Plaques, oblong shape, *pâte sur pâte* decoration on olive green ground, "Venus and Cupids," by F. Rhead. 11 x 7½ inches each, have ebonized and plush frames. 2 pieces.
180 00

1036 Very Large Plaques, Royal Vienna, round form, subject of decoration, "Aurora," by R. P., very rich crimson and gold border. Diameter 20 inches, mounted in plush frame.
335 00

1037 —— Another, same make, subject of decoration, "The Woman taken in adultery," from the original painting, by A. Beer, embossed gold ornamentation on borders of deep blue, and panels of copper red. Diameter 19 inches, has plush frame. *$205 00*

1038 PAIR LARGE PLAQUES, French porcelain, painting of peacock, golden pheasant, flowers, blossoms, etc., on silver ground, by N. Vivien. Diameter 20 inches, mounted in plush frames. 2 pieces. *110 00*

1039 DRESDEN PLAQUE, oblong form, decorated by E. Echardt, "The new Toy Book." 10 x 12½ inches, mounted in plush easel frame. *70 00*

1040 ROYAL VIENNA PLAQUE, oval shape, subject of decoration, "Vulcan gives Thetis the Arms of Achilles," by Jos. Zasche, crimson and white border with embossed gold ornamentation. 12 x 17 inches, has plush frame. *140 00*

1041 FRENCH PORCELAIN PLAQUE, decorated with Eastern scene after Gérôme, border painted in blue and red on gold and silver ground. Diameter 17½ inches, has plush frame. *135 00*

1042 —— Another, companion to above, subject of decoration, "Eastern Dancing Girl," after Giraud, mounted in plush frame to match above. *135 00*

1043 PAIR PLAQUES, Royal Vienna, round shape, decorated by Joseph Zasche, subject, "The Meeting on the Lake" and "Lesson in Geography." Diameter 10 inches, mounted in plush frames. 2 pieces. *80 00*

1044 FRENCH FAIENCE PLAQUE, *pâte sur pâte* decoration, "Egyptian Dancing Girl," by F. Rhead. Diameter 18 inches, has plush frame. *105 00*

1045 LARGE PLAQUE, royal Vienna, subject of decoration, "Mercury with Horse," copied by A. Beers from the original painting in the Belvedere, Vienna, rich ornamentation on borders. Diameter 18 inches, mounted in maroon plush frame. *195 00*

1046 LARGE MINTON PLAQUE, decorated by H. W. Foster, "Ideal Head," gold back ground. Diameter 19 inches, has plush frame. *95 00*

1047 DRESDEN PLAQUE, decorated by Frank Till, subject, "The Vigil," after the original painting by Angelica Kauffmann. 12 x 10 inches, mounted in maroon plush easel frame. *60 00*

1048 PAIR PORCELAIN PLAQUES, oblong shape, dark green glaze, with ornamentation in *pâte sur pâte*, "He loves me, He loves me not," by F. Rhead. 13 x 6 inches each, ebonized and gilt
$155 00 frames. 2 pieces.

1049 VERY LARGE PLAQUE, by "Minton," round form, decorated by H. W. Foster, subject, "The Pet Kitten," gold back
145 00 ground. Diameter 23 inches, mounted in maroon plush frame.

1050 FRENCH PORCELAIN PLAQUE, diameter 22 inches, decorated by T. LeRoy, "Young Lady of the XVI. Century," has plush
80 00 frame.

1051 OVAL PLAQUE, royal Vienna, decorated by Gestner, subject, "Samson and Delilah," copied from the original painting in the Belvedere, richly ornamented border. 15 x 19 inches
262 50 (slightly defective), has plush frame.

1052 DRESDEN PLAQUE, oblong form, subject of decoration, "Moses in the Bulrushes," copied from the original painting, by P. Delaroche. 20 x 14 inches, mounted in carved gilt frame, plush
175 00 mat.

1053 PAIR PLAQUES, French porcelain, decorated by J. Pascault. "Girls of the XVI. Century." Diameter 9 inches, have maroon
60 00 plush frames. 2 pieces.

1054 —— Another pair, larger, "Ideal Heads," painted on rough
75 00 gold ground. Diameter 12 inches, plush frames. 2 pieces.

1055 LARGE PLAQUE, royal Vienna. Diameter 19 inches, subject of decoration, "Jesus and the Woman of Samaria," copied by A. Beers from the original painting by Annebarle Caracci, borders
372 50 richly ornamented in gold and colors, has maroon plush frame.

1056 ROYAL VIENNA PLAQUE, same size as above, decorated with "Portrait of Rembrandt in his 45th year," mounted in plush
145 00 frame.

1057 PAIR PLAQUES, by Deck, round shape, decorated by R. Janvier, 1867, "Nymphs and Cupids." Diameter of each 11
140 00 inches, have carved ebonized frames. 2 pieces.

1058 SMALL DRESDEN PLAQUE, decorated by F. Till, after G. Hom,
100 00 subject, "Good Night." 9 x 6 inches, mounted in plush frame.

1059 LARGE PLAQUE, Dresden, decorated by A. L. Eckardt, copy of painting by Franz Deffregger, "Off for the Hunt." 19 x 15
200 00 inches, has carved gilt frame.

1060 ROYAL VIENNA PLAQUE, diameter 14 inches, subject of decoration, "Abraham and Hagar," after P. Van Dyke, border richly ornamented with embossed gold and enamels, has plush frame. *$177 50*

1061 —— Another, same size as above, subject of decoration, "Thetis brings his Armor to Achilles," maroon plush frame. *180 00*

1062 LARGE PLAQUE, French porcelain, decorated by Boullinière, after Lefèbvre, subject, "Mignon, Regretting her Country." Diameter 22 inches, mounted in plush frame. *115 00*

1063 ROYAL VIENNA PLAQUE, diameter 12 inches, subject of decoration, "The Rape of Dejanira," has ebonized, gilt and plush frame. *100 00*

1064 —— Another, larger, subject of decoration, "Diana," richly ornamented border. Diameter 14 inches, has plush frame. *130 00*

1065 —— Another, companion to the above, subject of decoration, "Venus and Adonis," mounted in plush frame. *125 00*

1066 VERY LARGE PLAQUE, Dresden, oblong form, a subject of decorative "Art and Liberty," after the original painting by Gallait. 26 x 20 inches, has gold leaf frame. *210 00*

1067 FRENCH PORCELAIN PLAQUE, "Ideal Head," painted on gold ground. Diameter 9½ inches, has plush frame. *35 00*

1068 DRESDEN PLAQUE, oblong form, decorated by C. Meinnelt, subject, "Marguerite." 16 x 9 inches, has gold leaf frame. *105 00*

1069 ROYAL VIENNA PLAQUE, decorated by A. Beer, subject, "Ariadne Waking," richly ornamented border in gold and colors. Diameter 11 inches, has plush frame. *92 50*

MISCELLANEOUS SMALL OBJECTS.

IN ENAMEL, SILVER, BRONZE, ETC.

1070 MINIATURE, in enamel, neatly framed. *omitted from sale.*

1071 PAPER WEIGHT, nickel, with enameled frog in relief. *2 00*

1072 BRONZE KITTENS, enameled. 3 pieces. *16 50*

1073 PORTABLE INKSTAND, sterling silver, hammered, finished Japanese designs in applied metals. *20 00*

$11 50 1074 MATCH BOX, French cloisonné, enamel.

7 00 1075 JEWEL TRAY, lapis-lazuli.

7 50 1076 BRONZE DOG, enameled.

15 00 1077 MINIATURE ARM CHAIR, in sterling silver.

4 50 1078 MATCH STAND, bronze boot, figures of mice in relief.

85 00 1079 SCENT BOTTLE, cameo glass, by Webb.

12 00 1080 MINUTE BIRDS, in bronze and enamel. 2 pieces.

13 50 1081 CACHOU BOX, French enamel ornamentation, gold lined.

4 00 1082 BRONZE TRAY, *repoussé* ornamentation.

12 00 1083 THERMOMETERS, silver plated. 2 pieces.

13 00 1084 JEWEL TRAY, cornelian, finely polished.

12 00 1085 PAPER KNIFE AND TRAY, bronze, carved ornamentation gold and oxidized finish. 2 pieces.

17 00 1086 SCENT BOTTLE, design of parrot, crystal glass body with gold gilt bronze mountings.

10 50 1087 MATCH STAND, silver dog, with hat.

4 50 1088 OBJECT GLASS, bronze and gilt, claw handle.

17 00 1089 BRONZE ORNAMENTS, cat with violoncello and boy on chair. 2 pieces.

50 00 1090 BRONZE PIECE, reclining bear.

25 00 1091 CACHOU BOX, enameled ornamentation, gold lined.

155 00 1092 PAIR TALL CANDLESTICKS, sterling silver, *repoussé* ornamentation, oxidized finish.

15 00 1093 SMALL VASE, cylindrical shape, French cloisonné in imitation of Chinese.

17 00 1094 POSTAGE STAMP BOX, gold gilt, and jeweled ornamentation.

10 00 1095 MATCH STAND AND TRAY, bronze and enamel owl's head.

14 50 1096 POCKET MATCH BOX, sterling silver, " Here's the last."

23 00 1097 PERFUME SPRINKLER, sterling silver, shape of watering pot.

20 00 1098 BOX AND COVER, old satsuma ware, black glaze with crests in white reserve.

15 00 1099 MATCH BOX, sterling silver, shape of dog house.

1100 GALLERY GLASS, mounted in platina. *$37 50*

1101 —— Another, mounted in German silver, ebonized handle. *17 50*

1102 —— Another, larger, similar mounting. *25 00*

1103 —— Another, larger, gold plated mounting, ivory handles. *62 50*

1104 —— Another, same size, mahogany mounting. *20 00*

1105 —— Another, larger, similar mounting. *27 50*

1106 ANTIQUE IVORY TANKARD, battle scene in bold relief, *repoussé* and chased silver mountings, gold finished, figures in relief on cover. Height and diameter 11 x 7 inches. *370 00*

1107 BRONZE CAT, enameled ornamentation. Height $7\frac{3}{4}$ inches. *26 00*

1108 —— Another, similar. *27 00*

1109 BRONZE AND ENAMELED KITTEN. Height $4\frac{3}{4}$ inches. *13 00*

1110 INK STAND, silver bronze fox. Height 7 inches. *14 00*

1111 NIGHT LAMP, silver bronze cat, with gold gilt base. Height 9 inches. *22 50*

1112 SILVER BAS-RELIEF, Pope Pius IX., by Sinédo, mounted on black polished marble. *60 00*

1113 VASE, satsuma ware, hexagonal shape, decorated with Japanese figures in medallions, in gold and colors, embossed diaper, arabesque and other designs surrounding. Height and diameter $6\frac{1}{2}$ x 4 inches. *40 00*

1114 OLD GREEK GLASS AMPULLA, in fine state of preservation, has morocco case. *75 00*

1115 BOTTLE WITH LONG NECK, old Greek glass, finely preserved, iridescent luster. *omitted from sale.*

1116 ANTIQUE CHOCOLATE POT, "Hochst," decorated in gold and colors. *55 00*

MINIATURE OBJECTS IN SILVER.

OLD DUTCH TOYS.

1117 SET FURNITURE, sofa, chairs, tables, etc. 9 pieces. *135 00*

1118 LANTERN, tall cone shape. *26 00*

1119 CENTRE TABLE, filigree work. 2 pieces. *16 00*

1120 COFFEE URN AND TEA POT. 2 pieces. *20 00*

$28 00 1121 TEA SET AND TRAYS. 2 pieces.

1122 WINDMILLS, specimens of old Dutch and filigree work.
44 00 2 pieces.

25 00 1123 PAIR CANDLE BRANCHES. 2 pieces.

70 00 1124 STATE CARRIAGE AND SLEIGH. 2 pieces.

12 00 1125 GONDOLA.

12 00 1126 CANDLESTICK, filigree work.

25 00 1127 REVOLVING STARS, figures in relief. 2 pieces.

36 00 1128 COFFEE URN AND TEA POT, filigree work. 2 pieces.

14 00 1129 ORNAMENTS. 2 pieces.

20 00 1130 WHEEL OF FORTUNE.

16 00 1131 SPINNING WHEEL.

16 00 1132 CANDLE STAND AND CANDLESTICK. 2 pieces.

40 00 1133 KITCHEN UTENSILS. 10 pieces.

8 00 1134 PERFUME BOXES. 2 pieces.

10 00 1135 BELLOWS AND TEA CANISTER. 2 pieces.

12 00 1136 TREASURE CHEST, etc., filigree work. 2 pieces.

14 00 1137 PAIR CANDLESTICKS. 2 pieces.

7 00 1138 FIGURES AND SET MINUTE SPOONS. 2 pieces.

27 00 1139 DOG HOUSE, ETC. 3 pieces.

---

55 00 1140 GALLERY GLASS, gold plated mounting, ivory handle.

26 00 1141 —— Another, german silver mounting, ebonized handle.

LARGE COLLECTION OF PLATES,

MANY OF UNIQUE DESIGNS, MADE AND DECORATED TO ORDER, AND NEVER DUPLICATED.

1142 ROYAL VIENNA PLATES, deep form, painting, of Biblical subjects, rich borders of applied gold on dark blue and maroon
65 00 ground. Diameter 10 inches. 2 pieces.

1143 ROYAL VIENNA PLATES, subject of decoration, "Spring" and "Summer," jeweled, and gold ornamented borders. 2 pieces. *$80 00*

1144 —— Others, decorated with mythological subjects, borders of various designs in gold and colors. 12 pieces. *360 00*

1145 —— Others, decorated with portraits of the "Queens of England." 12 pieces. *420 00*

1146 —— Others, decorated with portraits of Peter 1st of Russia, and Gustave Adolph 1st of Sweden, painted by Schröbel, borders ornamented in gold and fine colors. Diameter 9½ inches. 2 pieces. *90 00*

1147 —— Others, portraits of Frederick the Great, and Carl VI., painted by A. Beer, rich borders. 2 pieces. *95 00*

1148 —— Others, portraits of Sigismund of Sweden, and Carl 1st, painted by A. Beer and Berger, floral and other designs on borders in gold and delicate colors. 2 pieces. *85 00*

1149 —— Others, portraits of Louis XIV., by A. Beer, and Louis XVI., by Schröbel, borders of very rich design in gold and colors. Diameter 9½ inches. 2 pieces. *90 00*

1150 —— Others, portraits of King Ferdinand 1st, and Carl the Great, by A. Drest, and Gustave 1st of Sweden, by Grüner, borders ornamented with rich designs in applied gold over delicate colors. Diameter 10 inches. 3 pieces. *120 00*

1151 —— Others, decorated with mythological subjects by Joseph Zache, and others, "The Judgment of Paris," "Dœdalus und Icarus," and "Offerings of Venus," borders richly ornamented. 3 pieces. *150 00*

1152 —— Others, decorated by Männish, "Venus and Æneas," and "School of Love," richly ornamented borders of designs in gold on King's blue ground. 2 pieces. *70 00*

1153 —— Others, mythological and other subjects, "The Choice of Hercules," "Angelica and Medora," "The Departure of Hector," "Death of Achilles," and "Saul as King," borders richly ornamented in various designs. Diameter 10 inches. 6 pieces. *300 00*

1154 —— Others, decorated with mythological and other subjects, borders of rich designs in gold and colors. Diameter 10 inches. 8 pieces. *280 00*

1155 ROYAL VIENNA PLATES, "Cupid sharpening his Arrows," etc., borders of designs in gold on King's blue ground. Diameter
$88 00 10 inches. 2 pieces.

1156 —— Others, portrait of Henry VIII. of England, by Werner, and "Springtime," after Raphael, borders of very rich designs in embossed gold and colors. Diameter 9½ inches.
70 00 2 pieces.

1157 —— Others, "Venus and Troja," and "Hippolytus and Phœdra," borders of applied gold and colors. Diameter 9½ inches.
78 00 2 pieces.

1158 —— Others, subject of decoration "Rebecca at the Well" and
80 00 "Muse of Painting," richly ornamented borders. 2 pieces.

1159 —— Others, "Thetis brings his Armor to Achilles," "Thetis bathing Achilles in the Styx," "Pluto carrying off Proserpine," "Achilles disguised as a Woman," and "Boreas carry-
210 00 ing off Orythia." Diameter 9½ inches. 5 pieces.

1160 SÈVRES PLATES, *pâte tendre*, mark of the factory, 1768, and of Chulot decorator, in medallions are painted portraits of Court beauties: Duchesse de Bourgoyne, Duchesse de Pompadour, Diane de Poitiers, Marie Stuart, Gabrielle d'Estrées, Madame de Montesson, Anne d'Angleterre, Comtesse de Grignan, Madame Elizabeth, Marie de Médicis, Madame de Lamballe, Madame Dubarry. Rich jeweled borders with flowers painted
990 00 in medallions. 12 pieces.

1161 —— Others, same marks, hard paste, painted with portraits of Duchesse du Maine, Madame de Mailly, Madame de Longueville, Madame de Genlis, Madame de Parabère, Madame de Sévigné, jeweled and decorated borders to match
360 00 above. 6 pieces.

1162 MINTON PLATES, open work borders, decorated with floral designs, various roses, painted in natural colors. Diameter 9
360 00 inches. 18 pieces.

1163 —— Others, same pattern and size, decorated with figures of
468 00 Cupids, flowers, etc., by A. Boullemier. 18 pieces.

1164 —— Others, pierced border of Grecian pattern, rose pink glaze.
522 00 with floral designs and butterflies painted in white. 18 pieces.

1165 MINTON PLATES, for game, lattice design borders, various dogs, horses, birds, deer, etc., painted in medallions, on which is a band of turquoise glaze. 12 pieces. *$204 00*

1166 —— Others, of similar design and decoration, pink band around medallions. 12 pieces. *216 00*

1167 —— Others, lattice and turquoise blue borders, domestic scenes painted in medallions. Diameter 9½ inches. 24 pieces. *384 00*

1168 —— Others, cream glaze, with ornamentation in applied gold and platina, turquoise jeweled bands, and medallions. Diameter 10 inches. 18 pieces. *270 00*

1169 —— Others, white centre, with border of sea green, richly ornamented with floral and other designs in applied gold and white enamel, same shape and size as above. 18 pieces. *297 00*

1170 —— Others, open work borders of Grecian design, band of turquoise glaze, Cupids and floral designs in medallions, painted by A. Boullemier. Diameter 9½ inches. 18 pieces. *342 00*

1171 —— Others, gold embossed borders, decorated with various rare orchids in bloom, painted by W. Mussillé. Diameter 9½ inches. 18 pieces. *450 00*

1172 —— Others, cream color glaze, with various birds and plants, painted in natural colors. Diameter 9½ inches. 12 pieces. *132 00*

1173 —— Others, open work borders, with turquoise and gold ornaments, decorated by A. Boullemier with pastoral and other subjects in medallions. Diameter 9 inches. 12 pieces. *312 00*

1174 —— Others, same pattern and size, decorated by same artist, scenes from childhood, etc. 12 pieces. *288 00*

1175 —— Others, panels decorated with marine views and landscapes in sepia, by J. Evans, canary yellow glaze, with gold ornamentation. Diameter 9½ inches. 18 pieces. *432 00*

1176 —— Others, rich embossed gold enameled borders, roses and other flowers painted in centre by C. F. Hürtin. Diameter 9½ inches. 18 pieces. *720 00*

1177 —— Others, larger, King's blue border, with floral designs in applied gold and turquoise, white centre with star medallions. Diameter 10 inches. 18 pieces. *282 00*

1178 Minton Plates, pierced panels and cameo medallions on borders, with turquoise blue and gold ornamentation, pastoral and other subjects, painted in medallions by A. Boullemier.
$1,485 00 Diameter 10 inches. 18 pieces.

1179 —— Others, cameo medallion on borders, with floral design painted in colors, and vine design in gold on turquoise raised panels, in centre medallions, emblematical designs, band of
738 00 turquoise blue surrounding. Diameter 10 inches. 18 pieces.

1180 —— Others, open work borders of Grecian pattern, gold ornamentation, decorated by A. Boullemier. Diameter 9½ inches.
432 00 18 pieces.

1181 —— Others, same pattern borders as above, turquoise blue centres, with cameo medallions and gold and silver ornamentation of vine and floral designs, bands of cream color, with
414 00 festoons in gold. Diameter 9½ inches. 18 pieces.

1182 —— Others, turquoise blue borders, with bands of blossoms, white centre medallions, decorated with Chinese and Japanese vases and ornaments, plants, etc., in colors and gold. Diam-
225 00 eter 9½ inches. 18 pieces.

1183 —— Others, ivory finish, with embossed gold ornamentation, and *pâte sur pâte* medallions of various designs, shapes and
495 00 colors. Diameter 9½ inches. 15 pieces.

1184 —— Others, deep form, borders of floral designs with cameo medallions, centre of turquoise blue, with letter M in flowers
708 00 on white ground, Diameter 10 inches. 24 pieces.

1185 —— Others, ivory finish, with ornamentation of various rare orchids in bloom, insects, etc., in gold, platina and enamels.
462 00 Diameter 9½ inches. 22 pieces.

1186 —— Others, embossed gold borders, painted in medallions, Cupids, and nude figure, surrounding which a band of turquoise blue, with floral and other designs in white *pâte sur pâte*.
768 00 Diameter 9½ inches. 24 pieces.

1187 —— Others, for game, sunk panels, decorated with various domestic and wild animals, ground of turquoise blue, with floral ornamentation in imitation of Chinese cloisonné enamel.
360 00 Diameter 9½ inches. 18 pieces.

1188 MINTON PLATES, turquoise blue medallions, with Japanese ornaments and other designs, painted in colors and gold, cream color band and turquoise borders, rich enameled ornaments. Diameter 9½ inches. 22 pieces. *$332 00*

1189 ROYAL WORCESTER PLATES, ivory finish centres, with embossed medallions, centre decorated with four peacocks in penciled gold and colors, very rich borders in gold and turquoise enamel. Diameter 10 inches. 18 pieces. *492 00*

1190 —— Others, same make, rich embossed borders of jeweled and other designs, white centres with floral designs, painted in natural colors. Diameter 9 inches. 18 pieces. *288 00*

1191 —— Others, larger, ivory finish, Japanese style of decoration, storks, plants, etc., in gold matte and platina. Diameter 10 inches. 22 pieces. *264 00*

1192 —— Others, similar to above, smaller. Diameter 9½ inches. 10 pieces. *110 00*

1193 —— Others, smaller, similar in design to above. Diameter 9 inches. 12 pieces. *168 00*

1194 DRESDEN PLATES, open work borders, decorated with penciled gold over King's blue glaze, various heads painted in medallions, "Neapolitan Boy," etc. Diameter 9½ inches. 12 pieces. *336 00*

1195 —— Others, same shape and size as above, decorated with various subjects, copied from paintings by Gerard Douw and other famous painters. 11 pieces. *440 00*

1196 —— Others, same shape as above, pastoral scenes painted in centre medallions. 2 pieces. *76 00*

1197 —— Others, pierced borders with blue and gold ornamentation, painted with subjects after paintings by Caspar Netscher and others. Diameter 9 inches. 3 pieces. *120 00*

1198 —— Others, open work borders and scalloped edges, penciled gold ornamentation, centre panels painted with "The Goddess of Fairy Tales," etc. Diameter 9 inches. 2 pieces. *78 00*

1199 SÈVRES PLATES, *pâte tendre*, mark of 1769, decorated with floral wreaths around borders, gold ground centre with decoration in blue. Diameter 9½ inches. 18 pieces. *992 00*

1200 SÈVRES PLATES, mark of 1753, and Le Gay decorator, medallion portraits of court beauties and celebrated women of France, jeweled and painted ornamentation, turquoise blue and white ground, scalloped edges. Diameter 10 inches.
$798 00 18 pieces.

1201 —— Others, smaller, mark of 1883, decorated by E. Sieffert,
774 00 "Marionettes." Diameter 9 inches. 18 pieces.

SALE SATURDAY AFTERNOON, MARCH 13,

BEGINNING AT 2.30 O'CLOCK.

AT THE AMERICAN ART GALLERIES.

LARGE COLLECTION OF PLATES.

1202 "CROWN DERBY" PLATES, white centres with birds and flowers painted in natural colors, borders of various colors, and ornamented with floral panels, crests and other designs in gold and delicate colors, scalloped edges. Diameter 9½ inches.
18 pieces. *$288 00*

1203 BERLIN PLATES, centre medallion. decorated with ideal female heads, green and gold borders. Diameter 9½ inches.
18 pieces. *450 00*

1204 MINTON PLATES, richly ornamented with embossed gold and *pâte sur pâte* on turquoise and dark blue, white centre with gold crest. Diameter 10 inches. 18 pieces. *504 00*

1205 PLATE, "Brownfield's china," decorated with domestic and other scenes, by Boullemier, and Hartmann, subjects of decoration inscribed on back of plates. Diameter 9 inches.
19 inches. *874 00*

1206 —— Others, same make, ornamented with figure of Cupids in *pâte sur pâte*, vine and other designs in gold, dark blue and pink ground. Diameter 9 inches. 18 pieces *396 00*

1207 PLATES, of French porcelain, decorated with "Peasant Boys," by Jean and Georges Poitevin. Diameter 9 inches.
12 pieces. *168 00*

1208 FAIENCE PLATES, same as above, decorated by Georges Poitevin, "Peasant Children." 9 pieces. *117 00*

1209 COPELAND PLATES, scalloped edges, with embossed gold ornamentation, white centres with floral designs painted by C. F. Hürstin. Diameter 8 inches. 12 pieces.

$312 00

1210 —— Others, same make, similar shape, applied gold ornamentation, female heads in centre medallions. Diameter 8 inches. 12 pieces.

372 00

1211 —— Others, similer shape as above, turquoise border, delicate pink ground centre, rich jeweled and gold ornamentation. Diameter 8 inches. 12 pieces.

276 00

1212 PLATES, "Brownsfield China," open work borders with gold ornaments, decorated by Hartmann, domestic, pastoral, and other subjects, title inscribed on back of each plate. Diameter 9½ inches. 18 pieces.

756 00

1213 MINTON PLATES, pink and gold ornamented borders, orchids in bloom painted in centre on white ground. Diameter 9½ inches. 22 pieces.

252 00

1214 ROYAL WORCESTER PLATES, Persian borders, white centres, with various flowers and butterflies painted in natural colors. Diameter 9 inches. 18 pieces.

378 00

1215 —— Others, lotus leaf design, ivory texture, decorated with Japanese and other designs in applied metals and colored enamels. Diameter 9 inches. 18 pieces.

270 00

1216 MINTON PLATES, very intricate pierced borders, of floral and lattice designs, with gold ornamentation, decorated with subjects after Angelica Kauffmann by A. Boullemier. Diameter 10 inches. 18 pieces.

2,175 00

Finest and most expensive Plates ever produced by Minton.

1217 —— Others, white *soufflé* borders with gold bands, monogram on turquoise medallion. Diameter 9 inches. 18 pieces.

90 00

1218 —— Others, lemon yellow and gold borders, white centre, monogram in dark blue panels. Diameter 9 inches. 18 pieces.

90 00

1219 —— Others, same shape and size as above, turquoise and gold gilt border, monogram on gold ground panel. 18 pieces.

117 00

1220 —— Others, same shape and size as above, crimson and gold borders, monogram on gold ground panel. 18 pieces.

117 00

1221 MINTON PLATES, rich crimson and gold borders, monogram in centre. Diameter 10 inches. 25 pieces. *$187 50*

1222 —— Others, same size and shape as above, rich blue and gold borders, monogram in white ground centre. 25 pieces. *225 00*

1223 —— Others, same as above, turquoise and blue borders, with monogram in centre. 25 pieces. *187 50*

1224 —— Others, very richly ornamented borders of dark blue, with decoration in gold and crimson. Diameter 10 inches. 25 pieces. *262 50*

1225 —— Others, same shape and size as above, celadon borders with gold ornamentation. 25 pieces. *175 00*

1226 —— Others, turquoise borders with gold band, monogram in centre. Diameter 10 inches. 25 pieces. *162 50*

1227 —— Others, gilt band around edges, decorated with various Oriental vases, ornaments and flowers painted in natural colors. Diameter 9½ inches. 12 pieces. *132 00*

1228 —— Others, similar to above. 25 pieces. *237 50*

1229 —— Others, lapis-lazuli borders, jeweled ornamentation, "Cupid" subjects, painted in centre medallions. Diameter 9½ inches. 22 pieces. *660 00*

1230 —— Others, turquoise blue and gold borders, with pierced medallions and *pâte sur pâte* festoons, white centre, ornamented with flowers, grasses, and insects in applied gold and silver. Diameter 9½ inches. 22 pieces. *374 00*

1231 —— Others, open work borders, turquoise blue band, with fruits, blossoms and crests, in bright enamels, penciled gold medallions. Diameter 9½ inches. 22 pieces. *392 00*

1232 —— Others, same shape as above, white *soufflé* band, children's heads painted in medallions. 18 pieces. *306 00*

1233 —— Others, similar shape and size, floral designs, painted in medallions. 18 pieces. *270 00*

1234 —— Others, same shape and size as above, turquoise blue glaze, with ornamentation of birds, flowering plants, etc., in white *pâte sur pâte*. 22 pieces. *594 00*

1235 —— Others, gilt edges, white ground, with decoration of female heads. Diameter 9½ inches. 18 pieces. *378 00*

1236 MINTON PLATES, turquoise rough glaze, with enameled birds, grasses, etc., in natural colors. 22 pieces.
$364 00

1237 —— Others, for fish, same shape and size as above, decorated by W. Mussillé, with various species of fish, marine plants, etc. 25 pieces.
325 00

1238 —— Others, smaller, decorated by H. Mitchell, various fish painted in natural colors. Diameter 9 inches. 18 pieces.
270 00

1239 —— Others, for game, same size as above, decorated by H. Mitchell, with various birds, deer, and other game, painted in natural colors. 19 pieces.
304 00

1240 CROWN DERBY GAME PLATES, penciled and embossed borders in crimson and gold, centre panels painted with various domestic and wild birds, foliage, etc., in natural colors. Diameter 9½ inches. 25 pieces.
425 00

1241 PÂTE TENDRE PLATES, Sèvres style of decoration, pastoral and other subjects painted in centre medallions, turquoise borders, with birds and flowers, in panels, gold ornamentation. Diameter 9⅛ inches. 18 pieces.
486 00

1242 MINTON PLATES, pierced design on borders filled in with glaze, Chinese rice grain effect, painting of floral designs in centre panels, gold edge. Diameter 9⅛ inches. 22 pieces.
308 00

1243 —— Others, same size as above, similar design borders, Cupids painted in centres, penciled gold edges. 22 pieces.
440 00

1244 —— Others, open work borders with gold ornaments, decorated with female heads in medallion, turquoise band surrounding. Diameter 9 inches. 18 pieces.
378 00

1245 —— Others, larger, gold ground borders, with water and flying storks in Nankin blue, monogram in centre. Diameter 10 inches. 25 pieces.
200 00

MISCELLANEOUS.

1246 ROYAL VIENNA DESSERT SERVICE, decorated by K. Wildner and others, with subjects from famous paintings, very rich blue and gold borders, comprises 2 high compotes, 6 plates, and 6 after dinner coffee mugs and saucers. 20 pieces.
375 00

1247 Bowl and Saucer, Sèvres porcelain, decorated with flowers and butterflies, painted in natural colors. *$24 00*

1248 After-dinner Coffee Cups and Saucers, "Minton," semi-egg-shell texture, richly decorated with Persian and other patterns, in crimson and gold. 12 pieces. *54 00*

1249 Bouillon Cups and Saucers, to match above. 13 pieces. *71 50*

1250 Royal Vienna Dessert Service, decorated by Berger with mythological and other subjects, many after celebrated paintings, very rich borders in crimson and gold, vine designs in panels in delicate colors, comprises 4 low compotes, 12 plates, and 12 after-dinner mugs and saucers, mugs gold lined. 40 pieces. *1,600 00*

1251 Pair Minton Compotes, tall form, with Cupids for support, turquoise blue glaze, with gold and jeweled ornaments, Cupids painted in medallions. 2 pieces. *62 00*

1252 —— Another pair, similar shape as above, crimson glaze, with Cupids in medallions. 2 pieces. *42 00*

1253 —— Same. 2 pieces. *54 00*

1254 After Dinner Coffee Cups and Saucers, "Minton," celadon band, with floral and other designs in applied gold and white enamels. 17 pieces. *153 00*

1255 —— Others, same make, rich gold and enameled decoration with cameo medallions. 12 pieces. *204 00*

1256 —— Others, egg-shell texture, same make as above, "Minton," gold embossed ornamentation with painted floral band. Watteau subjects in medallions. 13 pieces. *273 00*

1257 —— Others, "Copeland" square shape with incised corners, rich jeweled and gold ornamentation on crimson glaze. 6 pieces. *84 00*

1258 —— Others, same make and shape, similar style of ornamentation on King's blue glaze. 6 pieces. *96 00*

1259 Tea Cups and Saucers, "Minton," decorated with fan shape medallions in turquoise blue, flowers, birds, and other designs in natural colors and gold. 12 pieces. *90 00*

1260 —— Others, same make, King's blue glaze with jeweled and gold ornamentation, Cupids painted in medallions, semi-egg-shell texture. *240 00*

1261 MINTON TEA CUPS AND SAUCERS, same make, bowl shape, gold ground, band with flying storks in nankin blue and white enamel. 12 pieces. $120 00

1262 AFTER DINNER CUPS AND SAUCERS, "Crown Derby," egg-shell texture, rich jeweled and embossed decoration over rose pink and canary yellow glaze. 12 pieces. 156 00

1263 TEA CUPS AND SAUCERS, "Minton," pierced designs filled in with glaze, Chinese rice grain effect, butterflies and blossoms in gold and silver. 12 pieces. 192 00

1264 —— Others, same make, turquoise floral glaze, with flying storks, bamboo branches and other designs painted in natural color enamels. 90 00

1265 CHOCOLATE MUGS AND SAUCERS, decorated medallions, turquoise band, embossed gold ornamentation. 12 pieces. 300 00

1266 ROYAL WORCESTER TRAY, leaf shape, decorated with flying storks, bamboo branches, etc., in gold and platina. 31 00

1267 SALAD PLATES, "Minton," ornamented with floral and other designs in bright colors, in imitation of Chinese cloisonné enamel. 24 pieces. 252 00

1268 PORCÉLAIN MENU STANDS, decorated with game subjects. 36 pieces. 42 00

1269 —— Others, similar. 9 pieces. 15 75

1270 —— Others, decorated with heads. 34 pieces. 68 00

1271 —— Others, same shape, decorated with scenes from childhood. 13 pieces. 22 75

RICH CUT ENGLISH GLASSWARE.

1272 LARGE FRUIT BOWL, high form, heavy texture, bold diamond pattern. 30 00

1273 PAIR FRUIT BOWLS, to match, low form. 26 00

1274 PAIR PRESERVE DISHES, to match, oval shape. 2 pieces. 30 00

1275 ICE CREAM DISH, oval shape, scalloped edge, fine diamond pattern. 16 x 11½ inches. 25 00

1276 FRUIT BASKET, antique pattern, oval shape, diamond design. 20 00

1277 ROUND PRESERVE DISH, heavy texture, bold cut. Diameter 10 inches. *$15 00*

1278 PAIR PRESERVE DISHES, to match. Diameter 9 inches. 2 pieces. *21 00*

1279 —— Another pair, smaller. Diameter 8 inches. 2 pieces. *20 00*

1280 ICE CREAM DISH, flat oval shape, scalloped edge, diamond and star pattern. 13½ x 9½ inches. *24 00*

1281 PAIR HIGH FRUIT BOWLS, fine diamond pattern. 2 pieces. *32 00*

1282 CHEESE DISH AND COVER, to match. *27 00*

1283 PRESERVE TRAY, to match, shell shape. *11 00*

1284 —— Another, oval shape, with handles at ends, heavy texture. 14 x 8 inches. *16 00*

1285 ICE CREAM TRAY, oblong form with handles at ends, heavy texture. 14 x 8 inches. *23 00*

1286 PRESERVE DISH, oval shape, bold diamond pattern. *14 00*

1287 PAIR JELLY DISHES, oval shape, heavy texture, bold cut. 2 pieces. *25 00*

1288 BERRY DISH, round shape with indented sides, heavy texture, bold cut. 12½ x 10 inches. *45 00*

1289 PAIR PRESERVE DISHES, to match. 2 pieces. *38 00*

1290 ICE CREAM TRAY, oval shape, with handles at ends, antique pattern. 14 x 8 inches. *22 00*

1291 FRUIT TRAY, to match, oval shape. 12 x 7 inches. *20 00*

1292 PAIR JELLY TRAYS, to match. 2 pieces. *40 00*

1293 —— Another pair, smaller. 2 pieces. *42 00*

1294 SALAD BOWL, antique shape, diamond pattern. *25 00*

1295 ICE CREAM TRAY, to match, oblong shape, with shell shape handles at ends. 13½ x 7½ inches. *30 00*

1296 PAIR JELLY TRAYS, to match, diamond shape. 2 pieces. *32 00*

1297 PAIR ROUND TRAYS, to match. 2 pieces. *16 00*

1298 OVAL TRAY, to match, with rim. 11 x 9 inches. *16 00*

1299 PAIR SHELL-SHAPE TRAYS, to match. 2 pieces. *16 00*

$10 50 1300 OBLONG TRAY, with rim, to match. 11 x 5 inches.

15 00 1301 PAIR PRESERVE DISHES, to match, oval, deep form. 2 pieces.

1302 FRUIT BASKET AND TRAY, antique shape, diamond pattern,
30 00 heavy texture. 11 x 6½ inches.

1303 PAIR PRESERVE TRAYS, to match, round, deep form. Diameter
28 00 10 inches. 2 pieces.

1304 PAIR FRUIT BASKETS, with trays, to match above, diamond
62 00 shape. 2 pieces.

32 00 1305 PAIR LARGE TRAYS, leaf shape, diamond pattern. 2 pieces.

21 00 1306 JELLY TRAY, oblong, deep form, boldly cut. 11 x 7 inches.

1307 PRESERVE TRAY, oval shape, with scalloped edge, diamond pattern.
16 00 11 x 8 inches.

1308 —— Another, similar shape and size, but different pattern,
15 00 heavy texture.

40 00 1309 RELISH TRAYS, antique shape, diamond pattern. 4 pieces.

1310 PAIR JELLY TRAYS, deep diamond shape, cut in squares.
40 00 9 x 4½ inches. 2 pieces.

1311 LARGE FRUIT STAND ON PEDESTAL, elaborate antique design, heavy texture. Height and diameter 12 x 9½ inches, can be
70 00 used with or without pedestal.

20 00 1312 SMALL FRUIT STAND, heavy texture, diamond pattern.

1313 PAIR CLARET FLAGONS, heavy texture, bold diamond pattern.
[illegible] 00 2 pieces.

50 00 1314 PAIR QUART DECANTERS, to match. 2 pieces.

144 00 1315 GOBLETS, to match. 36 pieces.

59 50 1316 CHAMPAGNE BOWLS, to match. 34 pieces.

85 00 1317 HOCK GLASSES, to match. 34 pieces.

63 00 1318 CLARET GLASSES, to match. 36 pieces.

45 00 1319 SHERRY GLASSES, to match. 36 pieces.

35 00 1320 LIQUEUR GLASSES, to match. 35 pieces.

88 00 1321 ALE PITCHERS, to match. 12 pieces.

222 75 1322 FINGER BOWLS AND PLATES, to match. 35 pieces.

20 00 1323 PAIR PINT DECANTERS, bold cut. 2 pieces.

1324 ENGRAVED GLASS ALE PITCHERS. 12 pieces. $48 00

1325 ALE GLASSES, to match. 10 pieces. 32 50

1326 TUMBLERS, to match. 6 pieces. 25 50

1327 CHAMPAGNE GLASSES, to match. 12 pieces. 21 00

BRONZES, SCULPTURE, CABINETS, ETC.

1328 BAS-RELIEF, in Bronze, "Le Christ au Tombeau," by Jean Goujon, F. Barbedienne, *Fondeur*. Height 7½ inches, width 18½ inches, mounted in crimson plush frame. 100 00

1329 BRONZE FIGURE, "North Wind," by Moreau. Height 36 inches. 230 00

1330 PEDESTAL for same. 28 00

1331 BRONZE FIGURE, "Summer," by Gregoire. Height 27 inches. 175 00

1332 PEDESTAL for same. 25 00

1333 BRONZE BUST, "A Chief of Timbuctoo," by A. Stralzer, 1880, marble base. Height 24 inches. 215 00

1334 TALL PEDESTAL for above, carved and polished brass. 165 00

1335 LIFE-SIZE FIGURE, in Carrara marble, "Reproof," by E. R. Thaxter, deceased. Height 36 inches. 1,050 00

1336 PEDESTAL for same, Verte antique marble. 150 00

1337 LIFE-SIZE BUST, in Carrara marble and bronze, "Othello," by Calvi, of Milan. 900 00

1338 PEDESTAL for same, carved onyx, with gold gilt ornaments and mountings. 375 00

1339 BRONZE FIGURE, "Eastern Dancing Girl." Height 28 inches. 200 00

1340 COMPANION to the above, "Eastern Dancing Boy." 200 00

1341 PAIR TALL PEDESTALS for the above, rose antique marble, with gold gilt mountings and ornaments. 2 pieces. 410 00

1342 BRONZE FIGURE, "The Fisher Girl," by B. Carpeaux. Height 28 inches, has black marble base. 165 00

1343 FIGURE IN BRONZE, "Psyche," by L. Gregoire. Height 38 inches. 225 00

1344 PEDESTAL for same, carved cherry, ebonized. 75 00

$1,700 00 1345 SCULPTURE IN IVORY, figure of "Fortune," by A. Moreau-Vauthier. Height of figure including Egyptian marble pedestal 33 inches, sold with hexagonal shape beveled glass case, with silver mountings, made to order by Tiffany & Co.

725 00 1346 FIGURE of "Andromeda," sculptured in ivory, by A. Moreau-Vauthier. Height, including Egyptian marble pedestal, 29 inches, has beveled glass case, with gold gilt mountings.

330 00 1347 MINIATURE BUST, in ivory, "Il Lazzarone," carved by A. Moreau-Vauthier. Pedestal of carved and polished agate, has silver and gold gilt stand, with glass shade.

425 00 1348 BUST, in Carrara marble, "Daisy," by C. Calverly. Height 15 inches.

525 00 1349 LARGE BRONZE, "Roman Boy Catching Crabs," by F. Moratilla, Rome. Height 52 inches, width at base 28 inches.

60 00 1350 PEDESTAL for same, carved cherry, ebonized, with black marble top.

1,000 00 1351 BRIC-À-BRAC CASE, beveled plate glass, with gold gilt bronze mountings, has movable shelf. Outside measurement height 28 inches, width 28 inches, depth 17 inches, made to order by Messrs. Herter Brothers.

1352 TABLE for the above, carved rosewood, with gold gilt mountings and ornaments, and shelf beneath, made to order by Messrs. Herter Brothers.

160 00 1353 BRIC-À-BRAC CASE, with side shelves, beveled plate glass, mounted in gold gilt bronze. Outside measurement 18 x 31 x 20 inches, made by Messrs. Herter Brothers.

90 00 1354 CARVED ROSEWOOD TABLE, for the above case, made to order by Messrs. Herter Brothers.

240 00 1355 ELABORATE CARVED OAK LIBRARY TABLE, with numerous drawers for etchings and engravings, made from original design by Messrs. Herter Brothers. Extreme outside measurement, 78 inches long, 48 inches wide, 30 inches high.

90 00 1356 ENGRAVING CASE, of carved oak, made to order by Messrs. Herter Brothers.

Fine Art and Other Books

Etchings and Engravings

SALE WEDNESDAY EVENING, MARCH 10,

BEGINNING AT 8 O'CLOCK.

AT THE AMERICAN ART GALLERIES.

FINE ART AND STANDARD BOOKS.

1357 ADVENTURES OF SAPPHO, POETESS OF MITYLENE: the text in Italian, with English translation facing each page. 2 vols. 8vo, calf, gilt. London, 1789. *$12 00*

Scarce and curious.

1358 AINSWORTH (W. H.). NOVELS. Best edition, *with numerous engravings by Cruikshank, H. K. Browne, Tony Johannot, etc.* 16 vols. 8vo, half mor. extra. London, n. d. *52 00*

Uniform library edition.

1359 ALCOCK (SIR R.). CAPITAL OF THE TYCOON; a narrative of a three years' residence in Japan. *Maps, and numerous illustrations on wood and in chromo-lithography.* 2 vols. 8vo, half calf extra. London, 1863. *5 50*

1360 ALDRICH (T. B.). POEMS. *Illustrated by the Paint and Clay Club, with the floral decorations in colors. Portrait.* 8vo, uncut. Boston, 1882. *13 00*

A fine specimen of American typography.

1361 ALGÆ. *Two hundred fine specimens,* carefully mounted and arranged in an album. Oblong 4to, mor., gilt edges and clasp. *30 00*

1362 ALISON (ARCHIBALD). HISTORY OF EUROPE. Both series *complete,* with Atlas. Large type, library edition. 24 vols. 8vo, *uniformly bound, calf extra, marbled edges, by Grieve.* Edinburgh, 1860. *96 00*

Fine copy.

1363 ALISON (SIR A.). ESSAYS, political, historical, and miscellaneous, 3 vols. 8vo, polished calf extra, by *Grieve.* London, 1850. *9 00*

Uniformly bound with the preceding and following items.

1364 ALISON (SIR A.). PRINCIPLES OF POPULATION, and their connection with human happiness. 2 vols. 8vo, calf extra, by *Grieve.* London, 1840.
$5 00

1365 AMERICAN CYCLOPEDIA. A Popular Dictionary of General Knowledge. Edited by George Ripley and Charles A. Dana, the ANNUALS to 1883 and INDEX. New edition, entirely revised and corrected. *Profusely illustrated.* 25 thick vols. roy. 8vo, tree calf extra, gilt edges, by *Mathews.* New York, *Appleton*, 1873.
137 50

1366 AMERICAN HISTORICAL AND LITERARY CURIOSITIES. Containing Fac-similes of some Plates, etc., relating to Columbus, and Original Documents of the Revolution, etc., etc. Edited and arranged by John Jay Smith and J. F. Watson. First series. Roy. 4to, half mor. Philadelphia, 1852.
7 50

1367 AMERICAN HISTORICAL AND LITERARY CURIOSITIES, etc., etc. with a Variety of Reliques, Antiquities, and Autographs. Second series complete, 64 plates. Roy. 4to, half mor. New York, 1860.
5 50

1368 AMERICAN PAINTERS. By G. W. Sheldon. *With 83 examples of their work engraved on wood.* 4to, mor., gilt edges. New York, 1879.
5 50

1369 ANTHON (CHARLES). CLASSICAL DICTIONARY, containing an account of the principal Proper Names mentioned in Ancient Authors. Thick roy. 8vo, sheep. New York, 1881.
2 75

1370 ARABIAN NIGHTS' ENTERTAINMENTS. Knight's pictorial Edition, translated, with copious notes by E. W. Lane. *Illustrated with several hundred woodcuts by Harvey.* 3 vols. roy. 8vo, brown crushed levant mor., gilt edges, by *Mathews.* London, 1841.
30 00

1371 ARGYLL (DUKE OF). THE REIGN OF LAW. 12mo, cloth. New York, 1879.
1 00

1372 ARMENGAUD (J. C. D.). THE PUBLIC GALLERIES OF ROME. *Several hundred woodcuts, illustrating the notable Galleries of Rome, with their treasures of art and antiquity. With numerous vignettes, culs-de-lampe,* etc., etc. Small folio, half red mor., gilt. Paris, 1859.
11 50

1373 ARTISTIC HOUSES, being a series of Interior Views of the most Beautiful and Celebrated Homes in the United States, with a description of the Art Treasures contained therein. *Over 200 fine photographs.* 4 vols. imp. folio, superbly bound in alligator skin, gilt edges, with velvet case. New York, 1883–84. *$200 00*

Only 500 copies printed. No. 338.

1374 ARTISTS AT HOME. 25 *fine portrait scenes in photo-engraving.* Edited by F. G. Stephens. Folio, cloth. New York (London), 1884. *5 00*

Comprises Millais, Alma-Tadema, Gilbert, Leighton, Redgrave, Webster, Cousins, Gladstone, etc.

1375 ART JOURNAL, complete from 1849 to 1883 inclusive. 35 vols. 4to, half red levant mor., extra, gilt edges. London, 1849–83. *148 75*

Uniform set, with an innumerable quantity of steel engravings and woodcuts—after the most celebrated modern painters. It includes all the plates contained in the Wilkie, Turner, Vernon, and Royal Galleries.

1376 ART TREASURES OF AMERICA, being the choicest works of art in the Public and Private Collections of North America. *With 93 plates and many woodcut illustrations.* Edited by Edward Strahan [Earl Shinn]. 12 large portfolios. Philadelphia, 1879. *78 00*

Edition de luxe, with proof impressions of the plates. No. 713.

1377 ATLAS.] COLTON'S ATLAS. *Colored maps.* Imp. 4to, half mor. New York, 1878. *5 50*

1378 ATLAS OF THE UNITED STATES AND ADJACENT COUNTRIES, by T. G. Bradford. *Colored maps.* Roy. 4to. half mor. Boston, 1838. *2 50*

1379 BALFE (M. W.). MEMOIR OF, by C. L. Kenney. *Portrait.* 8vo, half calf extra. London, 1875. *2 50*

1380 BARBER (J. W.). CONNECTICUT HISTORICAL COLLECTIONS. *Profusely illustrated.* 8vo, sheep. New Haven, 1836. *6 00*

1381 BARHAM. THE INGOLSBY LEGENDS; or, Mirth and Marvels, by Thos. Ingoldsby (Rev. R. H. Barham). Edited, with Notes, Introductory and Illustrative, by R. H. D. Barham. *Printed on heavy toned paper, with frontispiece and the celebrated series of plates by Cruikshank and Leech.* 2 vols. thick 8vo, polished calf extra, gilt edges. London, *Bentley,* 1876. *16 00*

1382 BARON MUNCHAUSEN, ADVENTURES OF. *With* 18 *colored plates by Bichard.* Folio, boards. London, n. d. — *$9 00*

1383 BARTLETT (J. R.). FAMILIAR QUOTATIONS: being at Attempt to Trace their Source. Passages and Phrases in Common Use. 12mo, mor. ant., gilt edges. Boston, 1875. — *5 50*

1384 BENTON (THOMAS H.). ABRIDGMENT OF THE DEBATES OF CONGRESS, 1789, vols. 1 and 2. Thick royal 8vo, cloth. New York, 1857. — *1 00*

1385 BERANGER (J. P. DE). ŒUVRES ET BIOGRAPHIE.

CHANSONS. 4 vols. 1865.
DERNIÈRES CHANSONS. 1 vol. n. d.
MUSIQUE. 1 vol. 1865.
MA BIOGRAPHIE. 1 vol. 1859.

UNIQUE SET, *having in addition to the plates by Tony Johannot, etc.* (*proofs on India paper*), *over* 275 *inserted plates, many proof impressions, and some woodcuts.* 7 vols. roy. 8vo, dark blue crushed levant mor. gilt backs, sides, and edges, and emblematic tooling, by *Marius Michel.* Paris, 1859. — *630 00*

An exceedingly fine set of books bound by the presiding bibliopegic genius.

1386 BERRY (MISS). EXTRACTS OF THE JOURNALS AND CORRESPONDENCE OF, from the year 1783 to 1852. Edited by Lady Theresa Lewis. *Portraits, etc.* 3 vols. 8vo, half calf, extra. London, 1865. — *8 25*

1387 BIRD (I. L.). SIX MONTHS IN THE SANDWICH ISLANDS. *Illustrated.* Crown 8vo, cloth. London, 1876. — *1 00*

1388 BISHOPS OF AMERICA. Album of Photographs. 4to, mor., gilt clasps. — *2 75*

1389 BOOK OF BEAUTY: complete from 1838 to 1849 inclusive: over 200 steel engravings. 12 vols. 8vo, half calf extra, gilt edges. London, 1838–49. — *36 00*

1390 BOOK OF GEMS; or, the Poets and Artists of Great Britain. Edited by S. C. Hall. Original Edition. Printed on thick paper, *and illustrated with* 150 *Engravings on Steel, from drawings by Mulready, Cooper, Eastlake, Prout, Stanfield, Collins, Stothard, David Cox, J. W. M. Turner, and other eminent artists.* 3 vols. 8vo, red mor. extra, gilt leaves. London, 1844, etc. — *21 00*

1391 BRIC-À-BRAC SERIES. Greville Memoirs, Anecdote Biographies of Dickens and Thackeray, Personal Reminiscences of Lamb, Hazlitt, Moore, Constable, Raikes, O'Keeffe, Kelly, Jerdan, etc., etc. 10 vols. 16mo, half calf extra.
New York, 1876, etc. *$25 00*

1392 BRITISH ESSAYISTS; with Prefaces, Historical and Biographical, by A. Chalmers. *Portraits on India paper.* 38 vols. 12mo, half red mor., extra gilt tops, uncut edges.
Boston, 1866. *85 50*

Large paper, 100 copies printed. No. 36. Comprises the Tatler, Spectator, Guardian, Rambler, Adventurer, World, Connoisseur, Idler, Mirror, Lounger, Observer, Looker-On, etc. etc., with index.

1393 BRITISH POETS. GILFILLAN'S LIBRARY EDITION, with Lives, Critical Dissertations and Notes. *Printed in large type with portraits.* 48 vols. 8vo, half calf extra. Edinburgh, 1868, etc. *96 00*

Comprises Akenside, Addison, Armstrong, Beattie, Blair, Bowles, Burns, Butler, Churchill, Collins, Cowper, Crashaw, Chaucer, Denham, Dryden, Dyer, Faulkner, Gay, Goldsmith, Graham, Gray, Greene, Herbert, Johnson, Kirke White, Milton, Parnell, Percy's Reliques, Prior, Pope, Quarles, Scott, Shakespeare, Somerville, Shenstone, Smollett, Spenser, Surrey, Thompson, Waller, Warton, Wyatt, Young, and less-known poets.

1394 BREWER (E. C.). READER'S HANDBOOK. 8vo, half mor.
Philadelphia, 1880. *3 00*

1395 BROGNIART ET RIOCREUX. Description du Musée Céramique, de la manufacture Royale de Porcelaine de Sèvres. *With over 100 colored plates.* 2 vols. roy. 4to, half red mor., gilt tops, uncut edges. Paris, 1845. *23 00*

1396 BRONTÉ (MISSES). LIFE AND WORKS. *Illustrated by numerous woodcuts.* 7 vols. crown 8vo, half calf extra. London, 1875. *24 50*

Includes: Jane Eyre, Shirley, Professor, Wuthering Heights, Agnes Grey, Tenant of Wildfell Hall, and Life.

1397 BRONTÉ (CHARLOTTE). POEMS. 16mo, mor., gilt edges.
New York, 1882. *2 00*

1398 BRONTÉ. SHIRLEY, AND VILETTE. 2 vols. 12mo, cloth. *1 00*

1399 BROWN (DR. JOHN). SPARE HOURS. 2 vols. 12mo, half calf extra. Boston, 1877. *5 50*

1400 Bruyère (Jean de la). The Characters of, newly rendered into English, with an Introduction, Biographical Memoir, and copious notes, by Henri Van Laun. *With 7 etched portraits by Damman, and 17 vignettes, etched by Foulquier and printed on China paper.* 8vo, half parchment, gilt top, uncut.
$9 00 London, 1885.

Only 500 copies printed, each of which is numbered. No. 45.

1401 Bryan (Michael). Biographical and Critical Dictionary of Painters and Engravers. Revised by Stanley.
15 00 *Portrait and Monograms.* Imp. 8vo, Russia. London, 1849.

1402 Bryant (W. C.). Poems. *Portrait and over 100 illustrations.*
4 25 8vo, mor. antique, gilt edges. New York, 1876.

1403 Buist (R.). American Flower Garden Directory. 12mo,
60 cloth. New York, 1858.

1404 Bulwer-Lytton. Novels and Tales. *Frontispieces.* 23 vols. 16mo, half calf extra, contents lettered.
74 75 Philadelphia, 1871.

Contents: My Novel, 2 vols.; What will he do with it, 2 vols.; Pilgrims of the Rhine and Lelia, Alice, Godolphin, Harold, Eugene Aram, Pompeii, Rienzi, Caxtons, Pelham, Disowned, Paul Clifford, Lucretia, Strange Story, Maltravers, Night and Morning, Last of the Barons, Devereux, Zanoni.

1405 Bunyan (John). Pilgrim's Progress. *With 100 illustrations on Japan paper, by Fred. Barnard, etc.* 4to, half vellum, un-
29 00 cut. London, 1880.

Only 500 printed. No. 226.

1406 Bunyan's Pilgrim's Progress, Holy War, etc. *Colored plates.*
12 50 4to, mor. ant., gilt edges. London, n. d.

1407 Burbidge (F. W.). The Gardens of the Sun. *Illustrated.*
1 00 8vo, cloth. London, 1880.

1408 Burton (Captain R. F.). The Lake Regions of Central Africa. *Map and plates.* Roy. 8vo, half calf extra.
3 00 New York, 1860.

1409 Byron (Lord). Poetical Works. *Portrait.* 6 vols. 8vo, red
34 50 mor. extra, gilt edges. London, *Murray*, 1855.

1410 Byron (Lord). Works, Life, and Contemporary Reminiscences, as follows:

I. Byron's Poetical Works. *Finden's plates.* 6 vols. 8vo.
137 50 1855.

II. BYRON (LORD). LETTERS AND JOURNALS OF LORD BYRON, with Notices of his Life, by Thomas Moore. 3d edition, *with a series of 44 engravings by Finden.* 3 vols. 8vo. 1833.

III. RECOLLECTIONS OF THE LIFE OF LORD BYRON, from 1808 to 1814, by R. C. Dallas. *Fac-similes.* 1824.

IV. CONVERSATIONS ON RELIGION WITH LORD BYRON AND OTHERS, by J. Kennedy. *Fac-simile.* 1830.

V. NARRATIVE OF BYRON'S LAST JOURNEY TO GREECE, by Count Gamba. 1825.

VI. CONVERSATIONS OF LORD BYRON, noted during a Residence with his lordship at Pisa, 1821–22. By T. Medwin. *Fac-simile.* 1824.

VII. MY RECOLLECTIONS OF LORD BYRON, by the Countess Guiccioli. *Portrait.* 2 vols. 1869.

VIII. GREECE IN 1823–24, with Reminiscences of Lord Byron, by Col. Stanhope. *Portrait*, etc. 1824.

IX. NARRATIVE OF A SECOND VISIT TO GREECE, by E. Blacquiere. 1825.

X. LETTERS ON THE CHARACTER AND POETICAL GENIUS OF BYRON, by Sir Egerton Brydges. 1824.

XI. LAST DAYS OF BYRON, by Wm. Parry. 1825.

XII. HISTORICAL ILLUSTRATIONS OF THE FOURTH CANTO OF CHILDE HARÓLD, by J. Hobhouse. 1818.

XIII. BYRON AND SOME OF HIS CONTEMPORARIES, by Leigh Hunt. *Portraits.* 2 vols. 1828.

Together 22 vols. 8vo, crimson calf extra, gilt tops, uncut edges. London, 1818–69.

UNIQUE SET, *with over 250 inserted plates. No. IX is an autograph presentation copy from the author.*—BLACQUIER.

1411 BYRON.] MOORE (THOMAS). LETTERS AND JOURNALS OF LORD BYRON, with Notices of his Life. *Fine portrait.* 4 vols. 4to., red mor. extra, gilt edges, by *Riviere.*

London, *Murray*, 1830. *$132 00*

Original edition. UNIQUE COPY, *with over 350 plates added, including a set of the Finden illustrations on India paper, and very many rare portraits in fine condition, mostly proofs and on India paper.*

1412 CALEDONIA, described by Scott, Burns, and Ramsay. *Illus-*
$2 00 *trated by John Macwhirter.* 4to, cloth. London, 1878.

1413 CAMPBELL (THOMAS). POETICAL WORKS. Printed on thick paper, *and illustrated with 20 engravings from designs by Turner.* Square 8vo, blue mor. extra, gilt leaves, by *Chatelin.*
12 00 London, *Moxon,* 1837.

1414 CARLYLE (THOMAS). COMPLETE WORKS. Large type, library edition, comprising: MISCELLANEOUS ESSAYS, 6 vols. FRENCH REVOLUTION, 3 vols. LIFE OF SCHILLER, 1 vol. SARTOR RESARTUS, 1 vol. LECTURES ON HEROES, 1 vol. PAST AND PRESENT, 1 vol. CROMWELL'S LETTERS AND SPEECHES, *portraits,* 5 vols. LATTER-DAY PAMPHLETS, 1 vol. LIFE OF JOHN STERLING, *portrait,* 1 vol. HISTORY OF FREDERICK THE SECOND, 10 vols. GERMAN TRANSLATIONS, 3 vols. GENERAL INDEX to the Set, 1 vol. Together, 34 vols, 8vo,
127 50 half calf extra. London, 1869, etc.

Best edition.

1415 CATS AND FAIRLIE. MORAL EMBLEMS, including Aphorisms, Adages, and Proverbs of all Nations. *With 60 illustrations on wood, etc., by Leighton.* 4to, mor. extra, gilt edges.
7 00 London, 1865.

1416 CERVANTES (MIGUEL DE). DON QUIXOTE DE LA MANCHA. Cadell's beautiful large type edition, printed by Bulmer. Translated from the Spanish (by Mary Smirke). *Illustrated with the series of engravings and vignettes from pictures painted by Robert Smirke.* 4 vols. 8vo, crimped mor. extra, gilt edges.
47 00 London, *Cadell & Davies,* 1818.

1417 CHESTERFIELD (LORD). LETTERS WRITTEN TO HIS SON. Edited by C. S. Carey. *Portrait.* 2 vols. post 8vo, half calf
9 00 extra. London, 1872.

1418 CHOLMONDELEY-PENNELL (H.). FROM GRAVE TO GAY. Poems.
1 00 *Portrait.* 16mo, cloth, uncut. London, 1884.

1419 CHURCH (A. J.). STORIES FROM VIRGIL. 24 *illustrations.* Post
3 50 8vo, tree calf extra. London, 1879.

1420 CLAYTON (ELLEN C.). ENGLISH FEMALE ARTISTS. 2 vols.
5 00 8vo, half calf extra. London, 1876.

1421 CLEMENT AND HUTTON. ARTISTS OF THE NINETEENTH
4 00 CENTURY. 2 vols. 12mo, cloth. Boston, 1880.

1422 COLERIDGE (SARA). MEMOIR AND LETTERS. *Portrait.* 2 vols. crown 8vo, half calf extra. London, 1873. *$4 00*

1423 COMPENDIUM OF GEOGRAPHY. AFRICA, AND CENTRAL AND SOUTH AMERICA. *Colored maps, etc.* 2 vols. crown 8vo, half calf extra. London, 1878. *5 00*

1424 CONDÉ.] HISTOIRE DES PRINCES DE CONDÉ, PAR LE DUC D'AUMALE. *Portrait.* 2 vols. 8vo, uncut. Paris, 1863 (?) *2 50*

1425 COOPER (J. FENIMORE). WORKS. *Illustrated Library Edition* printed in large type. *Engravings from designs by F. O. C. Darley, woodcuts, etc.* With a Biographical Essay by William Cullen Bryant. 32 vols. 12mo, half calf extra. New York, 1872. *112 00*

1426 COSTELLO (LOUISA). PILGRIMAGE TO AUVERGNE, FROM PICARDY TO LE VELAY. *Tinted plates.* 2 vols. 8vo. 1842. *25 00*

BEARN AND THE PYRENEES, a Legendary Tour to the Country of Henry IV. *Tinted plates.* 2 vols. 1844.

SUMMER AMONG THE BOCAGES AND VINES. *Frontispieces.* 2 vols. 8vo. 1840.

TOUR TO AND FROM VENICE, BY THE VAUDOIS AND THE TYROL. *Tinted plates.* 8vo. 1846.

MEMOIRS OF MARY OF BURGUNDY. Post 8vo. 1853.

MEMOIRS OF ANNE OF BRITTANY. Post 8vo. 1853.

JACQUES CŒUR, THE FRENCH ARGONAUT. *Portraits.* 8vo. 1847.

Together 10 vols. half calf extra. London, 1840–53.

1427 COSTUMES OF VARIOUS COUNTRIES, ETC. *92 75*

I. THE COSTUME OF AUSTRIA, displayed in 50 *colored engravings;* with Descriptions and Introduction by M. Bertrand de Moleville. Translated by R. C. Dallas. 1804.

II. THE COSTUME OF CHINA. *Illustrated by* 60 *colored engravings,* with Explanations in French and English. By George Henry Mason. 1804.

III. THE PUNISHMENTS OF CHINA. *Illustrated by* 22 *engravings (colored),* with explanations in English and French. 1801.

IV. THE COSTUME OF GREAT BRITAIN. 60 *colored plates*, designed, engraved and written by W. H. Pyne. 1804.

V. THE COSTUME OF THE RUSSIAN EMPIRE. *Illustrated by a series of 73 engravings (colored)*, with descriptions in English. 1803.

VI. THE COSTUME OF TURKEY. *Illustrated by a series of 60 engravings (colored)*, and descriptions in English and French. 1804.

VII. THE MILITARY COSTUME OF TURKEY. *Illustrated by a series of 31 engravings (colored)*, from drawings made on the spot. 1818.

Together 7 vols. roy. 4to, mor. extra.

1428 COWPER (WM.). THE TASK. Illustrated by *Birket Foster.*
$3 00 8vo, cloth. New York, *London*, 1778.

1429 CRABBE (GEO.). POETICAL WORKS, with his Letters, Journals, and Life, by his Son. *Vignette illustrations by Finden.* 8 vols. foolscap 8vo, half red mor. extra, gilt tops, uncut edges.
13 00 London, 1834.

1430 CRABB (GEO.) ENGLISH SYNONYMS. 8vo, sheep.
2 00 New York, 1848.

1431 CROSBY (S. S.). EARLY COINS OF AMERICA; and the Laws governing their Issue. *Many hundred illustrations.* 4to, half
11 50 mor. Boston, 1878.

1432 CROWE AND CAVALCASELLE. HISTORY OF PAINTING IN ITALY, from the Second to the Fourteenth Century; drawn from fresh materials after recent researches in the archives of Italy. *Several hundred engravings on wood.* 3 vols. 8vo,
54 00 tree calf extra, gilt edges. London, *Murray*, 1864–6.

"*The Works of Messrs. Crowe and Cavalcaselle are by far the richest mine of information upon Italian Painting that has been opened to us for many a long day. In a judicious, philosophical way it associates picture with picture, artist with artist, and school with school, illustrating and drawing illustration from all, by showing their general connection with the general history and the social and political tendencies of their own times.*"—EXAMINER.

1433 CUNNINGHAM (PETER). STORY OF NELL GWYNNE AND THE SAYINGS OF CHARLES THE SECOND. Post 8vo. $175 00

EXTRA ILLUSTRATED. The text carefully inlaid to 4to, and neatly ruled throughout. *Over 200 fine and rare engravings inserted, comprising Portraits of Nell Gwynne and other celebrities, including the Portraits of Oliver Cromwell's Porter, Doctor Busby, Oldys, Betterton, Nell Gwynne by Bartolozzi, etc., Davenant, Sedley, Oughtred, Killegrew, Wm. Cartwright, Joe Harris, Mrs. Bracegirdle, Miss Fenton, Mrs. Behn, Tom D'Urfey, Mrs. Barry, Col. Blood, Chiffinch, Bp. Ken, Mohun, Jane Shore, Sir Wm. Temple, Cave Underhill, Sir Robt. Vyner*, and many others, *also a choice series of Views, etc.* One thick vol. 4to, elegantly bound in full crimson levant mor., crushed and polished, full gilt back, inside borders, gilt top, uncut edges, by *Mathews.*
London, *Bradbury & Evans*, 1852.

1434 DANTE (ALIGHIERI). DIVINE COMEDY. Translated by H. W. Longfellow. 3 vols. imp. 8vo, half calf extra. Boston, 1873. *15 75*

1435 D'ARBLAY (MADAME). [FANNY BURNEY.] DIARY AND LETTERS complete, including the period of her residence at the Court of Queen Charlotte. *Portraits.* 7 vols. post 8vo, half calf extra. London, 1842. *33 25*

Best Edition.

1436 DARWIN (CHAS.). MOVEMENTS AND HABITS OF CLIMBING PLANTS. *Illustrated.* Crown 8vo, cloth. London, 1875. *2 75*

1437 DARWIN (C.). INSECTIVOROUS PLANTS. *Illustrated.* 12mo, cloth. New York, 1875. *1 25*

1438 D'AVILLIER (BARON CH.). SPAIN. [A Picturesque Tour.] *Printed on heavy paper and illustrated by 240 engravings on wood by the best artists, after drawings by Gustave Doré.* Text translated by J. Thompson. Imp. 4to, cloth extra, gilt edges. New York, *London*, 1876. *10 50*

1439 DIBDIN (T. F.). BIBLIOGRAPHICAL ANTIQUARIAN AND PICTURESQUE TOUR IN FRANCE AND GERMANY. Second Edition. *Portrait and plates.* 3 vols. 8vo, calf extra, gilt tops, uncut edges. London, *Major*, 1829. *13 50*

1440 DICKENS (CHARLES). WORKS, Complete. The new and Elegantly printed STANDARD EDITION in large type, on heavy paper, *and most profusely illustrated with engravings on steel and wood.* 30 vols. 8vo, half calf extra.

$112 50 London, *Chapman & Hall*, 1873, etc.

1441 DIEULAFAIT (L.). DIAMONDS AND PRECIOUS STONES. 126

2 00 *woodcuts.* 12mo, cloth. New York, 1876.

1442 D'ISRAELI, BENJAMIN (*Earl of Beaconsfield*). Collected WORKS. New edition. *Portrait, etc.* 10 thick vols. crown

20 00 8vo, cloth. London, 1875.

Comprising: Henrietta Temple, Tancred, Young Duke, Coningsby, Vivian Grey, Ixion, Lothair, Alroy, Sibyl, Venetia, Contarini Fleming.

1443 DIXON (W. H.). FREE RUSSIA. *With colored illustrations.* 2

3 50 vols. 8vo, half calf gilt. London, 1870.

1444 DORAN (DR.). WORKS. *Portraits.* 10 vols. post 8vo, calf extra.

47 50 London, 1855–60.

Comprises: Lives of the Queens of England, 2 vols.; Monarchs retired from Business, 2 vols.; Table Traits; Habits and Men; Knights and their Days; Princes of Wales; New Pictures in Old Panels; and Court Fools. All very scarce.

1445 DORÉ (GUSTAVE). LA FONTAINE FABLES DE, avec un notice sur la Vie de Jean La Fontaine, par Geruzez. *Illustrated with upwards of 300 large engravings and vignettes from designs by Doré.* 2 vols. roy. folio, half red levant mor. extra, gilt edges.

44 00 Paris, 1867.

Prefaced with India proof impression of the portrait of La Fontaine, engraved on steel by Delonnoy.

1446 DORÉ (GUSTAVE). LA SAINTE BIBLE. *With fine impressions of the 230 engravings from the celebrated designs by Doré.* 2 vols.

56 00 roy. folio, half red levant mor. extra, gilt edges. Tours, 1866.

1447 DORÉ. THE RAVEN, by E. A. Poe. *Illustrated by Gustave*

6 25 *Doré.* Atlas 4to, cloth extra. New York, 1884.

1448 DRAKE (J. R.). THE CULPRIT FAY. *Illustrated.* Small 4to,

4 50 tree calf extra. New York, 1879.

omitted 1449 DRURY (VICTOR). HISTORY OF ROME. Translated by W. J.
from Clarke, edited by J. P. Mahaffy. *Profusely illustrated.* 5 vols.
sale. imp. 8vo, half red mor., gilt tops. Boston, 1884.

Edition de Grand Luxe. No. 159.

1450 DU CHAILLU (PAUL B.). JOURNEY TO ASHANGO-LAND; and further penetration into Equatorial Africa. *Map and illustrations.* 8vo, half calf extra. New York, 1867. *$3 25*

1451 DUMAS (ALEX.). LE COMTE DE MONTE-CRISTO. *Plates and woodcuts.* 2 vols. roy. 8vo, half mor. Paris, 1846. *14 00*

1452 DUNCAN (PROF. P. M.). TRANSFORMATIONS (or Metamorphoses) OF INSECTS, second edition: *with very numerous plates.* Roy. 8vo, half calf extra. London, n. d. *2 75*

1453 EDGEWORTH (MISS). TALES AND NOVELS, Complete. *frontispieces and vignettes.* 18 vols. foolscap 8vo, mor., gilt tops. uncut edges. London, 1832. *45 00*

Best edition. Including Moral Tales, Popular Tales, Belinda, Castle Rackrent, Irish Bulls, Self-Justification, Tales of Fashionable Life, Patronage, Ormond, etc.

1454 EDWARDS (C.). HISTORY AND POETRY OF FINGER RINGS. *Woodcuts.* 12mo, cloth. New York, 1880. *1 50*

1455 ELIOT GEORGE (MARIAN C. EVANS, MRS. G. H. LEWES.) WORKS: viz., Adam Bede, 2 vols.; Mill on the Floss, 2 vols.; Scenes of Clerical Life, 2 vols.; Felix Holt, 2 vols.; Romola, 2 vols.; Silas Marner, 1 vol.; Middlemarch, 3 vols.; Daniel Derondo, 4 vols. Spanish Gipsy, and poems. Together 19 vols. post 8vo, uniformly bound in half blue mor., gilt top, uncut edges. Edinburgh, *Blackwood,* 1878, etc. *59 38*

1456 ELLIOTT (C. W.). POTTERY AND PORCELAIN. 165 *illustrations.* 4to mor. antique, gilt edges. New York, 1878. *6 25*

1457 EMERSON (G. B.). REPORT ON THE TREES AND SHRUBS OF MASSACHUSETTS. *Numerous colored plates and other illustrations.* 2 vols. roy. 8vo, half red mor. extra, gilt tops, uncut edges. Boston, 1875. *15 50*

1458 EZEKIEL AND OTHER POEMS, by B. M. 16mo, russia extra, gilt edges. *2 12*

1459 FALKE (J. VON). ART IN THE HOUSE. Translated and edited by C. C. Perkins. *Profusely illustrated, some plates in colors.* Imp. 8vo. cloth, gilt. Boston, 1879. *6 50*

1460 FÉNELON. ADVENTURES OF TELEMACHUS. 100 *illustrations.* 8vo, half calf extra. New York, n. d. *4 25*

1461 FERGUSSON (JAMES). HISTORY OF ARCHITECTURE in all Countries, from the earliest times to the present day; also, HISTORY OF THE MODERN STYLES OF ARCHITECTURE AND INDIAN AND EASTERN ARCHITECTURE. *Upwards of* 1,500 *engravings on wood.* 4 vols. 8vo, half mor., gilt tops, uncut.
$41 00 London, *Murray*, 1841.

1462 FIGUIER (LOUIS). THE INSECT WORLD; being a popular account of the Orders of Insects, the Habits and Economy of some of the most interesting species. *Profusely illustrated, upwards of* 579 *engravings on wood.* 12mo, half calf extra.
5 50 New York, n. d.

1463 FLIGHT (E. G.). ST. DUNSTAN AND THE DEVIL. *Plates by*
2 50 *Geo. Cruikshank.* Small 4to, cloth. London, 1871.

1464 FONVIELLE (W. DE). ADVENTURES IN THE AIR. *Illustrated.*
2 75 Post 8vo, half calf extra. London, 1877.

1465 FORD (JOHN). DRAMATIC WORKS, with Notes by William Gifford. Additions, etc., by Alex. Dyce. 3 vols. crown 8vo, half
12 00 mor. extra, gilt tops, uncut edges. London, 1869.
Best edition.

1466 FOREST (J. B. DE), SHORT HISTORY OF ART. *Illustrated.*
1 25 12mo, cloth. New York, 1881.

1467 FREER (MISS MARTHA W.). HISTORICAL NOVELS: comprising: Henry III., 3 vols.; History of Henry IV. of Navarre, 3 *plates*, 6 vols.; Life of Jeanne D'Albret, Queen of Navarre, 2 vols.; Elizabeth of Valois, Queen of Spain, 2 vols.; Marguerite D'Angoulême, Queen of Navarre, 2 vols. *Numerous portraits.* Together, 15 vols. post 8vo, uniformly bound in
52 50 half calf extra. London, 1854.

1468 FRIENDSHIP'S OFFERING FOR 1846 AND 1849, and the GIFT.
3 75 1843. *Illustrated.* 3 vols. 12mo, roan. Boston, 1843–49.

1469 FROISSART (SIR JOHN). CHRONICLES of England, France, Spain, etc., from Edward II. to Henry IV. Translated by Johnes. *Numerous illustrations, and the illuminated plates selected from the MS. in the British Museum, by H. N. Humphreys.* 36 *colored plates.* 2 vols. roy. 8vo, half mor., gilt
39 00 edges. London, 1874.

1470 FROMENTIN (EUGENE). PAINTER AND WRITER. By Louis Gonse. Translated by Mary C. Robbins. Small 4to, cloth. Boston, 1883. $2 00

1471 FROUDE (J. A.). HISTORY OF ENGLAND, from the Fall of Wolsey to the Defeat of the Spanish Armada. 12 vols. 8vo, tree marbled calf extra, by *Rivière.* London, 1875. 72 00
Best edition.

1472 FRY (W. H.). ARTIFICIAL FISH BREEDING. *Woodcuts.* 12mo, cloth. New York, 1866. 30

1473 FULLER (DR. THOS.). WORKS, comprising the Worthies of England, Church History of Britain, History of Cambridge University and Waltham Abbey, and the Holy and Profane State; BEST EDITIONS, edited by Nichols and Nuttall. *Portraits and engravings.* 8 vols. 8vo, calf extra. London, 1837–40. 32 00

1474 GALERIE DURAND-RUEL. 300 *etchings.* Preface par Armand Silvestre. 3 vols. 4to, half red mor., gilt tops. Paris, 1873. 39 75
Only a small edition printed on Holland paper.

1475 GARDEN (THE). An illustrated weekly Journal. *Profusely illustrated with woodcuts and colored plates.* 18 vols. 4to, cloth. London, 1872–80. 18 00
Complete from the commencement to 1880 inclusive, with some additional numbers, and 2 duplicate vols.

1476 GAY (J.). FABLES, WITH LIFE. Stockdale's fine Edition, printed in large type. 70 *plates by Blake, Audinet, Wilson, etc.* 2 vols. in one, imp. 8vo, tree calf extra. London, 1793. 15 50
Fine tall copy.

1477 GIRAULT DUVIVIER. Grammaire des Grammaires. 2 vols. 8vo, half mor. Paris, 1859. 2 00

1478 GOETHE. WORKS. Comprising Autobiography, 2 vols.; Novels and Tales, 1 vol.; Poems, 1 vol.; Dramatic Works, 1 vol.; Conversations, 1 vol.; Wilhelm Meister, 1 vol.; Translated from the German. *Portraits, etc.* 7 vols. foolscap 8vo, half calf extra, marbled edges. London, 1874. 31 50
The only uniform English Edition.

1479 GOETHE. FAUST: a Tragedy. Translated, in the Original Metres, by Bayard Taylor. 2 vols. roy. 8vo, half mor. extra, gilt tops, uncut edges, by *Smith.* Boston, 1871. 14 00

1480 GOLDSMITH (OLIVER). COMPLETE WORKS. Library Edition, Edited by Peter Cunningham. *Frontispiece.* 4 vols. 8vo, red calf extra, gilt tops, uncut edges. London, *Murray*, 1854. — $24 00

Best edition.

1481 GOLDSMITH (O.). POETICAL WORKS, with Life and Notes by Bolton Corney. *Profusely illustrated by wood engravings after Cope, Creswick, Horsley, Redgrave, and Tayler.* Sq. 8vo, mor. extra, gilt leaves, by *Mathews.* London, 1845. — 9 50

1482 GOLDSMITH. THE VICAR OF WAKEFIELD. *With 32 illustrations by William Mulready, R.A.* 8vo, red mor. extra, gilt edges. London, 1843. — 13 00

Very Scarce.

1483 GOODALE (ELAINE AND DORA READ). APPLE BLOSSOMS, and IN BERKSHIRE WITH THE WILD FLOWERS. *Illustrated.* 2 vols. 4to, cloth. New York, 1878–80. — 4 25

1484 GREAT ARTISTS (THE). BIOGRAPHIES, by eminent writers. *Illustrated.* 33 vols. small 8vo, cloth. London, 1880, etc. — 33 00

Includes: Tintoretto, Correggio, Murillo, Raphael, Giotto, Da Vinci, Masaccio, Fra Angelico, Michael Angelo, Titian, Romney, Lawrence, Wilkie, Hogarth, Turner, Gainsborough, Constable, Landseer, Reynolds, Del Sarto, Rubens, Meissonier, Watteau, Velasquez, Rembrandt, Hals, Dürer, Vandyke, Vernet, Delaroche, Holbein, etc., etc.

1485 GREAT MUSICIANS. Edited by F. Hueffner. 12 vols. 12mo, cloth. New York (London), 1883, etc. — 9 00

Includes: Handel, Mozart, Haydn, Mendelssohn, Schumann, Bach, Weber, Wagner, Rossini, Schubert, Purcell, and English Church Composers.

1486 GREENWOOD GEMS: 28 photographs of cheerful tomb-stones, and graveyard scenes, with interesting details relative to cost of erection, etc., oblong 4to, cloth. New York, 1868. — 8 00

1487 GROTE (GEORGE). HISTORY OF GREECE. From the Earliest Period to the close of the generation contemporary with Alexander the Great. *Portrait, maps,* and a complete Index. 12 vols. 8vo, tree calf extra. London, 1851, etc. — 72 00

Best edition.

1488 GUIZOT (F.) POPULAR HISTORY OF FRANCE, from the Earliest Times. Translated by R. Black, *with 300 illustrations by A. de Neuville.* 5 vols. roy. 8vo, half red mor., gilt tops, uncut edges. London, 1872–76. — 33 75

1489 HARTWIG (G.). THE AERIAL WORLD 8 *tinted plates, map and numerous woodcuts.* 8vo, half calf extra.
New York (London), 1875. *$3 75*

1490 HAVERGAL (F. R.). POEMS. 3 vols. 32mo, calf extra.
New York (London), 1879. *5 25*

1491 HAWTHORNE (NATHANIEL). COMPLETE WORKS. *Elegantly printed, and illustrated with portraits and etchings.* 12 vols. roy. 8vo, cloth uncut. Boston, 1883. *96 00*

Edition de luxe. Only 500 copies printed. No. 126.

1492 HAWTHORNE (NATHANIEL). WORKS. Little Classic Edition. 23 vols. 16mo, half mor. extra. Boston, 1876. *41 40*

1493 HAZLITT (W. C.). ENGLISH PROVERBS AND PROVERBIAL PHRASES. 8vo, half mor. extra. London, 1869. *4 25*

1494 HERCULANEUM AND POMPEII. 151 *beautiful outline illustrations of paintings etc. in the Museo Nazionale.* 4to, boards.
Napoli, 1863. *13 50*

1495 HIBBERD (S.). AMATEUR'S GREENHOUSE AND CONSERVATORY, also the ROSE BOOK. *Colored plates and woodcuts.* 2 vols. crown 8vo, cloth. London, 1873–74. *2 25*

1496 HISTORIC GALLERY OF PORTRAITS AND PAINTINGS, with Lives, Notes, etc., *and a large number of outline engravings.* 4 vols. 8vo, cloth, uncut. London, n. d. *7 20*

1497 HOLE AND WHEELER. BRIEF BIOGRAPHICAL DICTIONARY. 16mo, cloth. New York, 1866. *1 00*

1498 HOMER. ILIAD AND ODYSSEY. Translated into English verse by W. Sotheby. *Illustrated by* 73 *designs by Flaxman, engraved in outline by Moses, fine original impressions.* 4 vols. 8vo, half red mor. extra, gilt tops, uncut edges.
London, 1834. *22 00*

Sotheby's translation is equally remarkable for its poetic feeling and fidelity. Only a small edition was printed, at the expense of the translator.

1499 HOOD (THOMAS). WORKS. Comic and Serious, in Prose and Verse. *With all the original illustrations and portrait.* 10 vols. post 8vo, half calf, gilt. London, 1869. *30 00*

Best library edition of the works of this inimitable writer.

1500 HOOKER AND BAKER. SYNOPSIS OF ALL KNOWN FERNS. *Colored plates.* 8vo, cloth. London, 1874.
$4 25

1501 HORNBY (ADMIRAL). CRUISE ROUND THE WORLD IN THE FLYING SQUADRON 1869–70. *Maps and colored plates.* 8vo, half calf extra. London, 1871.
2 50

1502 HOWITT (W.). WORKS. VISITS TO REMARKABLE PLACES; Old Halls, Battle-Fields, and Scenes illustrative of striking passages in English History and Poetry, BOTH SERIES, *with numerous wood engravings.* 2 vols. 1840–42.
59 50

RURAL LIFE OF ENGLAND. *With woodcuts by Bewick and Williams.* 2 vols. 1844.

HOMES AND HAUNTS of the most eminent BRITISH POETS. *With 41 engravings of famous houses, localities, etc.* 2 vols. 1847.

RURAL AND DOMESTIC LIFE IN GERMANY. 50 *woodcuts.* 1842.

NORTHERN HEIGHTS OF LONDON. *Profusely illustrated.* 1869.

Together, 7 vols. 8vo, calf extra, gilt edges. London, 1840–69.

Fine uniform set.

1503 HUEFFER (F.). THE TROUBADOURS. A History of Provençal Life and Literature in the Middle Ages. 8vo, half calf extra. London, 1878.
4 00

1504 HUGO (VICTOR). NOTRE DAME. *Illustrated.* 8vo, cloth. London, n. d.
2 50

1505 HUMBERT (A.). JAPAN AND THE JAPANESE. Illustrated. Translated by Mrs. Hoey, and edited by H. W. Bates. *Illustrated by nearly 200 exquisite woodcuts.* 4to. half mor. extra gilt edges. New York (London), 1874.
9 00

1506 HUME (D.). HISTORY OF ENGLAND. *Woodcuts.* 12mo, cloth. New York, 1863.
1 50

1507 IRVING (WASHINGTON). COMPLETE WORKS, with Life and Letters. *Portraits and other engravings.* 28 vols. 12mo, half calf extra. Philadelphia, 1871.
70 00

1508 ITALY FROM THE ALPS TO MOUNT ETNA. Translated by F. E. Trollope, edited by T. A. Trollope. *With upwards of* 100 *full-page engravings, and* 300 *woodcuts from designs by Keller, Closs, Bauenfeind, Heilbuth, etc.* Roy. 4to, half mor. extra gilt edges. New York (London), 1877. *$13 50*

1509 JAMES (G. P. R.). NOVELS. Best edition, *with frontispieces.* 21 vols. roy. 8vo, half calf extra. London, 1844–49. *68 25*

Includes: Gipsy, Mary of Burgundy, Huguenot, One in a Thousand, Philip Augustus, Henry of Guise, Morley Ernstein, Robber, Darnley, Brigand, King's Highway, Gentleman of the Old School, Henry Masterton, Forest Days, Little Ball o' Fire, Delorme, Gowrie, Thirty Years Since, Arabella Stuart, Agincourt, and Castleneau.

1510 JAMESON (MRS.). ART WORKS. LEGENDS OF THE MADONNA. *With* 55 *drawings by the author and* 152 *woodcuts.* LEGENDS OF THE MONASTIC ORDERS. *With* 11 *etchings by the author and* 88 *woodcuts.* SACRED AND LEGENDARY ART. *Illustrated with* 16 *etchings and numerous woodcuts,* 2 vols. EASTLAKE'S HISTORY OF OUR LORD. 31 *etchings and* 281 *wood engravings* of Paintings, Mosaics, Ancient Ivory Carvings, Byzantine and other Miniatures, 2 vols. Together, 6 vols. square 8vo, blue mor. extra, gilt edges, by *Rivière.* London, 1865–72. *55 50*

1511 JAMESON (MRS.). WORKS. *48 00*

I. CHARACTERISTICS OF WOMEN, Moral, Poetical, and Historical. *With* 50 *vignette etchings.* 2 vols. 1858.

II. VISITS AND SKETCHES AT HOME AND ABROAD, with Tales and Miscellanies now first collected [Papers on Art and Literature, etc.], and a new edition of the Diary of an Ennuyée. *Etchings by the authoress.* 4 vols. 1840.

III. MEMOIRS OF CELEBRATED FEMALE SOVEREIGNS. 2 vols. 1840.

Comprising: Memorials of Semiramis, Cleopatra, Zenobia, Joanna I. and II., Isabella of Castile, Mary Queen of Scots, Queen Elizabeth, Queen Christina, Queen Anne, Maria Theresa, Empress of Germany, and Catherine II.

IV. COMPANION TO THE PUBLIC AND PRIVATE GALLERIES in London. *Frontispiece.* 3 vols. 1842–44.

Includes: Her Majesty's, the Bridgewater, Sutherland, Grosvenor, Lansdowne, Sir R. Peel's, and S. Rogers' Galleries.

JAMESON (MRS.). WORKS. (*Continued.*)

V. COMMONPLACE BOOK of Thoughts, Memories, and Fancies. *With illustrations.* 1854.

VI. LIVES OF THE POETS. *Frontispiece.* 2 vols. 1829.

VII. SOCIAL LIFE IN GERMANY. 2 vols. 1840.

Together 16 vols. small 8vo, half blue calf extra. London, 1829–54.

1512 JAMESON (MRS.). CHARACTERISTICS OF WOMEN. 12 *fine plates.* Roy. 8vo, cloth. New York, 1847. *$3 00*

1513 JARDINE (SIR W.). NATURALIST'S LIBRARY Complete, containing valuable works on every branch of Animated Nature, by the most eminent naturalists. *With upwards of* 1200 *colored plates.* 42 vols. foolscap. 8vo, half red mor. London, n. d. *73 50*

In the preparation of this valuable series, Sir Wm. Jardine was assisted by Swainson, Waterhouse, Magillivary, Bushnan, Selby, Schomburgh, Col. Hamilton Smith, Dr. Hamilton, and others.

1514 JENNINGS (S.). ORCHIDS and how to Grow them in India and other Tropical Climates. 48 *colored plates.* 4to, half mor. London, 1875. *7 00*

1515 JESSE (J. H.). LONDON: ITS CELEBRATED CHARACTERS AND REMARKABLE PLACES. *Frontispiece.* 3 vols. 8vo, calf extra, gilt tops, uncut edges. London, 1871. *18 00*

Very rare.

1516 JOHNSON (G. W.). THE GARDENER'S DICTIONARY. Crown 8vo, cloth. London, 1875. *2 50*

1517 JONES (WM.). FINGER-RING LORE. *Numerous illustrations.* Crown 8vo, half calf extra. London, 1877. *5 00*

1518 KANE (DR. E.). ARCTIC EXPLORATIONS OF 1853–55, in search of Sir John Franklin, *with portrait, maps, and upwards of* 300 *graphic illustrations on steel and wood from sketches by the author.* 2 vols. 8vo, cloth. Philadelphia, 1856. *7 50*

1519 KEATS (JOHN). POETICAL WORKS, with a Memoir by Lord Houghton, and 120 *woodcuts. Portrait.* Crown 8vo, cloth, *scarce.* London, *Moxon*, 1866. *4 25*

1520 KEATS (J.) POETICAL WORKS. *Illustrated.* Post 8vo, half calf, extra. London, n. d. *4 50*

1521 KEBLE. THE CHRISTIAN YEAR. Post 8vo, half calf extra. London, 1873. *$3 25*

1522 KING (C. W.). ANTIQUE GEMS AND RINGS. *Illustrated by 66 plates, containing representations of several hundred gems, and by numerous woodcuts in the text.* 2 vols. roy. 8vo, half mor. gilt edges. London, 1872. *21 00*

1523 KIT-KAT CLUB. Memoirs of the Celebrated Persons composing the . . . *With 48 fine portraits from the original paintings by Sir Godfrey Kneller.* Folio, red mor. extra, gilt edges. London, 1821. *31 00*

Includes portraits of Jacob Tonson, Congreve, Buckhurst-Dorset, Steele, etc.

1524 KNIGHT (Chas.). HALF-HOURS WITH THE BEST AUTHORS. 52 *illustrations.* 4 vols. post 8vo, half calf extra. London, n. d. *16 00*

1525 LACROIX (PAUL). ART WORKS; on the Manners, Customs, Costumes, Military Life, Arts, Dress, Religious Life, Science, and Literature of the Middle Ages, Period of the Renaissance, and the Eighteenth Century in France. *Illustrated with 90 plates in gold, silver and colors, and over 2,000 woodcuts.* 5 vols. imperial 8vo, tree calf extra, gilt edges, by *Mathews.* London, 1870–76. *50 00*

"These books have no equal in the annals of Art and Literature."

1526 LAMB (CHAS.). LIFE, LETTERS, AND WRITINGS. Edited with Notes and Illustrations by Percy Fitzgerald. *Portraits.* 6 vols. post 8vo, half calf extra. London, 1876. *22 50*

1527 LAMB (CHAS.). COMPLETE CORRESPONDENCE AND WORKS, with an Essay on his Life and Genius, by T. Purnell. *Portraits.* 4 vols. post 8vo, half calf extra. London, *Moxon*, n. d. *12 00*

1528 LANDSEER'S GREAT ANIMAL PAINTINGS. Pictures by Sir Edward Landseer, R.A., a New Series, with Descriptions by W. Cosmo Monkhouse. 17 *steel plates.* 4to, new cloth, bevelled sides, gilt edges. London, *Virtue*, n. d. *13 00*

1529 LANDSEER (SIR E.). PICTURES. 20 *steel engravings*, with Descriptions, etc., by J. Dufforne. Royal 4to, cloth. London, n. d. *13 00*

1530 LANDSEER (SIR E.), STUDIES OF. 116 illustrations from the Collection of Queen Victoria, etc., with a History of his Art Life, by Monkhouse. Royal 4to, cloth. London, n. d. *13 00*

1531 LANDON (L. E.). COMPLETE WORKS. Royal 8vo, cloth.
$2 00 Boston, 1856.

1532 LATHAN (D.). GENERAL HISTORY OF BIRDS, being the Natural History and Description of all the Birds (above four thousand) hitherto known or described by Naturalists. With Index, *and upwards of 200 colored plates.* 10 vols. 4to, blue
80 00 mor. extra. London, 1781–1802.

Fine subscription copy. "This is undoubtedly the most useful and valuable work of its class that has yet appeared, as it contains exact scientific descriptions of every bird known at the time."—NEVILLE WOOD.

1533 LEAFLETS OF MEMORY FOR MDCCCXLVII. *Numerous plates.*
2 50 8vo, mor. Philadelphia, 1847.

1534 LE MAOUT, DECAISNE, AND HOOKER. GENERAL SYSTEM OF BOTANY. *Many hundred woodcuts.* 4to, cloth.
5 00 London, 1873.

1535 LENNOX (LORD WILLIAM). CELEBRITIES I HAVE KNOWN, with Episodes, Political, Social, Sporting, and Theatrical. *2d*
4 50 *series.* 2 vols. 8vo, half red mor. extra. London, 1877.

1536 LE SAGE. ADVENTURES OF GIL BLAS of Santillane, translated by Smollett. *Numerous plates.* 3 vols. 8vo, half calf extra.
11 25 London, 1819.

SALE THURSDAY EVENING, MARCH 11,

BEGINNING AT 8 O'CLOCK.

AT THE AMERICAN ART GALLERIES.

1537 LEVER (CHARLES). WORKS. New and Revised Edition. *With upwards of 150 humorous etchings from designs by Phiz.* 26 vols. crown 8vo, half calf extra, marbled edges. London, n. d. *$58 50*

Complete Edition. Comprising: Dodd Family, Charles O'Malley, Harry Lorrequer, The O'Donoghue, Knight of Gwynne, Daltons, Roland Cashel, Jack Hinton, Martins of Cro Martin, Fortunes of Glencore, One of Them, Davenport Dunn, Barrington, Tom Burke, Luttrel of Arran, etc., etc.

1538 LE VERT (MAD. OCT. W.). SOUVENIRS OF TRAVEL. 2 vols. 12mo, cloth. New York, 1859. *1 00*

1539 LINDLEY AND MOORE. TREASURY OF BOTANY. *Illustrated.* 2 vols. post 8vo, cloth. London, 1873. *2 75*

1540 LIVINGSTONE (D. AND C.). EXPEDITION TO THE ZAMBESI. *Map and illustrations.* 8vo, half calf extra. New York, 1866. *2 75*

1541 LLOYD (L.). GAME BIRDS AND WILD FOWL OF SWEDEN AND NORWAY. *Colored and other illustrations.* Roy. 8vo, half mor. extra. London, 1867. *5 00*

1542 LODGE (E.). PORTRAITS OF ILLUSTRIOUS PERSONAGES OF GREAT BRITAIN. 240 *portraits of authentic pictures in the Galleries of the Nobility and in Public Collections.* With Biographical and Historical Memoirs. 10 vols. imp. 8vo, half mor., gilt edges. London, 1840. *42 50*

1543 LONDON (OLD AND NEW), a Narrative of its History, People, and Places, by Walter Thornbury and the Rev. E. Walford. *With 1200 illustrations and maps, from the most authentic sources.* 6 vols. imp. 8vo, half mor., gilt. London, n. d.
$42 00

1544 LONGFELLOW (H. W). POETICAL WORKS. *Portrait.* 4 vols. 12mo, red mor. extra gilt edges, by *Mathews.* Boston, 1866.
17 50

1545 LONGFELLOW (H. W.). PROSE WORKS. 3 vols. 12mo, red mor. extra gilt edges, by *Mathews.* Boston, 1866.
11 25
Uniform with the above.

1546 LONGFELLOW (H. W.). MICHAEL ANGELO, a Dramatic Poem. *Illustrated.* 4to, cloth extra. Boston, 1884.
4 50

1547 LONGFELLOW. POEMS. Song of Hiawatha, Masque of Pandora, In the Harbor, Ultima Thule, Keramos, and Aftermath. 6 vols. 16mo, cloth. Boston, v. y.
4 80

1548 LONGFELLOW (H. W.). HANGING OF THE CRANE. *Illustrated.* 8vo, mor. ant., gilt edges. Boston, 1874.
3 75

1549 LOTHIAN (R.). DANTE AND BEATRICE, from 1282 to 1290. *Portrait.* 2 vols. 8vo, half calf extra. London, 1876.
6 50

1550 LOUDON. ENCYCLOPÆDIA OF PLANTS. *Many hundred illustrations.* Thick 8vo, cloth. London, 1866.
5 25

1551 LOWE (E. J.). BEAUTIFUL LEAVED PLANTS. 60 *colored plates.* Royal 8vo, half mor. extra, gilt edges. London, 1872.
6 00

1552 LOWE (E. J.). NATURAL HISTORY OF NEW AND RARE FERNS. 72 *colored plates.* Royal 8vo, cloth, uncut. London, 1871.
7 25

1553 LOWER (M. A.). ESSAY ON FAMILY NOMENCLATURE. 2 vols. post 8vo, half red mor. extra. London, 1875.
4 50

1554 LÜBKE'S HISTORY OF ART, translated from the German and Edited by Clarence Cook. *Profusely illustrated with engravings on wood.* 2 vols. roy. 8vo, brown levant mor., gilt tops, uncut edges. New York, 1878.
16 00
Best Edition.

1555 LUXEMBOURG GALLERY. LES CHEFS D'ŒUVRE D'ART AU LUXEMBOURG, Publiées sous la direction de M. Eugène Montrosier, avec le concours littéraire de MM. Allard, Champfleury, Claretie, F. Coppée, Daudet, T. Gautier, Houssaye, Janin, Mistral, G. Sand, etc., etc. 41 *large Photogravures by the Goupil Process, of the most notable examples of Modern French Art, now in the Luxembourg Gallery; also* 50 *Vignettes, Portraits of the Artists, Views, Ornamental Letters, etc. etc., in the Text, mostly from designs specially made for this work,* with Text, descriptive, critical, and historical. Folio, cloth, gilt, uncut edges. Paris, 1880–81. *$50 00*

Gives a selection of 41 of the most notable examples by Bouguereau, Chaplin, Fromentin, Victor Giraud, J. P. Laurens, Gérome J. Bertrand, Guillemet, Lehman, Salmson, Cabanel, Carrier-Belleuse, Lévy, Rosa Bonheur, Meissonier, Corote, Hagborg, Marchal, Zeim, Pils, Coubert, Muller, Corot, Duval, Tissot, Ribot, Signol, Bida, etc, etc, etc. These pictures have all been purchased by the French Government from the yearly exhibitions of the Salon, and may be considered as representative of the best qualities of each artist.

1556 McCABE (J. D.). PARIS BY SUNLIGHT AND GASLIGHT. 150 *woodcuts.* 8vo, cloth. Philadelphia, 1869. *1 50*

1557 MACAULAY (T. B.). COLLECTED WORKS, comprising History of England, 4 vols.; Essays and Biographies, 3 vols.; Speeches and Poems, 1 vol., with Life, etc. *Portrait, etc.* Together, 8 vols. thick 8vo, half calf extra, marbled edges. New York, 1875. *44 00*

1558 MACAULAY. LIFE AND LETTERS. Edited by his Nephew George Otto Trevelyan. *Portrait.* 2 vols. 8vo, half calf extra. New York, 1878. *8 00*

1559 MAHONY (FATHER). RELIQUES OF FATHER PROUT, late P. P. of Watergraphill. Collected and arranged by Oliver Yorke. *Profusely illustrated by Maclise.* Post 8vo, half calf extra. London, 1878. *3 75*

1560 MARK TWAIN [SAM'L CLEMENS]. INNOCENTS ABROAD; or, The Pilgrim's Progress. *With* 234 *illustrations on wood.* Thick 8vo, half mor. Hartford, 1869. *5 13*

1561 MATHEWS (J. M.). THE BIBLE AND MEN OF LEARNING. 8vo, cloth. New York, 1855. *50*

$2 00 1562 MAUNDER. TREASURY OF BIBLE KNOWLEDGE. *Numerous woodcuts.* Thick post 8vo, half calf. London, 1872.

9 00 1563 MENARD (R.). LA MYTHOLOGIE DANS L'ART ANCIEN ET MODERNE. 823 *woodcuts.* Imp. 8vo, half mor., gilt tops. Paris, 1878.

2 00 1564 MEN OF PROGRESS. Sketches by J. Parton, B. Taylor, A. Kendall, and others. *Numerous steel portraits.* Roy. 8vo, cloth. New York, 1870–71.

2 00 1565 MEN OF PROGRESS. Another copy, cloth.

2 00 1566 MICHELET'S "LOVE" AND "WOMAN." Translated. 2 vols. 12mo, cloth.

27 00 1567 MILLET (J. F.). LA VIE ET L'ŒUVRE DE . . . par Alfred Sensier. *Numerous illustrations.* Small folio, crushed levant mor. extra, inside panels of red mor., gilt tops, uncut edges, by *Chatelin.* Paris, 1881.

21 00 1568 MILLET. Another Copy, uncut. Paris, 1881.

2 25 1569 MILLET (JEAN FRANÇOIS). PEASANT AND PAINTER. Translated by Helena de Kay from the French of Alfred Sensier. 4to, cloth. Boston, 1881.

400 00 1570 MINIATURE PAINTINGS ON VELLUM. 23 *exquisite portraits of the* BARTH FAMILY, from George in 1494 to Joseph 1760. *Painted on vellum, with coats-of-arms and inscriptions.* Small 8vo, mor. Silver rims, clasps, and shields.

A curious and interesting relic of the Barths. The portraits are most delicately finished.

3 50 1571 MITFORD (MARY R.). OUR VILLAGE. *Etching and numerous woodcuts.* 4to, uncut. London, 1879.

18 00 1572 MOLIÈRE (J. B. P.). DRAMATIC WORKS. Rendered into English by Henry Van Laun; with a Prefatory Memoir, Introductory Notices, Appendices, and Notes. *Portrait.* 6 vols. 8vo, half red mor. extra, gilt tops, uncut edges. Edinburgh, 1878.

4 75 1573 MOORE (TOM). POETICAL WORKS. *Portrait and plates.* Roy. 8vo, mor. ant., gilt edges. New York, 1875.

1574 MOORE (TOM). LALLA ROOKH: an Oriental Romance. *Numerous engravings on wood from drawings by Tenniel, etc.* Sq. 8vo, red mor. extra, gold borders and gilt edges, by *Rivière.* London, 1868. *$11 50*

1575 MORE (HANNAH). COMPLETE WORKS. *Portrait and vignettes.* 11 vols. small 8vo, half calf extra. London, 1830. *17 88*

1576 MORGAN (LADY SYDNEY OWENSON). FRANCE [Sketches of Parisian Society, Manners, etc.]. 2 vols. 8vo, calf. London, 1817. *6 25*

1577 MORGAN (LADY). FRANCE IN 1829–30. *Portrait.* 2 vols. 8vo, half calf gilt. London, 1381. *4 50*

1578 MORGAN (LADY). PASSAGES FROM MY AUTOBIOGRAPHY. *Portrait.* 8vo, half calf, gilt. London, 1859. *3 00*

1579 MORLEY (JOHN). ROUSSEAU. 2 vols. 8vo, half red mor. extra, gilt tops, uncut edges. London, 1872. *38 00*
Unique copy, with 50 portraits and views inserted.

1580 MOTLEY (JOHN LATHROP). WORKS. History of the United Netherlands, 2 vols.; and Rise of the Dutch Republic, 3 vols. *Portraits, maps, etc.* 5 vols. 8vo, half calf antique. New York, 1861–62. *26 25*

1581 MOUNSEY (A. H.). JOURNEY THROUGH THE CAUCASUS AND THE INTERIOR OF PERSIA. *Map.* 8vo, half calf extra. London, 1872. *3 00*

1582 MOWATT (ANNA C.). AUTOBIOGRAPHY OF AN ACTRESS; or, Eight Years on the Stage.. 12mo, cloth. Boston, 1854. *2 00*

1583 MURRAY (ALEX S.). MANUAL OF MYTHOLOGY. Greek, Roman, Norse, Old-German, Hindoo, and Egyptian. 45 *plates.* 8vo, cloth. New York, n. d. *3 25*

1584 NAPOLEONIC MEMOIRS, etc., as follows:

I. NAPOLEON'S OWN HISTORICAL MEMOIRS, dictated by him at St. Helena to Counts Montholon, Gourgaud, etc., and published from the Original Manuscripts, corrected by himself. *With maps, plans, and fac-similes.* Complete in 7 vols. 1823. *234 00*

NAPOLEONIC MEMOIRS, etc.

II. LAVALLETTE (COUNT). MEMOIRS OF, by Himself, with a biographical sketch, 2 vols. 1831.

III. NEY (MARSHAL). MEMOIRS OF, published by his Family. *Illustrated with portrait, map, and plans.* 2 vols. 1833.

IV. LAFAYETTE, LOUIS PHILIPPE, AND THE REVOLUTION OF 1830. By B. Sarrans, Jr. *Portrait.* 2 vols. 1832.

V. LAMBALLE (PRINCESS). SECRET MEMOIRS OF THE ROYAL FAMILY OF FRANCE DURING THE REVOLUTION. *Portraits and plates.* 2 vols. 1826.

VI. CAYLA (COMTESSE DE). PRIVATE MEMOIRS OF THE COURT OF LOUIS XVIII. 2 vols. 1830.

VII. CHARLES X, AND LOUIS PHILIPPE; the Secret History of the Revolution of July, 1830. 1839.

Together 18 vols. 8vo, half red mor. extra, gilt tops, uncut edges. London, 1826–39.

UNIQUE SET, *with over 200 extra portraits and views inserted.*

1585 NAPOLEON FORSYTH (W.). HISTORY OF THE CAPTIVITY OF NAPOLEON AT ST. HELENA; from the Letters and Journals of Sir Hudson Lowe. *Portrait and map.* 3 vols. 8vo, half calf extra. London, 1853.

$12 00

Containing a large number of curious facts relating to Napoleon, hitherto unknown.

1586 NAPOLEON. MEMOIRS OF NAPOLEON, his Court and Family, by the Duchess D'Abrantes (Madame Junot). *Portraits.* 2 vols. 8vo, half red mor. extra. New York, 1873.

12 00

1587 NATIONAL PORTRAIT GALLERY OF EMINENT AMERICANS, with Biographical and Historical Narratives. By Evert A. Duyckinck. *Steel engravings from the full-length portraits by Alonzo Chappel.* 2 vols. 4to, mor. antique, gilt edges. New York, n. d.

10 00

1588 NEW DICTIONARY OF QUOTATIONS. 12mo, cloth. Philadelphia, 1864.

2 25

1589 NEW TESTAMENT of Our Lord and Saviour Jesus Christ. *Illustrated with Borders, Ornaments, and Initial Letters, copied from Italian MSS. of the 15th and 16th Centuries, and by numerous other engravings on wood from the Old Masters;* viz.: Fra Angelico, Leonardo da Vinci, Pietro Perugino, Francesco Francia, Fra Bartolomeo, Albertinelli, Titian, Raphael, Fra Sebastiano del Piombo, Andrea del Sarto, Paolo Veronese, Bassano, Annibale Carracci, Guido Reni, Poussin, Van Dyck. Small 4to, morocco antique, gilt leaves, by *Matthews.* London, *Longman's*, 1865. *$18 50*

In addition to the large subjects, which are numerous, each page is decorated with borders, ornaments, initial letters, copied from the Italian Manuscripts of the fifteenth and sixteenth centuries, and numerous Medallions are introduced in the margins. The work was produced under the general superintendence of Mr. Henry Shaw."

1590 OGILVIE (JOHN). IMPERIAL DICTIONARY OF THE ENGLISH LANGUAGE. Edited by Geo. Annandale. 3,000 *woodcuts.* 4 vols. imp. 8vo, half mor. London, 1883. *11 00*

1591 OLD CASTLES AND ABBEYS. The History and Legends of. *Profusely illustrated.* 4to, cloth, gilt. London, n. d. *7 25*

1592 OLIPHANT (MRS.). THE MAKERS OF FLORENCE. Dante, Giotto, Savonarola, and their City. *Portrait of Savonarola, and illustrations by Delamotte.* 8vo, cloth, gilt top. London, 1876-81. *6 75*

1593 OLMSTEAD (F. L.). JOURNEYS AND EXPLORATIONS IN THE COTTON KINGDOM. *Map.* 2 vols. crown 8vo, half red mor., extra, gilt tops. London, 1861. *3 50*

1594 OPIE (AMELIA). WORKS. 3 vols. 8vo, sheep. Philadelphia, n. d. *6 00*

1595 "OUIDA" (LOUISE DE LA RAMÉ). NOVELS. Comprising: Chandos, Strathmore, Held in Bondage, Cecil Castlemaine's Gage, A Dog of Flanders, Tricotrin, Idalia, Puck, Under Two Flags, Pascarel, Wooden-Shoes, and Folle-Farme. 12 vols., post 8vo, half vellum extra. London, *Chatto*, v. d. *30 00*

1596 OXFORD ENGLISH CLASSICS. Complete set of these valuable and finely printed editions, comprising: *165 00*

OXFORD ENGLISH CLASSICS.—(*Continued.*)

HUME AND SMOLLET'S HISTORY OF ENGLAND, with Lives. *Fine series of portraits of the Kings by Worthington.* 13 vols.

GIBBON'S DECLINE AND FALL OF THE ROMAN EMPIRE. *Portrait.* 8 vols.

JOHNSON'S WORKS, WITH PARLIAMENTARY DEBATES. 11 vols.

BOSWELL'S LIFE OF DR. JOHNSON. 4 vols.

ROBERTSON'S (Dr.) HISTORICAL WORKS, complete, with Life. *Portrait.* 8 vols. Together 44 vols. 8vo, calf extra, gilt tops, uncut edges.

Oxford, *Talboys*, 1825, etc.

Some of the volumes have been "stilted" in binding to secure uniform size.

1597 PALGRAVE (W. G.). YEAR'S JOURNEY THROUGH CENTRAL AND EASTERN ARABIA (1862–63). *Portrait, map, and plans.* 2 vols. 8vo, half calf, gilt. London, 1865. *$4 00*

1598 PARDOE (JULIA). BIOGRAPHICAL WORKS, comprising LOUIS XIVth and the COURT OF FRANCE, 3 vols. LIFE OF MARIE DE MEDICIS, Queen of France, 3 vols. COURT AND REIGN OF FRANCIS I., 2 vols. *All profusely illustrated with portraits and engravings on steel.* Together 8 vols. 8vo, half blue calf extra, marbled edges. London, 1847–52. *81 00*

Fine uniform set. Very scarce.

3 75 1599 PARIS: 26 *fine steel-plate views of.* Oblong 4to, cloth.

1600 PAXTON (SIR J.). MAGAZINE OF BOTANY AND FLOWERING PLANTS, *with 700 colored plates of the most beautiful Flowers, and an immense number of woodcuts.* 16 vols. royal 8vo, half morocco, gilt edges. London, 1834–49. *64 00*

A fine complete set.

1601 PAXTON. BOTANICAL DICTIONARY. Revised and corrected by S. Hereman. Royal 8vo, cloth. London, 1868. *7 00*

1602 PEAKS, PASSES, AND GLACIERS: a Series of Excursions by Members of the Alpine Club. Edited by J. Ball and E. S. Kennedy. *Illustrated by numerous plates and maps, some colored.* 3 vols. 8vo, half mor. extra. London, 1859–62. $27 00
Both series complete. Scarce

1603 PERCY ANECDOTES, original and select, by Sholto and Reuben Percy, Brothers of the Benedictine Monastery, Mont Benger [Thomas Byerley, of "Mont Benger," in Scotland, editor of *The Star* newspaper, and J. C. Robertson, editor of *The Mechanics' Magazine*], *with* 40 *portraits.* 20 vols. 18mo, half calf extra. London, 1823. 22 50

1604 PETRARCH. SONNETS, TRIUMPHS, AND OTHER POEMS. Translated, with Life by T. Campbell. 16 *plates.* Post 8vo, half mor. extra. London, 1875. 3 25

1605 PICTORIAL SUNDAY BOOK. Edited by John Kitto. *Many hundred illustrations.* Folio, mor. gilt. London, n. d. 10 50

1606 PLUNKETT (FRED.). HERE AND THERE AMONG THE ALPS. Post 8vo, half red mor. extra. London, 1876. 2 00

1607 PLUTARCH. LIVES. The Translation called Dryden's, corrected from the Greek, and revised by A. H. Clough. 5 vols. 8vo, half red mor. extra. Boston, 1875. 26 25

1608 PLUTARCH. MORALS. Translated from the Greek by several hands, corrected and revised by W. W. Goodwin, with Introduction by Emerson. 5 vols. 8vo, half red mor. extra. Boston, 1874. 26 25

1609 POE (EDGAR ALLAN). WORKS. With Biographical Sketch by J. R. Lowell. 4 vols. foolscap 8vo, half calf extra. New York, 1876. 22 00

1610 POET AND PAINTER; or, Gems of Art and Song. *Numerous steel portraits and views.* Imperial 8vo, mor. antique, gilt leaves. New York, 1878. 6 00

1611 POETS OF AMERICA. Edited by John Keese [Auctioneer]. *Illustrated.* 2 vols. 16mo, half mor. New York, 1840–2. 5 50

1612 PORTRAITS. GALLERY OF BRITISH AND FOREIGN PORTRAITS (KNIGHT'S), with Memoirs by distinguished Biographers. 168 *portraits, engraved on steel.* Original impressions. 7 vols. im-
$38 50 perial 8vo, half red mor. extra, gilt edges. London, 1833–38.

An unusually fine copy, bound from the numbers; the impressions are unexceptionable.

The memoirs to this very interesting series were written by Arthur Malkin, Arthur Hallam, De Quincey, and other distinguished authors.

1613 PRAED (W. MACKWORTH). POEMS; with a Memoir by the Rev. Derwent Coleridge; new edition. 2 vols. foolscap 8vo, half mor.
4 50 extra, gilt tops, uncut edges. London, 1869.

1614 PRESCOTT (W. H.). HISTORICAL WORKS, complete. Large type, with *portraits.* 15 vols. 8vo, half calf extra.
75 00 Philadelphia, 1869.

Comprises: Reign of Ferdinand and Isabella, 3 vols.; Conquest of Mexico, 3 vols.; Conquest of Peru, 2 vols.; Reign of Philip II., King of Spain, 3 vols.; Charles V., 3 vols.; and Biographical and Critical Miscellanies.

1615 PRIME (S. I.). TRAVELS IN EUROPE AND THE EAST. *Wood-*
2 00 *cuts.* 2 vols. 18mo, cloth. New York, 1856.

1616 PUNCH. A COMPLETE SET of this famous Journal, from its commencement in 1841, to December, 1878, inclusive. *Many thousand humorous engravings by Leech, Doyle, etc.* 75 vols. in
180 50 38, 4to, half mor., gilt. London, 1841–78.

1617 RAND (E. S.). ORCHIDS; a Complete Manual of Orchid Culture, and description of the varieties grown near Boston, etc.,
2 00 etc. 12mo, cloth. New York, 1876.

1618 REICHENBACH (H. G.). XENIA ORCHIDACEA. 200 *plates, some partly colored.* 2 vols. 4to, mor. (vol. 1), unbound (vol. 2).
14 00 Leipzig, 1858.

1619 RELIGIOUS DENOMINATIONS IN THE UNITED STATES. *Por-*
2 00 *traits.* 8vo, roan. Harrisburg, 1849.

1620 REMBRANDT. L'ŒUVRE DE REMBRANDT. Commenté et décrit par Charles Blanc. *Printed on Holland paper, and illustrated with 75 etchings in fac-simile of the original examples by Rembrandt (including the Hundred Guilder Print).* 2 vols. imp. 4to, red levant mor. extra, gilt tops, uncut edges, by *Mathews.*
114 00 Paris, 1873.

Large paper, limited to 50 copies.

"*The illustrations etched by M. Flameng for M. Chas. Blanc's Catalogue of the Works of Rembrandt, have long been familiar to the students of art; and we have known for years that M. Flameng could copy Rembrandt with a degree of life and truth which left little to be desired. Still it is probable that the* élite *of the general art public will not be quite prepared for the great technical triumph which M. Flameng has just achieved. He has produced a copy of one of Rembrandt's most difficult and complicated etchings*—a copy, which, if we balance one quality against another, certainly exceeds the most perfect photography in accuracy, *while at the same time it possesses, as a piece of execution in etching, all those technical merits for which Rembrandt was famous. . . . In a certain sense, and for some peculiar reasons which will be given in support of the assertion, it may be boldly affirmed that, as a technical performance merely, such a copy as this is even more wonderful than the original plate itself.*"—HAMERTON.

1621 REMBRANDT. CATALOGUE RAISONNÉ de toutes les Estampes qui forment l'Œuvre de, par A. Bartsch. *Portrait.* 2 vols. in 1, small 8vo, half calf. Vienne, 1797. *$10 50*
Very scarce.

1622 REYNOLDS (SIR JOSHUA). LIFE AND TIMES, with Notices of some of his Contemporaries, by C. R. Leslie and Tom Taylor. *Portraits and engravings.* 2 vols. 8vo, half red mor. extra, gilt tops, uncut edges. London, 1865. *10 00*

1623 RHINE (THE), FROM ITS SOURCE TO THE SEA. Translated by G. C. T. Bartley. *With 425 illustrations.* Royal 4to, cloth. Philadelphia (London), 1878. *13 00*

1624 RICH (A.). DICTIONARY OF GREEK AND ROMAN ANTIQUITIES. 2,000 *woodcut illustrations.* 8vo, half mor., extra. New York, 1874. *6 25*

1625 RICHARDSON (SAMUEL). WORKS, with Life, by Mangin. *Portrait.* 19 vols. post 8vo, half blue mor. extra. London, 1811. *33 25*
Includes: Pamela, Clarissa Harlowe, and Sir Charles Grandison.

1626 RICHARDSON (SAMUEL). THE CORRESPONDENCE OF. *Portrait.* 6 vols. post 8vo, half blue mor. extra. London, 1804. *5 40*
Uniformly bound with the Works.

1627 ROGERS (S.). ITALY AND POEMS. The beautiful illustrated editions, *with 128 exquisitely finished engravings by Finden and others from Drawings by Turner and Stothard.* 2 vols. crown 8vo, red levant mor. extra, gilt edges, by *Chatelin.*

$70 00 London, 1834–36.

The enormous wealth of the author enabled him to command the best talents of the best artists of his time, and it is stated that he spent £10,000 in the illustration of his "Italy" alone. J. M. W. Turner, Prout, and Thos. Stothard rivalled themselves, and the genius of design was in turn rivalled by marvellously skilled engravers.

1628 ROGET (P. M.). THESAURUS of English Words and Phrases. Revised by B. Sears. 12mo, cloth.

1 00 New York, 1878.

1629 ROLLIN (CHAS.). ANCIENT HISTORY of the Egyptians, Carthaginians, Assyrians, Babylonians, Medes and Persians, Macedonians and Grecians. *Portrait and maps.* 4 vols. 8vo, half *12 00* mor. extra, gilt top. New York, 1885.

1630 ROMANCE OF HISTORY. ENGLAND, FRANCE INDIA, ITALY AND SPAIN. *Numerous illustrations.* 15 vols. 12mo, half mor. ex- *33 75* tra, gilt tops, uncut edges. London, 1832–36.

Sets as the above are exceedingly scarce.

279 00 1631 RUSKIN'S MODERN PAINTERS.

Vol. I. Modern Principles and Truth. 1873.
II. Imaginative and Theoretic Faculties.
III. Of Many Things. 17 *plates.*
IV. Mountain Beauty. 34 *plates.*
V. Leaf and Cloud Beauty, and Ideas of Relation. 34 *plates.*

—— STONES OF VENICE.

Vol. I. The Foundations. 21 *plates.* 1874.
II. The Sea Stories. 20 *plates.*
III. The Fall. 12 *plates.*

—— SEVEN LAMPS OF ARCHITECTURE. 14 *plates.* Second edition, 1855. Together 9 vols. royal 8vo, red mor. extra, gilt tops, uncut edges. London, 1855–74.

A superb set.

1632 RUSKIN (JOHN.) POEMS. Reprinted from Various Sources. *Printed on heavy laid paper, with India proof impression of the etched frontispiece.* Royal 8vo, tree calf extra, gilt edges, by *Mathews.* New York, 1882. *$14 50*

LARGE PAPER COPY, *only 50 printed. No. 33.*

1633 SALON CATALOGUE FOR 1884. 300 *illustrations.* 8vo, cloth. Paris, *Baschet*, 1884. *3 25*

1634 SALON OF 1884. 100 *fine plates in photogravure.* Texte par A. Dayot. Imp. 8vo, cloth. Paris, 1884. *25 00*

Only 533 copies printed.

1635 SARATOGA IN 1901. By Eli Perkins. 200 *illustrations.* Sq. 12mo, cloth. New York, 1872. *1 60*

1636 SCHILLER (FREDERICK). WORKS. Comprising Poems, 1 vol.; Historical, 1 vol.; Histories and Dramas, 2 vols.; Early Dramas, 1 vol.; Essays, 1 vol. *Portraits, etc.* Together, 6 vols. foolscap 8vo, half calf extra. London, 1877. *28 50*

The only uniform English Edition.

1637 SCHWEINFURTH.] THE HEART OF AFRICA. Three Years' Travel in Unexplored Central Africa, 1868–71, by Dr. G. Schweinfurth, translated by Ellen E. Frewer, and Introduction by Winwood Reade. *Maps and woodcuts.* 2 vols. 8vo, half calf extra. London, 1873. *8 00*

1638 SCOTT (SIR WALTER). COMPLETE WORKS. The SPLENDID ABBOTSFORD EDITION, comprising the WAVERLEY NOVELS, 12 vols.; POETICAL WORKS, 1 vol.; LIFE OF NAPOLEON, 1 vol.; TALES OF A GRANDFATHER, 1 vol., and BIOGRAPHICAL MEMOIRS, 1 vol. *Upwards of* 200 *engravings on steel and* 2,000 *beautifully executed woodcuts.* Together, 16 vols. thick roy. 8vo, blue calf extra, gilt tops, uncut edges. Edinburgh, 1842–52. *144 00*

Fine early copy, with brilliant impressions of the plates and cuts; also the Cruikshank, Turner, and other illustrations added.

1639 SCOTT (SIR W.). WAVERLEY NOVELS. *With 96 steel engravings and several hundred woodcuts.* 48 vols. fcap 8vo, calf extra. Edinburgh, 1865. *156 00*

This favorite edition is easiest identified by the rubricated title-pages.

1640 SEGUIN (L. G.) PICTURESQUE TOUR IN PICTURESQUE LANDS. *With upwards of 160 fine illustrations, proofs on Japan paper.* Folio, original vellum binding, inlaid sides, gilt top.

$80 00 London, 1881.

Edition de Luxe. Only 600 copies printed. No. 1.

1641 SHAKESPEARE'S DRAMATIC WORKS. BOYDELL'S SPLENDID EDITION. *Printed in large type by Bulmer, with the series of* 100 *highly finished engravings by the best artists, from paintings by* STOTHARD, WESTALL, SMIRKE, OPIE, NORTHCOTE, ETC. 9 vols. folio, half dark-red levant mor. extra, gilt tops, uncut

135 00 edges, by *Mathews.* London, *Bulmer*, 1802.

Scarce in uncut condition. This edition is one of the most finely printed books ever produced in any country.

1642 SHAKESPEARE'S PLAYS AND POEMS. With Copious Notes and Illustrations, Notes of the Plays ascribed to Shakespeare, Biography, etc., by Charles Knight ("Imperial Edition.") *With portrait and 46 steel engravings after pictures by Cope, Frith, Leslie, Maclise, Ward, Clint, etc.* 2 large and thick vols. folio, half

21 00 Russia, gilt edges. London, 1875.

1643 SHAKESPEARE (WM.). WORKS. Edited by Charles and Mary Cowden Clarke. *With 66 illustrations from the Boydell Gallery.*

28 50 4 vols. 8vo, tree calf extra, gilt edges. London, 1876.

1644 SHAKESPEARE SCENES AND CHARACTERS. *Comprising 36 engravings on steel by Bankel, Bauer, Goldberg, etc, from drawings by Adams, Hofman, Pecht, Spiers, and other German artists.* With explanatory text, selected and arranged by Professor Dowden. 4to, half mor. extra, gilt top, uncut edges, by

15 00 *Mathews.* New York (London), 1876.

1645 SHAKESPEARE.] CLARKE (Mrs. Cowden). CONCORDANCE to Shakespeare; being a Verbal Index to all the Passages in the Dramatic Works of the Poet. Thick roy. 8vo, half calf extra.

7 00 Boston, 1877.

1646 SHAKESPEARE.] TALES FROM SHAKESPEARE, by Charles and Mary Lamb. 12 *plates from the Boydell Gallery* 8vo, red

7 25 mor. extra. London, 1876.

1647 SHELLEY (P. B.). POETICAL WORKS. Edited with Prefaces and Notes, by H. B. Forman, *with etched portraits and other plates.* 4 vols. 8vo, mor. antique, gilt tops, uncut edges, by *Hammond.* London, 1876. *$20 00*

1648 SHERIDAN (RICHARD BRINSLEY). WORKS. With Memoir by J. P. Browne. Containing extracts from the Life of Thomas Moore. *Portrait.* Best edition. 2 vols. 8vo, tree calf extra. London, 1873. *12 00*

1649 SIDNEY (SIR P.). WORKS, complete, in Verse and Prose, with Life. *Illustrations by Van der Gucht, and others. Portrait by Vertue.* 3 vols. crown 8vo, sprinkled calf extra, yellow edges. *Scarce.* London, 1725. *15 00*

1650 SIR ROGER DE COVERLEY. *Illustrated by C. O. Murray.* 8vo, cloth. New York, n. d. *1 25*

1651 SKEAT (REV. W. W.). ETYMOLOGICAL DICTIONARY OF THE ENGLISH LANGUAGE. 4to, half Russia, red edges. Oxford, *Clarendon Press,* 1882. *7 63*

1652 SMITH (JOHN). HISTORIA FILICUM. An Exposition of the Nature, Number, and Organography of Ferns. 30 *lithographic plates.* Post 8vo, cloth. London, 1875. *1 85*

1653 SMITH'S DICTIONARY OF GREEK AND ROMAN BIOGRAPHY AND MYTHOLOGY. *Several hundred woodcut illustrations* 3 vols. very thick 8vo, half calf, gilt. Boston (London), 1854. *18 00*

1654 SMITH (SYDNEY), MEMOIR OF, by his daughter, Lady Holland. 2 vols. 12mo, cloth. New York, 1856. *2 00*

1655 SMYTH (PROF. WM.). LECTURES ON MODERN HISTORY, from the Irruption of the Northern Nations to the Close of the American Revolution. Best edition. 2 vols. 8vo, polished calf extra, gilt tops, uncut edges. London, *W. Pickering,* 1840. *6 00*

1656 SOUTHEY (ROBERT). COMMON-PLACE BOOK, containing Choice Passages from English Authors, translations of interesting extracts from Portuguese and Spanish Authors, Analytical Readings, Original Memoranda, etc., edited by J. W. Warter. *Portrait.* 4 vols. thick 8vo, calf extra. London, 1850. *13 00*

1657 SPEKE (J. H.). JOURNAL OF THE DISCOVERY OF THE SOURCE OF THE NILE. *Maps and plates.* 8vo, half calf extra.
$4 00 New York, 1868.

1658 SPENCE (REV. JOS.). ANECDOTES, OBSERVATIONS, AND CHARACTERS OF BOOKS AND MEN, collected from the Observations of Mr. Pope and other eminent persons of his time. Edited, with Notes and a Life of the Author, by Sam'l Weller Singer. *Illustrated by the insertion of over two hundred and twenty-five portraits, views, etc., all fine impressions.* 2 vols. thick folio,
172 00 red mor. extra, gilt tops, uncut edges. London, 1820.

Largest paper; few printed.

Includes: Autograph memoranda of Pope, signed March 19, 1721, and rare portraits of Horace Walpole, Sir Wm. Davenant, Dodsley, Bp. Corbet, John Dennis, Farquhar, Drayton, Faber's Mezzo of George I., Dr. Newton, Sir Wm. Temple, Martha Blount, Sedley, Penn, Ld. Hervey, Arabella Fermor, Prince of Wales, etc., etc., and Pope's Will.

1659 SPIERS AND SURENNE. FRENCH AND ENGLISH PRONOUNCING DICTIONARY. Enlarged by G. P. Quackenbos. Royal 8vo,
4 00 half morocco. New York, 1856.

1660 STANLEY (H. M.). THROUGH THE DARK CONTINENT. 10
5 50 *maps and* 150 *woodcuts.* 2 vols. 8vo, cloth. New York, 1878.

1661 STERNE (LAURENCE). COMPLETE WORKS. With Life. Edited by James P. Browne. 4 vols. 8vo, half calf extra, gilt.
20 00 London, 1873.

Best edition of this standard work.

1662 STODDARD (C. W.). SUMMER CRUISING IN THE SOUTH SEAS. *Illustrated by Mackay.* Post 8vo, half calf, gilt.
2 00 London, n. d.

1663 STOTHARD (THOMAS). LIFE OF, with Personal Reminiscenses by Mrs. Bray. Extra illustrated copy, *having nearly* 100 *engravings from the works of the artist, comprising many of his choicest designs, all in fine condition and neatly arranged.* Very thick small 4to, elegantly bound in green crushed levant mor.,
33 00 super-extra, gilt leaves. London, 1851.

Unique copy, including many of the illustrations to the Pilgrim's Progress, Fairy Queen, Shakespeare's Plays, the Novels of Scott, Smollett, etc., etc.

1664 STRICKLAND, AGNES. LIVES OF THE QUEENS OF ENGLAND, from the Norman Conquest. Large type, library edition. *With portraits of every Queen.* 8 vols. 8vo, beautifully bound in red polished calf extra, marbled leaves, by *Mansell.* London, 1851. *$61 00*

Best edition, very scarce.

1665 STRICKLAND. LIVES OF THE QUEENS OF SCOTLAND and English Princesses connected with Regal Succession of Britain, complete. *Portraits.* 8 vols. post 8vo, tree calf extra, by *Grieve.* Edinburgh, 1850. *26 00*

1666 STRUTT (J.). SPORTS AND PASTIMES OF THE PEOPLE OF ENGLAND, including the Rural and Domestic Recreations, May Games, Mummeries, Shows, Processions, Pageants, and Pompous Spectacles, from the earliest period to the present time, new edition, by W. Hone. *With* 140 *woodcuts from ancient paintings.* Super-roy. 8vo, half calf extra. London, 1845. *8 00*

Large paper.

1667 SWIFT (DEAN). WORKS, containing additional Letters, Tracts, and Poems, not hitherto published; with Notes and a Life of the Author by Sir Walter Scott. *Portrait.* 19 vols. 8vo, polished calf extra, yellow edges, by *Riviere.* Edinburgh, 1824. *71 25*

The rare Second Edition.

"No author in the British language has enjoyed the extensive popularity of the celebrated Dean of St. Patrick's. Neither the local and temporary nature of the subjects on which his pen was frequently engaged, nor other objections of a more positive nature, have affected the brilliancy of his reputation."—SCOTT.

1668 SWITZERLAND, its Mountains and Valleys, described by W. Raden. *With* 418 *wood engravings (many full page) by eminent artists.* Roy. 4to, half mor., gilt edges. New York (London), 1879. *18 25*

1669 SWITZERLAND AND THE SWISS. Sketches of the Country and its Famous Men. 24 *illustrations.* Post 8vo, half red mor. extra. London, 1877. *2 00*

1670 SYNTAX (DR.). THREE TOURS IN SEARCH OF THE PICTURESQUE, in search of CONSOLATION, and in search of a WIFE (in Hudibrastic verse, by William Combe). *Illustrated with* 81 *humorous colored engravings by Rowlandson.* 3 vols. royal 8vo, half mor. extra, gilt edges. London, 1851. *20 25*

1671 TAINE (H. A.). HISTORY OF ENGLISH LITERATURE. Translated by Van Laun. 4 vols. 8vo, half red mor., gilt tops, uncut edges. London, 1877.
$12 00

1672 TAINE (H. A.). TOUR THROUGH THE PYRENEES. *Illustrated by Doré.* 4to, red mor., extra gilt edges, by *Smith.* New York, 1875.
8 00

1673 TASSO (T.). JERUSALEM DELIVERED. Translated by Hoole. 8vo, half mor., gilt. London, 1811.
3 50

1674 TENNYSON (ALFRED). WORKS OF. *Portrait.* 7 vols. post 8vo, cloth extra, uncut edges. London, 1884.
22 75

Macmillan's charming edition, which will probably remain the best.

1675 TENNYSON (ALFRED). WORKS. *Portrait.* 7 vols. 8vo, half calf extra. London, 1877.
26 25

1676 THACKERAY (W. M.). WORKS. New Library edition. *Printed on heavy paper, and profusely illustrated, including all of the author's original designs.* 22 vols. 8vo, tree calf extra, gilt edges. London, *Smith & Elder*, 1874.
93 50

1677 THACKERAY (MISS). NOVELS. *Vignettes.* 8 vols. crown 8vo, half calf extra. London, 1879.
20 00

Includes : Old Kensington, Village on the Cliff, Five Old Friends, To Esther, Bluebeard's Keys, Elizabeth, Toilers and Spinsters, Miss Angel, etc., etc.

1678 THOMAS AND BALDWIN. COMPLETE PRONOUNCING GAZETTEER. Roy. 8vo, sheep. Philadelphia, 1874.
3 25

16 00 1679 THORNBURY (WALTER). WORKS.

LIFE IN SPAIN, Past and Present. 8 *tinted plates.* 2 vols. 1859.

ART AND NATURE, at Home and Abroad. 2 vols. 1856.

A TOUR ROUND ENGLAND. *Frontispiece.* 2 vols. 1870.

BRITISH ARTISTS, from Hogarth to Turner. 2 vols. 1861.

Together, 8 vols. post 8vo, half calf extra. London, 1856–61.

1680 THORNWELL (J. H.). LIFE AND LETTERS OF, by B. M. Palmer. 8vo, cloth. Richmond, 1875.
1 25

1681 TIMBS (JOHN). ANECDOTE LIVES of Hogarth, Reynolds, Gainsborough, Fuseli, Lawrence, and Turner. Post 8vo, half calf extra. London, 1872. *$3 13*

1682 TOURGEE'S NOVELS. Fool's Errand, Royal Gentleman, Figs and Thistles (2), John Eax, Bricks without Straw, and Hot Plowshares. 7 vols. 12mo, cloth. *4 90*

1683 TUCKERMAN (H. T.). BOOK OF THE ARTISTS. American Artist Life, comprising Biographical and Critical Sketches of American Artists. *Portrait.* Royal 8vo, half calf extra. New York, 1870. *5 50*

1684 TUPPER (M. F.). PROVERBIAL PHILOSOPHY. *Illustrated.* Small 4to, mor., gilt edges. London, 1867. *5 50*

1685 TURNER (J. M. W.) LIFE OF. Founded on Letters and Papers furnished by his Friends and Fellow Academicians, by Walter Thornbury. *Fine portrait and engravings.* 2 vols. 8vo, half calf extra. *Scarce.* London, 1862. *6 50*

Contains a complete Catalogue of all Turner's Engraved Works, and of his Paintings exhibited at the Royal Academy and British Institution, etc.

1686 TURNER GALLERY. *A series of 120 large line engravings from the most famous paintings of J. M. W. Turner, by Willmore and other celebrated engravers,* with a Memoir and Descriptions by W. C. Monkhouse. 2 vols. folio, red mor., gilt edges. New York, n. d. *52 00*

1687 TRENCH (R. C.). ENGLISH, PAST AND PRESENT. Study of Words and Select Glossary. 3 vols. 12mo, cloth. London, 1873–78. *3 00*

1688 TRONSON (J. M.). PERSONAL NARRATIVE OF A VOYAGE TO JAPAN . . . and various parts of China. *Maps, charts, and views.* 8vo, half mor., gilt. London, 1859. *3 25*

1689 VAMBERY (A.). TRAVELS IN CENTRAL ASIA. *Illustrated.* 8vo, half calf extra. London, 1864. *4 25*

1690 VENISE. HISTOIRE, ART, INDUSTRIE, LA VILLE, LA VIE, par C. Yriarte. 525 *beautiful illustrations.* Folio, half mor. extra. Paris, 1878. *16 50*

1691 WALFORD (EDWARD). PLEASANT DAYS IN PLEASANT PLACES.
$2 50 *Illustrated.* 8vo, cloth. London, 1879.

1692 WALLACE (D. M.). RUSSIA. *Illustrated.* 8vo, cloth.
2 80 New York, 1878.

208 00 1693 WALPOLE'S CORRESPONDENCE AND WORKS, as follows:

I. WALPOLE. Royal and Noble Authors of England, Scotland, and Ireland, with Lists of their Works, enlarged and continued by T. Park. 150 *portraits, original impression,* 5 vols. 1806.

II. ANECDOTES of Painting in England, with some account of the Principal Artists; also a Catalogue of Engravers by Virtue; with additions by Dallaway; revised by Wornum. *Numerous portraits.* 3 vols. 1862.

III. MEMOIRS of the Reign of George II. Edited by Lord Holland. *Portraits.* 3 vols. 1846.

IV. MEMOIRS of the Reign of George III. Edited by Sir D. Le Marchant. *Portraits.* 4 vols. 1851.

V. LAST JOURNALS of the Reign of George III. Edited by Dr. Doran. 2 vols. 1859.

VI. WALPOLE. Letters to the Countess of Ossory, from 1769 to 1797. Edited with Notes by the Right Hon. R. Vernon Smith. *Portraits.* 2 vols. 1848.

VII. MEMOIRS of Horace Walpole and his Contemporaries, etc. Edited by Eliot Warburton. *Portrait.* 2 vols. 1852. *Very scarce.*

VIII. LETTERS to Sir Horace Mann. 4 vols. 1843–4.

IX. LIFE of Lord Herbert. 1826.

Together 26 vols. 8vo, polished calf extra, gilt edges. London, 1806–59.

1694 WALTON (ISAAC). LIVES OF DR. John Donne, Sir Henry Wotton, Richard Hooker, George Herbert, and Robert Sanderson. *Portraits and plates.* Post 8vo, full mor. extra.
7 00 Scarce. London, 1825.

1695 WARNER (ROBT.). SELECT ORCHIDACEOUS PLANTS, with Notes on Culture, by B. S. Williams. 80 *colored plates.* 2 vols. roy. folio, cloth, and 3 extra numbers. London, 1862–75. *$20 00*

1696 WARREN (CHAS.). UNDERGROUND JERUSALEM. *Numerous Illustrations.* Imperial 8vo, half mor. extra. London, 1876. *4 75*

1697 WEBSTER (NOAH). AMERICAN DICTIONARY OF THE ENGLISH LANGUAGE. The Entire Corrections and Improvements. Revised by Chauncey A. Goodrich. *Pictorial illustrations and portrait.* 4to, mor., gilt edges. Springfield, 1877. *10 50*

1698 WELLS (W. V.). EXPLORATIONS AND ADVENTURES IN HONDURAS. *Maps and numerous illustrations.* 8vo, cloth. New York, 1857. *2 13*

1699 WELLS. Another copy, half calf extra. New York, 1857. *4 50*

1700 WHARTON (GRACE AND PHILIP). WORKS. *39 00*

QUEENS OF SOCIETY. 2 vols.

WITS AND BEAUX OF SOCIETY. 2 vols.

LITERATURE OF SOCIETY. 2 vols.
Together 6 vols. crown 8vo. *Illustrated by Doyle, etc.* Tree calf extra, gilt leaves.
London, *Hogg, etc.*, 1862, etc.

1701 WHARTON (GRACE AND PHILIP). QUEENS, AND WITS AND BEAUX OF SOCIETY. *Numerous illustrations.* 2 vols. 8vo, half red mor. extra, gilt tops, uncut edges. London, n. d. *10 00*

1702 WHEELER (W. A.). NOTED NAMES OF FICTION. 16mo, cloth. Boston, 1866. *1 12*

1703 WHITE (JAMES). EIGHTEEN CHRISTIAN CENTURIES. 12mo, cloth. New York, 1879. *1 88*

1704 WHITTIER BIRTHDAY-Book; arranged by Elizabeth S. Owen. 16mo, mor. Boston, 1883. *2 00*

1705 WILLIAMS (B. S.). CHOICE STOVE AND GREENHOUSE FLOWERING PLANTS, Select Ferns and Lycopods, and Orchid Grower's Manual. *Colored and other illustrations.* 5 vols. post 8vo, cloth. London, 1870–77. *7 50*

1706 WILSON (JOHN W.). CATALOGUE of a COLLECTION of PICTURES, etc. Exposée dans la Galerie du Cercle Artistique et Littéraire de Bruxelles, au profit des pauvres de cette Ville. Troisième édition. *Printed on heavy paper, and illustrated with a series of* 68 *large etchings*, from the most remarkable pictures in this celebrated collection. Roy. 4to, cloth.
$100 00 Bruxelles, 1873.

This charming Catalogue was gotten up at the expense of the generous owner of the collection, and the money received from its sale donated to the fund for the relief of the poor of the city. The edition consisted of 1,000 copies. No. 324.

1707 WISTER'S (MRS.) TRANSLATIONS. Hulda, Second Wife, Only a
3 40 Girl, and Countess Gisela. 4 vols. 12mo, cloth.

1708 WOOD (REV. J. G.). HOMES WITHOUT HANDS, being a description of the Habitations of Animals, classed according to their principle of construction. *Profusely illustrated.* Roy.
4 75 8vo, half calf extra. New York, 1874.

1709 WOOD (J. G.). BIBLE ANIMALS: a description of every living creature mentioned in the Scriptures. 24 *full-page engravings,*
6 75 *and* 60 *woodcuts* 8vo, half calf extra. London, 1860.

1710 WOOD (REV. J. C.). INSECTS AT HOME. A Popular Account of Insects, their Structure, Habits, and Transformations. *Over*
7 50 700 *illustrations.* 8vo, half calf extra. New York, 1872.

1711 WORCESTER (J. C.). DICTIONARY OF THE ENGLISH LANGUAGE. Unabridged edition. *Numerous woodcuts.* Thick 4to, sheep.
6 00 Boston, 1867.

1712 WOMEN OF NEW YORK. *Written and illustrated by Marie L.*
1 00 *Hankins.* 12mo, cloth. New York, 1861.

1713 YONGE (CHARLOTTE M.). HISTORY OF CHRISTIAN NAMES. 2
8 00 vols. crown 8vo, half red mor. extra. London, 1863.

1714 YONGE (MISS). CAMEOS FROM ENGLISH HISTORY. 4 vols.
4 40 post 8vo, cloth. London, 1880.

1715 YOUNG (EDWARD). COMPLAINT, or, Night Thoughts on Life,
2 00 Death and Immortality. Post 8vo, mor., gilt. London, 1853.

1716 YOUNG (JENNIE). CERAMIC ART, a compendium of the History and Manufacture of Pottery and Porcelain. 404 *illustrations.* 4to, cloth. New York, 1879. *$4 50*

1717 ZINCKE (F. B.). [SWITZERLAND.] Walk in the Grisons and Swiss Allmends. *Illustrated.* 2 vols. post 8vo, half red mor. extra. London, 1874. *6 25*

COLLECTION OF ENGRAVINGS AND ETCHINGS.

NOTES BY MR. FREDERICK KEPPEL.

THIS collection has been made with the view of illustrating the whole history of the art, extending over a period of about four centuries.

The best examples of the greatest artists in engraving and etching are here included, in so far as it has been possible to procure them; and several of the prints are undoubtedly unique in America, being the only examples which have ever come here.

The great masterpieces of the old *painters* are now absolutely unprocurable. They are treasured in the public galleries of Europe, whence they will never come out; but such masters of painting as Albert Dürer, Rembrandt, and Claude Lorraine have engraved their own designs, either with the etching needle or the graver, and fine original impressions, printed from such plates, are just as *original*, just as *personal* to these artists as are the paintings themselves.

Thus there are in this collection precious relics of the infancy of art, which were not only engraved, but printed also by the hands of such masters as Israel von Mecken, Martin Schongauer, and Andrea Mantegna; and these identical sheets of paper having been religiously treasured by generation after generation of sincere art-lovers, have come down to the present day, and now take their place in the present collection.

And the wonder is—not that these early prints are costly—but that they are procurable at any cost.

It is not, however, every *old* print which is valuable, or even a work of art in the proper sense at all. It is only those which have genuine artistic merit to recommend them as well as antiquity—only the works of the true artists.

The relative value of each print is determined by its merit *and* its rarity; the best are usually, but not always, the dearest. In May, 1883, an impression of Rembrandt's etching, known as the "Advocate Tolling," was sold at auction in London for the enormons sum of £1,510 sterling ($7,500.00), and yet Rembrandt has etched better portraits than this, but, for some reason, very few impressions of it exist. In Charles Blanc's admirable book on Rembrandt there is a most dramatic account of an auction sale at which the Chevalier Claussin made incredible sacrifices to obtain this same print, and how he failed to get it.

Quite recently Marc Antonio's print of the poet Aretino was sold for £780 ($3,900.00), and Rembrandt's "Hundred Guilders Print" for £1,180 ($5,900.00); and these are not imaginary values, for the same prints would bring as much or more at auction to-day, for their value has steadily increased for the past two hundred years.

The high value of choice prints has caused many of them to be counterfeited. There are as many as four and five different counterfeits of some of Dürer's plates, mostly produced during the artist's own lifetime, or very shortly after his death. The same is true of the works of Marc Antonio, Lucas van Leyden and Rembrandt. Many of these counterfeits are very deceiving, and, were it not that we have in book form the researches of skilled connoisseurs to guide us, collectors of the present day would have good reason to fear that some of their treasures were in reality spurious. But each important print has been positively authenticated, and the slight differences between the originals and the copies have been accurately shown.

Among these critical books of reference one work is pre-eminent. It is "*Le Peintre-Graveur*," in 21 volumes, by Adam Bartsch, who was the curator of the public collection at Vienna, where he was born in 1756. This work is a monument of critical research. It gives a detailed and systematic list of the works of each of the Painter-Engravers, telling how the various "states" of each plate are known, and minutely describing all the dangerous counterfeits of these plates.

The different "states" of a plate are somewhat like the different editions of a book, and it must always be borne in mind that as each impression taken *wears* the plate a little, the earliest impressions are usually the best, and a late impression from a worn-out plate is never good. The first state of a plate is not *always* the best, though it is nearly always the dearest. In the etchings of Rembrandt especially the first state is often very much unfinished, and of course presents an incomplete picture.

In a recent book, Sir William Drake's catalogue of the etchings of Seymour Haden, the excellent plan has been adopted of calling the unfinished and experimental proofs, "*trial* proofs," numbering them a, b, c, etc., and afterwards counting the "first state" from the actual completion of the plate. But Bartsch, Robert Dumesnil, and the other authorities designate these unfinished trial proofs as "states."

The "states" of the older plates correspond to the different "proof" states of the later engravings.

In the later engravings the "artists' proofs" are a limited number of the first taken from the *finished* plate. They are printed with great care, and before any inscription whatever has been put into the lower margin of the plate. Within the last thirty years it has become a custom for the engraver to examine each one of these artists' proofs, and to affix his signature to those that he finds perfect and unexceptionable; such a signature is, therefore, an endorsement or guarantee of the proof which bears it.

After the artists' proofs comes a second printing of "proofs before letters," which by a contradiction of terms are *not* before letters—since they usually bear the name of the painter, engraver, and publisher—but they are "before letters" in the sense that they are before the *title*, which does not appear till the next later state. After the "proofs before letters" come the "open letter" proofs. These are impressions with the final title of print added—but sketched in outline only.

Last of all come the "lettered prints," in which the title is completed. These lettered prints are issued until the metal plate wears out from use, and are unlimited in number.

In addition to these various proof states of a plate, an extra modern refinement has created the "*épreuves de rémarque*." These are the choicest and finest of all: they are very few in number, and are issued from the finished plate *before* the artists' proofs. They are so named from the "*rémarque*" or little special sketch which the artist adds in the lower margin of the plate, and which is again burnished out of the plate before the printing of the regular edition of the artists' proofs begins.

"States" of etchings are not always indicated by the lettering in the lower margin, as is the case with line engravings and mezzotints, because very often there *is* no blank margin to an etching, the etched work filling up the entire space of the copper. In such cases the "states" are indicated by something added to or taken from the etched work itself. For example: in Rembrandt's renowned plate of Christ before Pilate, known as the "Great Ecce Homo," the various states are described by Charles Blanc thus: *First state*, only the figures of Pilate and of five Jews appear, the greater portion of the composition has not yet been even commenced. Only two impressions of this state are known to exist; both are in the British Museum. *Second state:* The plate is now finished, except that in the subsequent state Rembrandt has added some diagonal lines to the face of one of the Jews. "*Il est extrêmement rare*" (Blanc). This second state shows the plate in all its glory—(and a superb impression of it is in the present collection). *Third state:* With the aforesaid diagonal lines added to the face of one of the Jews. *Fourth state:* The name of the publisher Malbousc is added in the lower margin.

Rembrandt's plates, and also those of Claude, present a variety of "states; while in the line engravings of Martin Schongauer, Albert Dürer, and Lucas van Leyden, "states" are almost unknown, and the value is altogether determined by the quality of the impression—a very fine early one being worth twenty times more than a late and worn one.

The following extract from an article in *Harper's Magazine* gives some practical hints on this subject:

> "A word of suggestion as to the selection of engravings. It is not essential that they must be 'proofs,' though proofs, being the very earliest impressions taken from the plate, are naturally the finest. But a bad or worn impression should not be tolerated, no matter how cheap it is. Such a print is known by its general effect of weakness and paleness; the figures have lost their rotundity, and the perspective is almost gone. Especially among old engravings are bad impressions to be avoided.
>
> "Modern impressions taken from such old plates as still exist are also worthless. A print, to be as it should be, must have been printed at the time it was engraved. Modern impressions are readily known by the paper on which they are printed.
>
> "Another necessary warning is against 'retouched' impressions; many plates have been thus ruined, when, after they have begun to wear out from use, they have been re-cut in the worn parts by incompetent hands. The effect of a retouched impression is dull, heavy, and disagreeable; all the harmony and beauty of the plate are gone. It is only fine original impressions in good condition that worthily represent the great engravers."

While the works of the early "Painter-Engravers" and "Painter-Etchers" are the most valuable, still no collection would be complete without the best works of the later engravers, who have reproduced the masterpieces of painting, *translating* them—so to say—into black and white.

Thus Raphael never engraved or etched his Sistine Madonna; but Müller engraved it for him three centuries later. Rembrandt never etched his Night Watch; but Flameng has etched it for him in our own day. Turner did not engrave his Calais Pier; but Seymour Haden etched Turner's painting in a most masterly manner.

No doubt Raphael, Rembrandt, and Turner could have engraved these three paintings respectively—*but they did not do so;* and meanwhile the most satisfactory copies of them are the three plates just named.

Injudicious partisans of the beautiful art of etching have gone so far as to disparage all reproductive engraving as not being "original." But they forget that we do not *want* originality in a translation or a reproduction. What we want is fidelity.

In Müller's plate of the Sistine Madonna it is Raphael who furnishes us with the originality, and his translator Müller has no business to be "original." And while the painting is far away in Dresden, this satisfactory copy of translation of it may adorn an American home.

The great value then of these engravings after the paintings of other men is, that they are the most available and most satisfactory presentations of those paintings which are the recognized masterpieces of art.

It is an interesting fact that those masters, such as Dürer, Rembrandt, and Claude, seldom or never engraved the same designs which they painted, or painted those that they had previously engraved, so that their prints do not duplicate their paintings—and this is one reason more for admitting good reproductive engravings into a collection.

NOTE ON COLLECTORS' STAMPS AND MARKS.

For centuries it has been the custom of some eminent collectors to put a distinctive mark on the backs of such prints as have been found worthy to make part of their several collections.

When the mark of some renowned collector is found on a print it is always recognized as a certificate of high quality. In the older prints the highest possible endorsement is to find the name of "P. Mariette" written, with the date, ranging from 1660 to 1710. Mariette sometimes even wrote his name on the face of a print—but so great was his judgment of quality that even this disfigurement adds value to it. A book is now being compiled by Mr. Thibaudeau, of London, which will be devoted to explaining these collectors' marks.

In the best modern collections it is usual to stamp the initials of the owner neatly in small letters on the back of the print.

ENGRAVERS, AND SPECIAL WORKS BY THEM, IN THIS COLLECTION.

OLD SCHOOL.

MARTIN SCHONGAUER, painter, engraver, and goldsmith, was born at Ulm, in 1420, and died at Colmar on the 2d of February, 1488.

He was one of the earliest and one of the best painter-engravers whose names have been preserved. The art of etching was not yet known in his lifetime—the discovery of it being ascribed to Albert Dürer, who was born in 1471—51 years later.

Although the works of all the early German masters seem stiff and "gothic" to modern eyes, yet there is real taste and beauty in the engravings of Schongauer. Perhaps the finest of his prints is the Saint Anthony tormented by Demons. Vasari records that Michael Angelo in his youth took the pains to color an impression of this print.

This collection is very rich in the works of this master. Among the finest specimens in it are the "Coronation of the Virgin" (Bartsch No. 71); "Peasants going to Market" (Bartsch No. 88); and the Elephant (Bartsch 92). This last is of extreme rarity.

ISRAEL VON MECKEN (or Meckenen), born at Bocholt, according to Byran, "about" the year 1424. Died the 15th of March, 1503.

Like others of the earliest engravers, he was a goldsmith—the separate profession of a painter being unknown at that period.

The "Dance of Herodias" is considered his masterpiece (see Andreson). The present impression is superb, and it is most probably the only example of this very rare print that exists in America. The costumes in it are most interesting.

ANDREA MANTEGNA, born at Padua in 1431. Died on the 15th of September, 1506.

This famous artist was not a goldsmith, like some of the early Germans, but was only known as a historical painter and engraver, and both his paintings and his prints display a bold and masterly style which is very different from the stiff and laborious work of the early Northern school.

Fine impressions of his works are exceedingly scarce and are highly valued.

"La Sépulture" (Bartsch, Vol. 13, pp. 229, 230)—cette estampe, dont Vasari fait mention, est une des plus parfaites de l'œuvre, tant pour le dessein que pour l'expression de la gravure."

It is very rare.

"La Flagellation" (Bartsch No. 1). Fine original impression. There is an old counterfeit of this print, in which the pavement is somewhat different in design from the original.

ALBERT DÜRER.—This great master was born on the 20th of May, 1471, and died in his native town of Nurenberg on the 18th of April, 1528.

The books which have been written upon his works would form a small library in themselves, and the artist himself—like Leonardo da Vinci—is also a writer of books.

The greatest museums of the world compete in perfecting their collections of Dürer's engravings.

The present collection is especially rich in them, and many of the examples are absolutely *unsurpassed* as to quality.

"Adam and Eve" (Bartsch No. 1). The artist's masterpiece, "Saint Hubert," Dürer's largest plate. "St. Jerome in his Cell" (Bartsch No. 60), very fine. The "Melancholia"—a perfect impression of this celebrated print.

NOTE.—Dürer has put into this plate a curious tablet of numbers which, when added up in a line, give the total of 34. This tablet gives the same total (34) when added in ten different ways, viz.: perpendicularly, diagonally, or horizontally.

Of Dürer's plate of "St. Hubert," Bartsch records that the original copper-plate came into the possession of the Emperor Rudolph, who caused the engraved lines to be filled with gold, and in this condition the plate was put into the Emperor's museum. After this filling up of the lines, of course no more impressions could be taken.

This collection now contains no fewer than *thirty-eight* engravings by Dürer.

MARC ANTONIO (Raimondi).—This most celebrated of the Italian engravers was born at Bologna, in 1487.

He was not a "painter-engraver" in that he did not engrave his own designs, but inasmuch as his career was intimately associated with that of Raphael—the "prince of painters," and that Raphael never engraved or etched, Marc Antonio's prints take rank with those of Dürer and Rembrandt, as the choicest gems in the realm of engraving.

In early life this engraver executed several plates in which he counterfeited the works of Dürer—even to the adding of Dürer's monogram to them. But going to Rome he attracted the attention of Raphael, and thereafter his great achievements were his plates from Raphael's works.

An interesting fact is that in many cases these engravings differ in certain details from the master's well-known paintings, and from this circumstance it is concluded that Raphael furnished his engraver with drawings from which to engrave his plates. And so truly "Raphaelesque" are those prints that connoisseurs are of opinion that Raphael himself must have aided Marc Antonio in his work.

"Saint Paul preaching at Athens" (Bartsch No. 44). Brilliant impression of one of Marc Antonio's finest prints. "Mary Magdalen washing the Feet of Christ," (Bartsch 23). "La Vierge au Berceau" (Bartsch No. 63).

The above, among several others in this collection, may be cited as examples of Marc Antonio's beautiful and artistic work.

LUCAS VAN LEYDEN.—Born at Leyden, Holland, in 1494. Died in 1533. Eminent painter and line engraver; contemporary and friend of Dürer.

Fine impressions of this engraver's work are even scarcer than those of Dürer, because his plates were so delicately engraved that they yielded only very few good proofs before they began to wear out.

His print of Mary Magdalen enjoying the pleasures of the World, called "La Dance de la Madeleine," is his most admired work, and ranks as one of the masterpieces of engraving.

PARMIGIANO.—Born at Parma, in 1503. Died in 1540. The family name of this eminent painter was Mazzuoli. The collection contains a fine proof in the "first state" of his etching, "The Entombment."

CLAUDE LORRAINE.—This great master of landscape painting and etching was born in France in the year 1600, and died in Rome in 1682. His family name was Gelée. The parents of Claude were very poor and he was apprenticed to a pastry-cook. He afterwards became valet and cook to the Roman painter Tassi, and from this poor beginning he rose to be, perhaps, the greatest master of landscape.

In Smith's "Catalogue Raisonné of Claude," the writer says: "Upwards of two centuries have elapsed since the birth of this enchanting painter, and during this long period no successful rival has appeared. He therefore stands alone, preeminent in excellence."

The etchings of Claude are as highly esteemed as his paintings. The standard authority on the former is the work of Robert Dumesnil, "*Le Peintre-Graveur Français.*"

REMBRANDT.—Paul Rembrandt van Ryn, the supreme master of etching, was born on the 15th of July, 1606, and died in 1665.

Rembrandt's etchings are the choicest treasures in the portfolios of amateurs throughout the world. Their value has steadily increased during two and a half centuries. In May, 1883, the highest price ever paid for an etching was given at auction in London for Rembrandt's portrait of the "Advocate Tolling." The price was £1510 sterling, or about $7,500.00. The purchaser was Monsieur Dutuit of Rouen. The auction sale took place at Christie & Manson's.

In the important revival of true painter-etching, which began about the year 1860 with Meryon, Jacque, Seymour Haden, Whistler, etc., and which has continued with such splendid results to the present day, it is a fact that all the best etched is frankly modeled after the methods of Rembrandt, and that "inspired Dutchman" seems to have known and practiced all the processes which are now used.

The great diversity of the money value of this master's etchings is partly due to their comparative quality, but partly also to their comparative rarity, so that the costliest print is not always the finest work of art.

His acknowledged *chef d'œuvre* is the "Christ healing the Sick," known by the sobriquet of the "Hundred Guilders Print." It is so called because Rembrandt himself used to sell it for that price (about $60.00). This was at that time a price unprecedentedly high. Dürer sold his finest prints at about *twenty-five cents* each.

The present impression of the "Hundred Guilders Print" is especially fine. A few years ago Mr. Palmer of London paid $5,900.00 for the first state of this print.

"The Three Trees." This is perhaps the most celebrated, as it is the most valuable of all Rembrandt's landscapes. There are several counterfeits of this plate, but none of them approach the original in quality.

The "Great Ecce Homo." Magnificent proof in the first finished state (2d state according to the books of reference). The present impression is described on page 8. There is probably not a finer example of it in the world. Only one other proof in this second state exists in America.

The collection now contains no fewer than 109 of Rembrandt's etchings; all are fine, and many are of such extreme rarity that it would be impossible to find any others in this country.

Portrait of the "Burgomaster Jan Six."

This is admittedly the finest of Rembrandt's etched portraits. It is of great rarity and value in any state, but the present impression is of such beauty that it would be almost impossible to duplicate it.

While Rembrandt was still poor and obscure one of his first patrons was Jan Six, member of an old Amsterdam family, and who afterwards became Burgomaster of his native city.

When the great Jan Six first patronized the poor and unknown Rembrandt he little thought that Rembrandt's work would immortalize his own name, but so it has proved.

This portrait was etched in 1647, when Six was 29 years old. After more than two centuries the Six family reside in the same plain and comfortable old house, and the house is full of precious works of art.

CORNELIUS VISSCHER.—This interesting artist was born in Holland in 1629, and died at the early age of 28.

His print of the Pancake Woman is celebrated. A curious point in it is that there are *two* children eating pancakes, while any one would assert that there is only one. The second child can be found in the very middle of the print, near the woman's elbow.

The portrait of De Ryck is a masterpiece and very rare.

ANTOINE MASSON.—An eminent line engraver. Born at Orleans in 1636. Died in Paris, 1700.

His portrait of Brisacier, known as the "Gray-Haired Man," is considered one of the four finest portraits in line engraving. The other three being the Pompone de Bellièvre of Nauteuil, Philippe de Champaigne by Edelinck, and Bossuet by Drevet.

The present impression of the "Gray-Haired Man" is in a rare early state, in which there are two errors in the spelling of the inscription round the oval.

GERARD EDELINCK.—This greatest of portrait line-engravers was born at Antwerp in 1627, but his whole artistic career was in Paris.

ROBERT NAUTEUIL.—Born at Rheims, 1630. Died in Paris, 1678. One of the great portrait engravers. His portrait of Pompone de Bellièvre is considered to be the finest ever executed. His works are minutely described in the catalogue of M. Robert Dumesnil.

PIERRE DREVET.—Born at Lyons, 1664. Died in Paris, 1739.

One of the great portrait engravers. His large full-length portrait of Louis XIV. is considered his finest work. A fine impression of it is in the collection.

PIERRE IMBERT DREVET.- Son of Pierre. Born at Paris, 1697. Died there in 1739. The younger Drevet has never been surpassed and has hardly been equaled as a portrait engraver. His portraits of Bishop Bossuet and of Adrienne Lecouvreur are his most esteemed works.

This eminent engraver died insane at the age of 42.

G. B. PIRANESI.—This artist was by profession an architect, and this aided him in the branch of art to which he devoted himself and in which he was unequaled.

His complete etched works comprise a great number of volumes, but it is only a election of his most pictorial subjects which are sought by print collectors.

JOHN GEORGE WILLE.—Eminent master of line-engraving, born 1715. Died 1808.

A superb proof of the "Satin Gown" is one of the gems of the collection.

SIR ROBERT STRANGE.—Born in Scotland, in 1721. Died in London, 1792.

One of the very finest gems in the collection is the artist's proof of Strange's portrait of King Charles I. It bears an autograph dedication to a fellow artist.

WILLIAM WOOLLETT.—Born in England, 1735. Died in 1785.

Proofs of Woollett's prints are of great rarity. One such brought £70 sterling at auction in London recently.

There are several proofs of his finest works in the collection.

WILLIAM SHARP.—Born in England, 1746. Died in 1824.

A fine proof of the "Doctors of the Church" is one of the important plates in the collection.

The original painting was offered to the British Government, but while they delayed to secure it, Catharine the Great, of Russia, bought it along with other masterpieces.

GIUSEPPE LONGHI.—Born 1766. Died 1831.

A proof of the Reclining Magdalen is one of the loveliest things in engraving. It is very rare.

RAPHAEL MORGHEN.—Born near Naples, 1758. Died at Florence, 1833.

In the collection are the portrait of Leonardo da Vinci, and a proof of the small Madonna of the Chair, which Morghen engraved at the age of 72 years.

PAOLO TOSCHI.—Born at Parma in 1788. Died there in 1854.

This artist's two best plates are represented in the collection by unique proofs, both from his own collection. These plates are the Madonna della Scala, and the "Incoronata."

FRIEDRICH MÜLLER.—Born 1783. Died 1816.

A fine old impression of the great engraving of the Sistine Madonna also enriches the collection.

The plate is still in existence but very much retouched, and only the original impressions do justice to this masterpiece.

Other famous line-engravers are Porporati, Mandel, Calamatta, Schavoni, Richomme, Perfetti, François, Van Dalen, Bartolozzi, etc., all of whom, and several others, are well represented in the collection.

MODERN ETCHERS.

FRANCIS SEYMOUR HADEN.—This renowned etcher is not even an artist by profession, but has spent his life as a surgeon in London. He is one of the Fellows of the Royal College of Surgeons, and his etched work was only done as a recreation, and originally without any view to publication.

But yet no professional etcher of the 19th century ranks so high as Haden.

Mr. Hamerton's book, *Etching and Etchers*, devotes a very interesting chapter to this artist.

All his etchings are from his own designs, except one family portrait and the great plate of the Calais Pier, which is after Turner's painting.

The two large plates of Greenwich and Windsor are from his own designs. All three of these plates are destroyed and the proofs are very valuable.

Seymour Haden was born in 1818.

CHARLES MÉRYON.—Born at Paris in 1821. Died insane at Charenton, 1868.

Mr. Hamerton, in *Etching and Etchers*, eloquently tells the pathetic story of this wonderful artist's life.

Though he died so recently, his etchings to-day sell at nearly as high a price as those of Rembrandt; but he was driven insane by hunger, misery, and neglect, and in a paroxysm of madness he destroyed his precious copper-plates, so that his works are much scarcer than they otherwise would have been.

The collection is very rich in Méryon's prints.

CHARLES JACQUE.—Born in Paris the 23d of May, 1813.

This famous painter was one of the first to start the modern revival of true etching. His great plate, "La Grande Bergerie," is an acknowledged masterpiece.

JEAN FRANÇOIS MILLET.—This great artist was born at Gréville in 1814, and his etchings are as thoroughly characteristic of him as his paintings themselves.

It is stated that during the whole of his life Millet finished only about eighty oil paintings, many of which he retained in his studio for a long time, returning to work on them again and again in order to satisfy himself.

What a pity it is that he did not receive, during his life, the *tenth part* of the present value of any *one* of these paintings, in addition to the pittance that he sold them for! Such a sum would have made a rich man of him.

Millet sometimes repeated the subjects of his paintings in his etchings.

The collection contains several of his finest, notably "La Cardeuse," and a unique proof of "La Bergère," the latter being probably the only signed proof of it in the world.

DE GRAVESANDE.—This eminent etcher is the son of the late President of the Senate of Holland.

He went through the law course at the University of Leyden, but his overpowering bent toward art resulted in his adopting the profession of an artist. Mr. Hamerton devotes a highly laudatory chapter to him in the *second* edition of his *Etching and Etchers*, the first edition having appeared before his first etchings were published.

De Gravesande's etchings are highly esteemed in England and France. He now lives in Brussels.

AMERICAN ETCHERS.

Some of the very best and truest etchers of the present day are Americans.

The critics say that the practical *directness* of the American character is conducive to this result. In general these works are specially decorative and pictorial, and are well adapted to framing purposes.

Perhaps the most popular—and justly so—of American etchers, is

STEPHEN PARRISH.—He was born in Philadelphia, in 1846, and belongs to one of the old Quaker families there. Mr. Hamerton writes of him in the London *Portfolio*:

"Mr. Parrish is one of the most sincere and straightforward of living etchers."

The collection includes a set of his works, which is almost complete, and as many of the earlier plates are destroyed, many of those are rare.

PETER MORAN.—This celebrated painter of animals, etc., is President of the Philadelphia Painter-Etchers' Society. He was one of the first to practice the art in this country, and he has been eminently successful as a teacher.

Peter Moran is brother of Thomas and of Edward, the well-known New York painters, and is uncle of Percy and Leon Moran.

JOSEPH PENNELL.—Born in Philadelphia. A pupil of the Pennsylvania Academy of Fine Arts.

There is probably no living etcher who has achieved as high a reputation in so short a time as Mr. Pennell. He is now about twenty-five years old, but he has won the cordial approval of such masters as Haden, Whistler, and De Gravesande.

OTTO H. BACHER.—A native of Cleveland, Ohio. Studied art in Munich and Venice. Of his set of twelve views of Venice, Seymour Haden writes:

"The whole set, accessories and all, evinces a strong artistic feeling. Bold and painter-like treatment characterizes it throughout."

Mr. Bacher is not yet thirty years old.

SALE MONDAY MORNING, AFTERNOON, AND EVENING, MARCH 15.

BEGINNING AT 10.30 A.M., 2.30, AND 7.30 O'CLOCK P.M.

AT THE AMERICAN ART GALLERIES.

ENGRAVINGS AND ETCHINGS.

PART I.

ALDEGREVER.

1718 Portrait of himself. Bartsch 189. *$20 00*

1719 " " Albert van der Halle. " 186. *30 00*

ALTDORFER.

1720 Bible Scenes. 40 illustrations. *17 50*

ANDERLONI.

1721 Mater Dolorosa. *9 00*

BARTOLOZZI.

1722 Young Bacchus, after Franceschini. *12 00*

1723 Mary Queen of Scots, after Zuccheri. Large margin. *40 00*

BEAUVARLET.

1724 Telemachus in the Island of Calypso. Proof. *27 00*

1725 Le Comte d'Artois and Mlle. Clotilde. Proof. *35 00*

BEGA.

$6 00 1726 Dutch Peasants.

BEHAM.

9 00 1727 Vignette. Bartsch 228.

22 00 1728 The Well at Samaria.

BEISSON.

14 00 1729 St. Cecilia, after Raphael. Proof.

BERGHEM.

21 00 1730 Landscape, Pastoral.

10 00 1731 " Watering the Flock.

8 00 1732 " Evening. Returning from Work.

23 00 1733 Musicians. Fine Impression.

29 00 1734 Flageolet Player. " "

BERTINOT (G.).

13 00 1735 Marguerite, after Merle. Proof.

BERVIC (C.).

65 00 1736 Louis XVI., after Callet. First state.

17 00 1737 Le Repos. Proof.

50 00 1738 The Laocoon. Proof.

BETTELINI (P.).

6 00 1739 Matei Amabilis, after Allori. Proof.

BIOT (G.).

1740 Aglae, after Cábanel. *$14 00*

BLANCHARD.

1741 Isabella and the Pot of Basil, after Holman Hunt. Proof. *30 00*
1742 Eve of St. Agnes, " " " " *25 00*

BOL (F.).

1743 Philosopher. *18 00*

BOLSWERT.

1744 The Holy Family, after Vandyke. *7 00*

BOUILLARDT (J.).

1745 Comtesse de Provence. *10 00*
1746 The Holy Family, after A. Caracci. Open Letter Proof. *23 00*

BURT (CHAS.).

1747 Portrait of Longfellow. *7 00*

CALAMATTA.

1748 Madonna della Sedia. Rare Proof. *28 00*
1749 Vow of Louis XIII. *30 00*
1750 Portrait of George Sand. *15 00*

CAMPAGNOLA (G.).

1751 St. John the Baptist. Bartsch 3. *72 50*
1752 Woman of Samaria. *125 00*
1753 Assumption of the Virgin (D.). *62 50*

CARON (A.).

$8 00 1754 Duchess de Berri and her Children, after Gérard.

CHAILLOUX.

6 00 1755 Madonna of the Fish.

CHAMBERS (THOS.).

7 00 1756 Saint Martin, after Rubens.

CHATILLON.

7 00 1757 Genevieve of Brabant.

CLAESSENS (L. A.).

42 50 1758 Descent from the Cross, after Rubens. Proof.

32 00 1759 Night Watch, after Rembrandt. Proof.

CLAUDE.

17 00 1760 Flock Drinking.

19 00 1761 Crossing the Brook.

15 00 1762 Dance by the Water-side.

14 00 1763 Mercury and Argus.

17 00 1764 Shipwreck.

13 00 1765 The Four Goats.

12 00 1766 Campo Vaccino.

13 00 1767 The Three Goats.

10 00 1768 Rape of Europa.

23 00 1769 Seaport.

18 00 1770 "

1771 Le Temps Appollon, etc. *$9 00*

1772 " " *11 00*

1773 Goatherd. *16 00*

1774 Wooden Bridge. *10 00*

1775 Le Dessinateur. *14 00*

1776 Le Troupeau au Marche. *26 00*

1777 Le Depart pour les Champs. *17 00*

1778 Berger et Bergère. *21 00*

1779 Flight into Egypt. *17 00*

1780 The Apparition. *10 00*

COUSINS (S.).

1781 Chandos Portrait of Shakespeare. *17 00*

DANIELL (J.).

1782 Samuel and Eli (Mezzotint), after Copley. *19 00*

DE FREY.

1783 Supper at Emmaus, after Rembrandt. *12 00*

DENON (BARON).

1784 L'Abbe Zani. *12 00*

DESNOYERS.

1785 Belisarius, after Gérard. Rare open letter Proof. *65 00*

1786 Napoleon, in his Coronation Robes (with the mask), after Gérard. *110 00*

Proof before the name of the Artist.

DESSON.

$27 00 1787 Rheims Cathedral. Rare.

DREVET (PIERRE).

42 50 1788 Louis the Great, after Rigaud.
24 00 1789 Louis Alexander de Bourbon, "
32 50 1790 Bossuet, "
25 00 1791 Philip d'Anjou (Philip V. of Spain), "
25 00 1792 Adrienne le Couvreur, after Coybel.

DÜRER.

85 00 1793 Adam and Eve. Bartsch 1.
18 00 1794 The Man of Sorrow. " 20.
21 00 1795 Crown of Thorns. " 25.
23 00 1796 The Face of Christ carried by an Angel. Engraved on Iron. " 26.
50 00 1797 The Prodigal Son. " 28.
29 00 1798 Madonna and Child. " 35.
14 00 1799 Virgin and Infant Christ. " 36.
30 00 1800 " " " " " 36.
45 00 1801 Virgin crowned by an Angel. " 37.
51 00 1802 Madonna and Child. " 38.
27 50 1803 Virgin crowned by two Angels. " 39.
95 00 1804 Madonna by the Wall. " 40.
40 00 1805 Madonna of the Pear. " 41.
67 50 1806 Conversion of St. Hubert. " 57.
65 00 1807 St. Anthony. " 58.
100 00 1808 St. Jerome in his Cell. " 60.
47 50 1809 St. Jerome. " 61.
105 00 1810 Apollo and Diana. " 68.

1811	L'Enlèvement d'Amynone.	Bartsch	71.	$50 00
1812	Effects of Jealousy.	"	73.	67 50
1813	Melancholy.	"	74.	310 00
1814	Four Nude Women.	"	75.	31 00
1815	The Idler.	"	76.	50 00
1816	The Little Fortune.	"	78.	27 50
1817	Justice.	"	79.	32 50
1818	Lady on Horseback.	"	82.	55 00
1819	Peasant and Wife.	"	83.	80 00
1820	Hostess and Cook.	"	84.	47 50
1821	Three Peasants.	"	86.	17 50
1822	The Ensign.	"	87.	32 50
1823	Warriors.	"	88.	50 00
1824	The Madman.	"	92.	40 00
1825	Portrait of Melancthon.	"	105.	30 00
1826	Portrait of Erasmus.	"	107.	50 00
1827	Knight and Lady.			57 50
1828	St. Jerome, woodcut.	"	114.	20 00
1829	Portrait of Dürer, woodcut (1527).			22 50
1830	La Madonna dans Bethlehem.			12 50

EARLOM.

MEZZOTINTS.

1831	Newfoundland Dog Saving a Child from Drowning, after Eckstein.	15 00
1832	Companion to above, after Eckstein.	15 00
1833	The Forge, after Jno. Wright. Proof.	47 50
1834	Rembrandt's Portrait of himself. Proof.	30 00
1835	Concert of Birds, after Marie di Fiori. Proof.	30 00
1836	Flowers, after Van Huysom. Proof.	24 00
1837	Fruit, " " " Proof.	24 00

EICHEUS (E.).

$18 00 1838 Frederick the Great and his Sister as Children, after Pesne. Proof.

EDELINCK.

67 50 1839 Holy Family, after Raphael. Before the Coat of Arms.

50 00 1840 Louise de la Vallière, after Lebrun. Before the Border.

7 00 1841 Paul de Lionne.

5 00 1842 J. B. Santeuil.

32 50 1843 Nath. Dilgerus.

10 00 1844 J. H. Mansard, after Rigaud.

35 00 1845 Phillippe de Champagne.

47 50 1846 The Fight for the Standard, after Da Vinci.

☞ See also NANTEUIL.

FELSING.

8 00 1847 Poetry and Love, after Kaulbach.

25 00 1848 The Lorellei.

FICQUET.

11 00 1849 Madame Maintenon, after Mignard.

FLEISCHMAN.

17 00 1850 St. Paul in Prison, after Rembrandt. Proof.

FORSTER (F.).

14 00 1851 Dido and Æneas, after Guérin.

56 00 1852 The Three Graces, " Raphael.

7 00 1853 Albert Dürer, after Dürer. Proof.

FRANÇOIS (A.).

1854 Mother and Child. *$6 00*

1855 Portrait of Titian. *6 00*

1856 " " Raphael d'Urbino. *12 50*

1857 Marie Antoinette going to the Guillotine, after P. Delaroche. Proof. *52 50*

FRYE (THOS.).

1858 Portrait of himself, mezzotint. Fine and rare. *21 00*

1859 " " in Turban, mezzotint. Fine and rare. *12 50*

GANDOLFI (M.).

1860 Cupid Sleeping, after Raphael. Open Letter Proof. *7 00*

GARAVAGLIA.

1861 Jacob Meeting Rachel and Leah, after Appiani. Remarque Proof. Showing the *white* buckle on the left sandal of Jacob. *60 00*

1862 The Madonna. Proof. *15 00*

GHISI (GIORGIO).

1863 Dream of Raphael. *27 50*

GOLTZIUS.

1864 Portrait of Theodore Coernhert. *20 00*

1865 Christ before Pilate. *7 50*

GREATBACH (W.).

1866 The Winder, after Gerard Dow. Proof. *12 50*

1867 The Reader, " " " " *15 00*

HESS (C.).

$12 50 1868 "Suffer Little Children to come unto Me," after Rembrandt.

HOLLAR.

32 50 1869 The Dead Hare.

30 00 1870 Cup, after Andrea Mantegna.

30 00 1872 Cathedral (Antwerp).

16 00 1873 Study of Heads, after Da Vinci.

HUNTER.

13 00 1874 Hide and Seek, after Henrietta Ronner. Remarque Proof.

13 00 1875 A Fascinating Tale, " " " " "

KARL DU JARDIN.

9 00 1876 Landscape, Mules. Bartsch 27.

10 00 1877 " Peasant Crossing Stream. " 2.

15 00 1878 " Mules. " 29.

JACQUET (JULES).

18 00 1879 Madame Récamier, after David. Proof.

6 00 1880 The Sacrifice, " Leroux.

6 00 1881 The Invocation, " "

JOSEY (RICHARD).

13 00 1882 Whistler's Portrait of his Mother. Proof.

15 00 1883 " " " " Autograph copy.

32 50 1884 The Captain of the "Eleven."

27 50 1885 Artist's Child, after Greuze. Proof.

JOUANIN.

1886 Fortune Teller, after Becker. $5 00

JOUBERT.

1887 Il Penseroso, after Winterhalter. Proof. 12 00
1888 Nina, " Greuze. 13 00

KELLER.

1889 Holy Family, after Ittenbach. 16 00

KELLERHOVEN.

1890 An Oriental, after Rembrandt. 8 00

KNOLLE.

1891 Madonna and Christ, after Correggio. 11 00
1892 Christ and the Tribute Money. 11 00

LA CASAS.

1893 Baccio Bandinelli. 20 00

LECOMTE.

1894 Last Supper, after Da Vinci. 12 50

LEFÈVRE

1895 Holy Night, after Correggio. Proof. 30 00

LEQUAY.

$3 00 1896 Rabelais.

3 00 1897 Paul de Kock.

LEVY (G.).

5 00 1898 Anne of Austria.

4 00 1899 Cardinal de Retz.

7 00 1900 Pascal.

17 50 1901 Damocles in Prison, after Couture. Proof.

LIGNON (F.).

6 00 1902 Talma, after Pici. Proof.

10 00 1903 Mlle. Mars, after Gérard. Proof.

13 00 1904 St. Cecilia, after Domenichino. Proof.

LONGHI (GUISEPPE).

40 00 1905 Eugene Napoleon, after Gérard.

22 00 1906 The Holy Family, after Raphael.

130 00 1907 Magdalen, after Correggio. Very Rare Proof.

11 00 1908 Lady Burgesch and Child, after Lawrence.

15 00 1909 Genius of Music burning Cupid's Arrows.

LOWENSTEIN.

7 00 1910 In Confidence, after Alma Tadema.

LUCAS (A.).

17 00 1911 English Setters, after Hardy. Proof.

LUDY (F.).

1912 Congratulations, after Knaus. $25 00

MANDEL (E.).

1913 La Vedova, after L. Robert. 12 00

1914 Madonna of the Stars, after Carlo Dolci. Proof. 42 50

1915 La Bella di Tiziano. Proof. 45 00

ANDREA MANTEGNA.

1916 Triumph of Scipio. 22 50

1917 Entombment of Christ. 57 50

1918 Flagellation of Christ. 52 50

MARCUCCI (J.).

1919 Madonna of the Goldfinch, after P. Agricola. Proof. Private Plate never in Print. 40 00

MARI (GUISEPPE).

1920 St. John, after Carraci. 7 50

MARTINET (A.).

1921 Nativity, after Murillo. 15 00

1922 Charles I., after Paul Delaroche. 15 00

1923 Rembrandt, after himself. 17 00

MASSARD (JULES).

1924 Hippocrates refusing the Bribes of Artaxerxes, after Girodet. Proof. 20 00

1925 Burial of Atala. Proof. 20 00

1926 Homer. Proof. 42 50

$12 50 1927 Madame Le Brun and her Daughter. Remarque Proof.

26 00 1928 St. Cecilia, after Raphael. Proof.

9 00 1929 Study of Pointers, after Desporte. Proof.

MASSON.

72 50 1930 Portrait of Guilliaume de Brisacier. "The Gray-headed Man." Second state.

7 00 1931 Guido Patin.

25 00 1932 Henri de Lorraine, Comte D'Harcourt.

MELLAN (CLAUDE).

22 50 1933 St. Peter Nolasque, borne by Angels.

25 00 1934 Face of Christ. Engraved in a Single Line beginning at the tip of the nose. *Very Rare.*

MELLINI (C. D.).

27 50 1935 Savoyards.

MERCURI (P.).

26 00 1936 St. Amelia, after Paul Delaroche. Proof. The most minute engraving ever executed.

20 00 1937 Madame de Maintenon, after Petitot. Proof.

MEUNIER (J. B.).

22 50 1938 The Mouse Hunt, after Madon. Proof.

MICHELS.

7 50 1939 Peter the Great, studying Naval Architecture, after Wappers.

MILLER (J. D.).

21 00 1940 Friends now, Pussy!

21 00 1941 Modern Italy, after Turner. Proof.

RAPHAEL MORGHEN.

1942 Duke of Moncada, after Vandyke. Proof. $47 50

1943 Lorenzo di Medici, after Vasari. 7 50

1944 La Fornarina, after Raphael. 14 00

1945 Madonna della Seglia, after Raphael. Proof. Last work of Morghen. 20 00

1946 Boccaccio, after Gozzini. 6 00

1947 Tasso, after Ermini. 8 00

1948 Horace, after Tenderini. 2 00

1949 Christ, after Da Vinci. 6 00

1950 Leonardo da Vinci, after Da Vinci. Open Letter Proof. 37 50

1951 Raphael Morghen. 7 00

1952 Duchess of Alba. 5 00

MORIN (J.).

1953 Cardinal Bentivoglio, after Vandyke. 13 00

MOTTRAM.

1954 Pride and Humility, after Geo. Cole. Proof. 26 00

MÜLLER (FRED'K).

1955 Madonna San Sisto, after Raphael. Rare. Open Letter Proof. 500 00

1956 St. John, after Domenichino. Rare. 1808 edition. 40 00

MUNNICKHUYSEN.

1957 Henri Spiegel. 7 50

NANTEUIL (ROBT.).

$10 00 1958 Duc D'Espernon.

11 00 1959 Edouard Mole.

26 00 1960 Pompone de Bellievre. Engraver's Masterpiece.

19 00 1961 Van Steenberghen.

NANTEUIL & EDELINCK.

17 50 1962 Moses, after Philippe de Champagne.

NAUURENS (J.).

6 00 1963 The Rain has Ceased, after Verheyden.

PANNIER.

2 00 1964 Portrait of Malherbe.

2 00 1965 Portrait of Thiers.

PARKES (R. B.).

10 00 1966 A Cup of Coffee (Mezzotint), after Madrazzo. Proof.

23 00 1967 Viola (Mezzotint), after Gordon. Proof.

32 50 1968 A Winter Walk (Mezzotint), after Gordon. Proof.

PARMIGIANO.

17 00 1969 Entombment of Christ.

PENCZ (GEO.).

23 00 1970 Duke of Saxony.

PERFETTI (A.).

1971 Esperanza (Ellena Zanoni), after Carlo Dolci. *$6 00*
1972 Maria Carolina of Tuscany. *3 00*
1973 Cavaliere de Onis. *2 00*
1974 Raphael's Madonna Granduca. Remarque Proof. White cuff. *6 00*
1975 Cosmo di Medici. *2 00*

PETERSEN.

1976 Children in the Wood, after Embde. *4 00*

PIOTTI (CATRINA).

1977 Semiramis. Proof. *7 00*

PIRANESI.

1978 Temple of Peace. *10 00*
1979 Temple of Concord. Uncut Margins. *12 00*
1980 " " Janus. *21 00*
1981 " " Apollo. *12 50*
1982 Interior of the Colosseum. *15 00*
1983 " " " *17 50*
1984 Exterior " " *20 00*
1985 Island of the Tiber. *15 00*
1986 St. Paul's, Outside the Walls. *8 00*
1987 Arch of Septimus Severus. *19 00*
1988 " " Titus. *20 00*
1990 " " Constantine. *16 00*
1991 " " Benevento. *18 00*
1992 Hadrian's Villa. *15 00*
1993 " " *9 00*
1994 " " Temple. *9 00*

POILLY (F.).

$11 00 1995 The Virgin of the Cradle, after Raphael.

POLANZONI.

8 00 1996 Piranesi.

PORPORATI.

25 00 1997 Garde à vous, after Angelica Kauffman.

80 00 1998 Venus et l'Amour. Proof before the Border.

POTTER (PAUL).

35 00 1999 Cattle Scene. Cows. Bartsch 14.

34 00 2000 " " Sheep. " 15.

PREVOST (Z.).

6 00 2002 Venus de Milo.

PRIOR (T. A.).

52 50 2003 Heidelberg, after Turner. Proof.

MARC ANTONIO RAIMONDI.

120 00 2004 The Last Supper.

90 00 2005 St. Paul.

20 00 2006 The Sybil.

30 00 2007 Martyrdom of St. Lawrence.

11 00 2008 Notre Dame l'Escalier.

2009	Chasse aux Lions.			$12 00
2010	Massacre of the Innocents.	Bartsch	18.	40 00
2011	Martyrdom of St. Felicité.	"	117.	62 50
2012	La Vendage.	"	306.	32 50
2013	Jurisprudence.	"	381.	50 00
2014	Young Man with Lantern.	"	384.	40 00
2015	Woman with Long Hair.	"	427.	17 50
2016	Virgin with Cradle.			52 50
2017	Grimpours.			35 00
2018	Triumph of Galatea.			50 00
2019	Christ at the Table of Simon.			32 50

REMBRANDT.

2020	Portrait of himself. Mustachios.	Bartsch	2.	120 00
2021	" " in rich cloak.	"	7.	55 00
2022	Portrait of himself, with scarf round his neck.	"	17.	17 50
2023	" " plumed hat.	"	20.	32 50
2024	" "	"	21.	105 00
2025	" " with sabre.	"	23.	40 00
2026	" " " aigrette.	"	23*	42 50
2027	" " in white habit.	"	24.	9 00
2028	" " with flat hat.	"	26.	11 00
2029	Abraham Caressing Isaac.	"	33.	12 00
2030	Abraham and Isaac. The Sacrifice.	"	35.	23 00
2031	Joseph relating his Dreams.	"	37	11 00
2032	Triumph of Mordecai.	"	40.	75 00
2033	David Praying.	"	41.	15 00
2034	Tobit struck Blind.	"	42.	26 00
2035	Tobit and the Angel.	"	43.	29 00
2036	The Angels appearing to the Shepherds.	"	44.	80 00

Price	No.	Title	Note		Bartsch
$27 50	2037	The Nativity.		Bartsch	46.
100 00	2038	Presentation in the Temple.		"	50.
35 00	2039	Flight into Egypt.	Dark effect.	"	53.
95 00	2040	" " "		"	56.
25 00	2041	Repose in Egypt.		"	58.
75 00	2042	Jesus brought back from the Temple.		"	60.
11 00	2043	Virgin and Child.		"	61.
10 00	2044	Holy Family.		"	62.
11 00	2045	Christ and the Doctors.		"	64.
100 00	2046	Jesus Preaching.		"	67.
11 00	2047	Raising of Lazarus.		"	72.
575 00	2048	Christ Healing the Sick (the " 100 Guilder " print).		"	74.
30 00	2049	Christ in the Garden of Olives.		"	75.
625 00	2050	Ecce Homo.	Second State.	"	77.
40 00	2051	The Three Crosses.		"	78.
350 00	2052	Descent from the Cross.	First State.	"	81.
12 50	2053	" " "		"	82.
28 00	2054	" " "		"	83.
17 00	2055	Entombment of Christ.		"	84.
52 50	2056	" " "		"	86.
23 00	2057	The Supper at Emmaus.		"	87.
20 00	2058	Christ and Disciples at Emmaus.		"	88.
45 00	2059	Good Samaritan.		"	90.
16 00	2060	Tribute Money.		"	91.
24 00	2061	Prodigal Son.		"	91*
11 00	2062	Martyrdom of St. Stephen.		"	97.
22 00	2063	Philip and the Eunuch.		"	98.
42 50	2064	Death of the Virgin.		"	99.
55 00	2065	St. Jerome.		"	103.
120 00	2066	Marriage of Jason.	First State.	"	112.

2067	The Star of the Kings.	Bartsch	113.	$17 00
2068	Lion Hunt.	"	116.	15 00
2069	Battle Scene.	"	117.	14 00
2070	Jacob and Laban—with 2 copies.	"	118.	17 00
2071	Wandering Musicians.	"	119.	13 00
2072	Rat Catcher.	"	121.	50 00
2073	Pancake Woman.	"	124.	12 00
2074	The Card Player.	"	137.	11 00
2075	The Hunchback.	"	140.	10 00
2076	Philosopher.	"	148.	12 50
2077	The Shell (after).	"	159.	7 50
2079	Beggar.	"	162.	9 00
2080	Beggars.	"	177.	6 00
2081	"	"	178.	6 00
2082	" with wooden leg.	"	179.	10 00
2083	The Painter's Model.	"	192.	42 50
2084	Academy Model.	"	194.	12 00
2085	Bathers.	"	195.	17 00
2086	Academy Figure, reclining.	"	196.	14 00
2087	The Negress.	"	205.	38 00
2088	Amsterdam.	"	210.	60 00
2089	Three Trees.	"	212.	650 00
2090	Les Trois Chaumières.	"	217.	135 00
2091	La Passage à la tour.	"	218.	125 00
2092	Landscape.	"	219.	16 00
2093	The Shepherd and his Family.	"	220.	22 50
2094	Canal.	"	221.	30 00
2095	Le Bouquet de bois.	"	222.	100 00
2096	Passage à la tour, carré.	"	223.	115 00

$400 00	2097	Chaumière et la Grange a foin.	Bartsch	225.
45 00	2098	Chaumière au Grand arbre.	"	226.
90 00	2099	La Verger et la Grange.	"	228.
32 50	2100	Landscape. Grotto and Pool.	"	231.
150 00	2101	The Mill.	"	233.
37 50	2102	La Campagne du Péseur d'or.	"	234.
30 00	2103	Landscape. Cow and Water.	"	237.
25 00	2104	Old Man, with gray beard and black velvet coat.	"	262.
21 00	2105	Jan. C. Sylvius.	"	266.
80 00	2106	Head. Jeune Homme assis et réfléchessant.	"	268.
77 50	2107	Dr. Faustus.	"	270.
110 00	2108	Renier Avesloo.	"	271.
25 00	2109	Abraham Franz.	"	272.
35 00	2110	Jan Asselyn.	"	277.
165 00	2111	Ephraim Bonus.	"	278.
45 00	2112	Utenbogardus.	"	279.
145 00	2113	Jean C. Sylvius.	"	280.
225 00	2114	The great Coppenol.	"	283.
460 00	2115	Jean Six. Burgomaster. Fine margin.	"	285.
52 50	2116	Head. Young Man in velvet hat.	"	289.
12 00	2117	Old Man with large hat.	"	290.
	2118	Laughing Portrait.	"	294.
12 00	2119	Old Man with beard.	"	297.
13 00	2120	Head with cap.	"	304.
12 00	2121	" duplicate.	"	304.
14 00	2122	" in broad-brimmed hat.	"	311.
7 00	2123	Head.	"	316.
13 00	2124	" of Rembrandt.	"	319.
150 00	2125	The Jewish Bride. Rembrandt's Wife.	"	340.
28 00	2126	Rembrandt's Mother.	"	343.

2127 Rembrandt's Mother. Bartsch 344. $29 00
2128 " " " 354. 21 00
2129 Heads (six). " 365. 17 00

REYHER.

2130 Princess Potocka. Proof. 60 00

RICHOMME

2131 Henry IV. and the Spanish Ambassador, after Ingres 30 00
2132 Andromaque, after Guérin. 18 00
2133 Daphnio and Chloe, after Gérard. 12 00

RIVERA.

2134 St. John the Baptist. [illegible] 00

RUYSDAEL.

2135 The Wooden Bridge. 24 00
2136 The Stream. 21 00
2137 Trees. 22 00

SANGSTER (SAM'L).

2138 The Fair Student, after Newton. Proof. 6 00
2139 Belisarius, after Sir M. A. Shee. 7 00

SCHIAVONETTI (L.).

2140 Cartoon of Pisa. 10 00
2141 The Happy Reunion (colored), after Pellegrini 29 00

SCHIAVONI.

$115 00 2142 Assumption of the Virgin, after Titian. Proof.

SCHMIDT (G. F.).

17 50 2143 Handel.

13 00 2144 Portrait, after G. Flinch.

4 00 2145 The Good Friends.

6 00 2146 The Count de Gueldres threatening his Father, after Rembrandt.

10 00 2147 Presentation in the Temple.

7 00 2148 Mother of Rembrandt.

7 00 2149 Portrait of Schmidt.

SCHOENGAUER (MARTIN).

37 50	2150	St. John.	Bartsch 54.
37 50	2151	La Vierge au Piroquet.	" 28.
50 00	2152	Passion of Christ.	" 9.
105 00	2153	Coronation of the Virgin.	" 71.
75 00	2154	Flight into Egypt.	" 88.
40 00	2155	Arrest of Christ. Pilate washing his hands.	" 10.
70 00	2156	Elephant.	" 92.
80 00	2157	First of the Wise Virgins.	" 77.
32 50	2158	Fourth " " "	" 80.

SHARP.

55 00 2159 Doctors of the Church, after Guido Reni. Proof.

20 00 2160 Holy Family, after Reynolds.

17 00 2161 John Hunter, " "

14 00 2162 Diogenes, after Salvator Rosa.

STEINMULLER.

2163 Madonna of the Belvedere Gallery, after Raphael. *$11 00*

STEPHANUS.

2164 3 Niellos. *7 00*

STOCK (A.).

2165 Hans Holbein, after himself. *6 00*

STRANGE.

2166 Portrait of himself, after Greuze. *12 00*

2167 Infant Jesus, after Murillo. Proof. *25 00*

2168 " " after Vandyke. Proof. *21 00*

2169 Charles I., after Vandyke. Presentation Proof. Unique. *225 00*

2170 Henrietta Maria, after Vandyke. Proof. *70 00*

2171 Salutation, after Guido. *14 00*

SUYDERHOEF (JONAS).

2172 Burgomasters of Amsterdam, etc. *50 00*

TENIERS (D.).

2173 Dutch Interior. *14 00*

THEVENIN.

2174 Children of Charles I., after Vandyke. *17 00*

THOUVENIN.

$26 00 2175 Marriage of the Virgin, after Raphael.

TOSCHI (P.).

70 00 2176 Descent from the Cross, after Volterra. Proof.

62 50 2177 Madonna della Scala, after Correggio Proof.

80 00 2178 St. Thomas, after Correggio. Proof remarque.

52 50 2179 Madonne Incoronata, after Correggio. Proof signed.

16 00 2180 Diana returning from the Chase, after Correggio. Proof.

55 00 2181 Group of Cherubs and Angels, after Correggio. Proof.

TROSSIN (R.).

10 00 2182 Mater Dolorosa, after Guido Reni.

TURNER (C. W.).

7 00 2183 A Frosty Morning, Mezzotint, after Sharp.

6 00 2184 The Glow-Worm.

4 00 2185 The Glutton.

4 00 2186 At Fault !

VALLOT (P. J.).

3 00 2187 "Le Reveil" of Jesus, after Carraci.

VAN DALEN.

21 00 2188 Giorgio Barbarello, after Titian.

21 00 2189 Boccaccio, after Titian.

21 00 2190 Petro Aretino, after Titian.

21 00 2191 Sebastian del Piombo, after Titian.

VAN LEYDEN.

2192	Mahomet killing Sergius.	Bartsch 126.	$37 50
2193	Milkmaid.	" 158.	18 00
2194	Madonna and St. Anne.	" 79.	17 00
2195	Adam and Eve.	" 9.	10 00
2196	Pyramus and Thisbe.	" 135.	21 00
2197	Emperor Maximillian (after).	" 172.	16 00
2198	Man with Torch.	" 147.	34 00
2199	St. Jerome.	" 113.	11 00
2199*	St. Jerome.	" 113.	12 00
2200	Joseph and Potiphar's Wife.	" 20.	13 00
2201	Madonna and Joseph.	" 83.	13 00
2202	Agar and Abraham.		13 00
2203	Danse de la Madelaine.		62 50
2204	Virgin and Tree. Adam and Eve.		50 00
2205	Prodigal Son.		52 50
2206	Abraham and Three Angels.		32 50
2207	St. Anthony.		11 00
2208	Samson and Delilah.		34 00
2209	Virgin and Infant.		47 00
2210	Susannah and the Elders.		17 00
2211	Esther.		12 00
2212	Lazarus		16 00

VAN MECKEN.

2213	Genealogy of Christ.	Bartsch 202.	42 50
2214	Dance of Herodias.	" 9.	110 00

VAN OSTADE.

2215	Benedicité.	11 00
2216	La Gouter. .	9 00

$4 00 2217 The Empty Pitcher.

4 00 2218 Musician.

VAN VLIET.

17 00 2219 The Reader, after Rembrandt.

12 00 2220 St. Jerome, " "

VISSCHER (C.).

9 00 2221 Robert Junius.

45 00 2222 Pancake Woman.

62 50 2223 Guilliaume de Ryck.

6 00 2224 Jan Dousa.

12 00 2225 Aloynius.

7 00 2226 The Angel directing the Departure of Abraham, after Bassano.

6 00 2227 Arrival of Abraham at Sichem.

20 00 2229 Rat Catcher.

10 00 2230 Sleeping Cat.

4 00 2231 Portrait of Visscher.

5 00 2232 Portrait of his Mother.

25 00 2232* Wandering Musicians.

VOGEL.

7 00 2233 Saxon Courtship, after Lasch.

11 00 2234 Card Players, after Knaus.

VALLOT.

22 00 2235 Napoleon at the Battle of the Pyramids, after Gros. Proof.

VORSTERMAN (L.).

13 00 2236 Jerome de Brau.

WATSON (JAMES).

2237 Sir Joshua Reynolds, by himself. Mezzotint. Fine Impression. *$14 00*

WATTEAU.

2238 Female Head. *17 00*

WEBER (FRED'K).

2239 Portrait of Ammerbach, after Holbein. Proof. *14 00*

2240 Madame de Sevigne, after Petitot. *6 00*

2241 " " Grignan (Marquise de Simiane). *6 00*

WILLE (J. G.).

2242 The Aunt of Gerard Dow. *10 00*

2243 Family Concert. Proof. *65 00*

2244 The Good Friends. " *22 00*

2245 Death of Marc Anthony. Proof. *26 00*

2246 L'Instruction Paternelle. "The satin gown picture." Proof. *125 00*

2247 L'Observateur Distrait. Proof. *37 50*

2248 The Little Philosopher. *37 50*

2249 Le Petit Joueur d'Instrument. Rare Proof. *32 50*

2250 Agar presenting Abraham to Sara. Rare Proof. *14 00*

2251 Bonne femme de Normandie. " " *26 00*

2252 Soeur de la Normandie. Rare Proof. *26 00*

WILLMORE.

2253 Ancient Italy, after Turner. Rare Proof. *27 00*

2254 Grand Canal, Venice, after Turner. Rare Proof. *40 00*

2254* Mercury and Argus. Rare Proof. *25 00*

WILSON (D.).

$31 00 2255 Ancient Carthage, after Turner. Proof.

WOLF.

3 00 2256 Infant Jesus, after Carlo Dolci. Proof.

WOLGEMUTH.

9 00 2257 Æneus Pius II. and Frederick III.

WOOLLETT (W.).

12 00 2258 Roman Ruins, after Claude.
37 00 2259 Temple of Apollo, after Claude. Proof.
40 00 2260 Spanish Pointer, after G. Stubbs.
18 00 2261 Solitude, after R. Wilson. Proof.
13 00 2262 Ceyx and Alcione, after R. Wilson. Proof.
27 00 2263 Apollo and Sybil, " " "
21 00 2264 Dido and Æneas, " Jones and Mortimer. Open letter.

WORTHINGTON.

6 00 2265 Canterbury Pilgrims, after Stothard.

MISCELLANEOUS.

10 00 2266 Portraits of Fulton, Decatur, Porter, Jones, and Bainbridge.
8 00 2267 " of Madame de Sévigné. Proof.
3 00 2268 " of Madame de la Fontaine. "
6 00 2269 " of Molière. "
8 00 2270 " of Charles de Sévigné. "

2271	Portraits of Marquise de Simiane. Proof.	$4 00
2272	" of Pascal (Jacqueline). Proof.	2 00
2273	" of Boileau. Proof.	5 00
2274	" of Henri de Sévigné. Proof.	4 00
2275	" of La Fontaine. Proof.	6 00
2276	" of La Rochefoucauld. Proof.	5 00
2277	" of Volckaerdt. Woodcut.	4 00

ANONYMOUS.

2278 Coronation of the Virgin.

2279 Niello. One of the first impressions ever printed from an engraved-plate—about 1430. 20 00

2280 La Sybille.

ETCHINGS.

PART II.

APPIAN.

$6 00 2281 Source de l'Albane. Signed Proof.
5 00 2282 Une Mare.
11 00 2283 La Mère aux Canards. Signed Proof.
6 00 2284 Genoa. Signed Proof.

BACHER (H.).

5 00 2285 Bead Stringers.
50 2286 La Belvedere.
6 00 2287 Venetian Laundry.
5 00 2288 Making Fish-nets.
6 00 2289 The Ferry.
3 00 2290 Bridge of Sighs.
7 00 2291 Interior of St. Mark's.
9 00 2292 Lace Makers.
3 00 2293 Gondolier.
8 00 2294 Ponte de la Pistor.
5 00 2295 Venetian Well.
8 00 2296 Via Garibaldi.

BALL (W.).

20 00 2297 Light Thickens, etc. Signed Proof.

BELIN-DOLLET.

2298 Home of Millet. $7 00

2299 Hotel Dieu. 8 00

2300 Couseuse. 4 00

2301 Bergère. 5 00

BELLOWS (A. F.).

2302 Mill Stream. Signed Proof. 28 00

2303 The Inlet. " " 28 00

BRACQUEMOND.

2304 The Hare. 17 00

BRUNET-DEBAINES.

2305 Harfleur. 4 00

CHAMPOLLION.

2306 The Butterfly, after Fortuny. 12 00

CHURCH (F. S.).

2307 A Lesson in Wisdom. Signed. 10 00

COCK (C. de).

2308 Farm House. 4 00

COLEMAN.

2309 Mediterranean Balcony. Remarque, signed. 15 00

2310 Gathering Pampas Grass. " " 10 00

COOPER (G.).

$16 00 2311 Monarch of the Meadows, after T. S. Cooper. Remarque.

COROT.

7 00 2312 Souvenirs of Italy.

6 00 2313 Environs of Rome.

35 00 2314 "Dry Point," Landscape.

COUTIL.

15 00 2315 The End of the Day's Work, after Miller. Remarque.

COURTRY (C.).

27 00 2316 Milton Dictating Paradise Lost to his Daughter, after Munkacsy.

8 00 2317 Washing Day.

28 00 2318 Black Cow, after Von Marcke.

COX (WALTER).

15 00 2319 Moonlight on the Mole, after Page. Remarque.

CUCINNOTTA.

2 00 2320 Fan Design. The Bridge.

DAUBIGNY.

7 00 2321 Les Vendages.

DAUTREY.

8 00 2322 Near Orleans. A Farm. Parchment.

DELAUNEY.

2323 Landscape. *$1 00*

DENON.

2324 Young Bull, after Paul Potter. *21 00*

DESBROSSES.

2325 The Old Bridge. *7 00*

2326 Une Mare aux Vaches. *7 00*

2327 The Great Tree, after Corot. Parchment. *16 00*

DETAILLE.

2328 The Uhlan. *12 00*

DOVERA.

2329 The Model. *4 00*

DESCHENNIS.

2330 Twilight. Signed. *13 00*

2331 Moonrise. " *14 00*

DOWNARD.

2332 Hay Field. Remarque Proof. *17 00*

FLAMENG.

2333 Charles Darwin, after J. Collier. Signed. *18 00*

2334 Hassan and Namouna, after Regnault. Proof. *9 00*

2335 Sauvée. Proof. *26 00*

FOCILLON.

$16 00 2336 Old Tannery.

FORMSTECHER (A.).

4 00 2337 The Amateur.

FULLWOOD (J.).

26 00 2338 Belated Traveler. Parchment remarque.

11 00 2339 Old Mill. Remarque.

8 00 2340 Village Church. Remarque.

7 00 2341 Edge of a Moor.

10 00 2342 Twilight. Plate destroyed.

17 00 2343 Moonrise. " "

20 00 2344 Devonshire Hay Field. Remarque. Parchment proof.

GAUJEAN.

2 00 2345 Cherry Ripe, after J. Russel.

GAUTIER.

37 00 2346 The Seine at Paris. Parchment.

14 00 2347 Castle of St. Angelo.

27 00 2347* Loch Lomond.

GEDDES.

5 00 2348 Child with Pear.

3 50 2349 Study of Head.

GOURCY (BARON DE).

5 00 2350 Alone with Nature.

GRAVESANDE.

2351 Return of the Fishermen. Parchment. *$25 00*
2352 Forest Opening. " *33 00*
2353 Sawmill. " *31 00*
2354 Borders of Gien. *51 00*
2355 Riveirè d'Auray. Parchment. *13 00*
2356 Old Oak. " *18 00*
2357 Rotterdam. *14 00*
2358 Zandvoort. Parchment. *16 00*
2359 On the Yesel. *13 00*
2360 Flushing Old Pier. *15 00*
2361 Environs Dortrecht. *15 00*
2362 Set of 13 small subjects. *136 50*

GRAVIER.

2363 Rose Standish, after Boughton. Remarque. *16 00*
2364 Hesitation, " " " *16 00*
2365 The Fighting Téméraire, after Turner. Remarque. *16 00*
2366 Ship of Ulysses, after Turner. Remarque. *15 00*
2367 Going to Church. " *8 00*
2368 La Mare aux Canards. " *12 00*
2369 Moorish Garden. " *12 00*
2370 Egyptian Court. " *13 00*

GUERARD.

2371 Vive la Fidelité, after Hals. *2 50*

HALLYER.

2372 Daniel Webster. Signed. *16 00*

HADEN (SEYMOUR).

Price	No.	Title			
$300 00	2373	Calais Pier, after Turner.	First state.	Plate destroyed.	
41 00	2374	Windsor Castle.	Early state.	"	"
48 00	2375	Greenwich Harbor.	" "	"	"
95 00	2376	Shere Mill Pond.	First state.		
80 00	2377	Breaking up the "Agamemnon."	First state.		
50 00	2378	Sunset at Tipperary.	Proof on vellum.	Plate destroyed.	
41 00	2379	Lancashire River.	The artist's favorite Plate.		

HESTER.

10 00 2380 Cherry Ripe, after Millais.

JACQUE.

Price	No.	Title		
100 00	2381	Sheepfold.	Plate destroyed.	Only 98 printed.
28 00	2382	Evening.	Only 100 printed.	
16 00	2383	Watering the Flock.	" " "	
14 00	2384	Sheep.	" " "	
21 00	2385	Swineherd.	" " "	
15 00	2386	La Sortie.	" " "	

JACQUEMART.

5 00 2387 Le Cavalier, after Meissonier.

10 00 2388 Old Houses.

JACQUET.

250 00 2389 "1814," on vellum, after Meissonier.

JONGKIND.

10 00 2390 Two Marine Pieces.

KNAUS.

2391 Portrait of Ludy. *$13 00*

LALANNE.

2392 Environs of Paris. *4 00*

2393 The Canal. *4 00*

2394 Landscape, after Daubigny. *18 00*

2395 " " " *22 00*

LEGROS.

2396 Sir Frederick Leighton, R. A. *8 00*

LELOIR (L.).

2397 Head. *10 00*

LOWENSTEIN.

2398 Roman Dinner, after Alma Tadema. Remarque. *10 00*

2399 Roman Siesta, " " " " *9 00*

MARE.

2400 H. M. Stanley, with Autograph. Parchment. *23 00*

MARTIAL.

2401 The Cancalaises, after Feyin-Perrin. *80 00*

MACBETH (R. W.)

2402 Maud Müller. Remarque. *24 00*

McFADDEN.

$22 00 2403 Abingdon. Remarque Parchment.

11 00 2404 Cornfield.

14 00 2405 Black Fen.

8 00 2406 Roadside Çottages.

17 00 2407 Where the Pike Lies.

MERYON.

4 00 2408 New Zealand.

2 00 2409 Rebus "Vendetta."

24 00 2410 Rue des Etoilles.

8 00 2411 " " " Bourges.

22 00 2412 " " Mauvais Garçons.

28 00 2413 Tour de l'Horloge.

17 00 2414 St. Etienne du Mont.

20 00 2415 Le Petit Pont.

20 00 2416 Rue Peronette.

17 00 2417 Pont Notre-Dame.

95 00 2418 Notre-Dame.

34 00 2419 Morgue.

15 00 2420 Grand Châtelet.

13 00 2421 Pavillion de Mademoiselle.

9 00 2422 Oceanic.

40 00 2423 Pompe Notre-Dame.

32 00 2424 Pont Neuf.

62 50 2425 Pont au Change.

25 00 2426 Notre-Dame Gargoyle.

3 50 2427 Portrait.

24 00 2428 Galerie de Notre-Dame.

3 00 2429 Jean Besly.

2430	Boulay-Paty.	$4 00
2431	Tourelle.	21 00
2432	Rue de Chartres.	18 00
2433	Rene de Burgidale.	12 00
2434	San Francisco.	17 00
2435	Louis XI.	10 00
2436	François Viete.	3 00
2437	Verses.	5 00
2438	Portrait of Bizeal.	4 50
2439	L'Espérance.	3 00
2440	Bourges.	10 00
2441	Code of Laws.	2 00
2442	Petite Pompe.	11 00
2443	St. Martin.	5 00
2443A	Ministere de Marine.	8 00

MICHETTI.

2444	La Gardeuse de Durdens.	3 00

MILLET.

2445	Bergerè Signed. Rare and unique.	105 00
2446	Departure for Work.	37 50
2447	Bonfire.	18 00
2448	Trench Digger.	8 00
2449	Seamstress.	10 00
2450	Flax Spinner.	38 00
2451	Sower, after Millet.	12 00
2452	Churning.	15 00
2453	The Carder.	50 00

$32 00 2454 The Spaders.

7 00 2455 Milking.

13 00 2456 Too Hot!

MORAN (P.).

30 00 2457 Passing Storm. Proof on Vellum.

26 00 2458 Summer Afternoon. " "

28 00 2459 New England Orchard. " "

MORSE.

2 00 2460 Morning, after Greuze.

2 50 2461 Dead Bird, " "

1 00 2462 Girl and Dog, " "

NARGEOT.

2 00 2463 Study, after Hebert.

O'CONNELL (MAD.).

10 00 2464 Portrait d'un Cavalier.

PALMER (S.).

5 00 2465 The Willow.

8 00 2466 The Vine. 2 in 1.

PARRISH (S.).

25 00 2467 Evening on the Schroon. Satin. All signed. Proof

2 50 2468 " " " Small.

3 00 2469 Girard Point.

5 00 2470 In the Meadows.

2471	Canal, Trenton.	$3 00
2472	Belleville. No. 1.	10 00
2473	Lewisburg.	3 00
2474	Inner Harbor, Gloucester.	15 00
2475	Bay of Fundy.	16 00
2476	Fisherman's House, Cape Ann.	20 00
2477	Old Farm.	15 00
2478	Gloucester Ferry. No. 1.	12 00
2479	Southwark, Philadelphia.	3 00
2480	Acadian Night.	10 50
2481	Old Fish House. Gloucester.	6 00
2482	Portsmouth, N. H.	9 00
2483	Lobsterman's House.	3 00
2484	Lobster Cove, Annisquam.	4 00
2485	Left by the Tide.	5 00
2486	A Spring Day.	8 00
2487	A Windy Day.	4 00
2488	Rocks off Cape Ann.	8 00
2489	Fishing Hamlet.	4 50
2490	Carleton.	6 50
2491	Annisquam.	5 00
2492	Evening. Gloucester.	9 00
2493	On the Annisquam.	5 50
2494	Fishing Boats. Gloucester.	4 00
2495	Harbor Cove. "	6 50
2496	Getting under Weigh.	5 00
2497	Marblehead.	5 50
2498	Old Acadian Inn Yard.	8 00
2499	Rocky Neck.	12 00
2500	Trenton.	17 50
2501	A Showery Day	4 00

$5 00	2502	Spanish Garden.
5 00	2503	Twilight.
5 00	2504	Gloucester Harbor.
5 50	2505	By-way in Trenton.
5 50	2506	Bit of Marblehead.
4 50	2507	Market Day.
5 00	2508	Street Corner.
4 00	2509	Drifting.
10 50	2510	Northern Moorland.
3 50	2511	Portsmouth.
6 00	2512	Sunset.
4 00	2513	Evening Sketch.
4 50	2514	Twilight. No. 2.
2 50	2514A	On the Flats.
3 00	2515	Sunset. Gloucester Harbor.
9 00	2516	On the St. John.
7 00	2517	On the Schroon.
6 50	2518	Belleville. No. 2.
3 50	2519	Market Boats.
9 00	2520	Catching the Geese.
3 50	2521	Upper Hudson.
14 00	2522	Archer's Studio.
4 00	2523	Old Barn.
3 00	2524	Portland, N. B.
14 50	2525	Fish House.
5 00	2526	In the Meadows.
3 50	2527	In Port.
5 25	2528	Evening.
5 50	2529	Eastern Point, Cape Ann.
5 00	2530	Haunted House.

2531 Riding out a South-Easter. $4 00
2532 Gloucester Ferry. No. 2. 5 00
2533 Marblehead. 8 00
2534 Bethlehem. 2 50
2535 Windsor. 11 00
2536 Wood Boats. 6 00
2537 Shepherd's Christmas Eve. 4 00
2538 Fishing Boats. 4 00
2539 Ten Pound Island. 5 00
2540 Towing to Windward. 5 00
2541 Bethlehem. 4 00
2542 Winter, Trenton. 6 50
2543 Chester County, Pa. 3 00
2544 Annisquam. 3 50
2545 Calling the Geese. 6 00
2546 Acadian Inn. Small. 6 00
2547 Gloucester Harbor. 15 00
2548 Deserted Mill. 5 00
2549 Mills on the Schroon. 4 50
2550 Upper Delaware. 4 00
2551 November. 5 00
2552 Flooded Lands. 3 50
2552A Old Farm. 5 50

PENNELL (JOSEPH).

2553 Up and down Siena. All signed Proofs. 3 00
2554 Swing of the Arno. 8 00
2555 Washing Place. 6 00
2556 Gateway. 5 00
2557 Sienese Street. 6 00

$5 00 2558 Pisa.
8 00 2559 Fiesole.
4 00 2560 Siena.
5 00 2561 San Ghimignano.
4 00 2562 Mad. Delphine's.
5 00 2563 Organ Grinder.
4 00 2564 Brass Foundry.
10 00 2565 On the Arno.
6 00 2566 Ducal Urbino.
4 00 2567 Schuylkill Coal Wharves.
7 00 2568 Under the Bridges.
4 00 2569 Callow Hill St. Bridge.
3 00 2570 An Inner Court, New Orleans.
4 00 2571 Covered Street, Florence.
5 00 2572 A Narrow Way, Florence.
5 00 2573 Plow Inn Yard.
7 00 2574 Water Street Stairs. (No. 1 and No. 2.)
6 00 2575 Porto Romano.
14 00 2576 An American Venice.
7 00 2577 Philadelphia Public Buildings.
4 00 2578 Chancery Lane.
2 00 2579 Alley-way.
6 00 2580 Atlantic City.
6 00 2581 Yesterday and To-Day, Venice.
6 00 2582 Scaffolding.
5 00 2583 Street Sweeper.
11 00 2584 Pilot Town, La.
12 00 2585 In the Twilight.
6 00 2586 Sauerkraut Row.
6 00 2587 Archways.

2588 Doorway, Venice. *$7 00*
2589 Sieur Georges. *3 00*
2590 In the Piazza. *4 00*
2591 Lynchburgh, Va. *11 00*
2592 Chestnut Street Bridge. *5 00*
2593 Towers, San Ghimignano. *4 00*
2594 Little Venice. *3 00*
2595 Old Market, Florence. *4 00*
2596 Landing Place, Leghorn. *4 00*

PLATT (C. A.).

2597 Ebb Tide at St. John's, N. B. Plate destroyed. *15 00*

RAJON.

2598 Mrs. Siddons. *5 00*
2599 The Bath, after Alma Tadema. Proof. *20 00*
2600 The Blue Boy, after Gainsborough. Proof. *15 00*

RIVIÈRE.—L'HUILLIER.

2601 The Last Meeting, after L'Huillier. Remarque. *23 00*

RUDAUX.

2602 The Sportsman's Find. *6 00*

SEWELL (R. W.).

2603 Dortrecht. *6 00*
2604 Canal at Dortrecht. Upright one. *8 00*

SHORT (F.).

$8 00 2605 Old London, Street Scene.

SLOCOMBE (F.).

14 00 2606 Noonday Rest, after Birket Foster. Proof.
18 00 2607 Wooden Bridge.
13 00 2608 Chalfont Village.
10 00 2609 Street in Rye.
10 00 2609* Street in Rye.

TAECE (A.).

3 00 2610 The Old Bridge.

TEYSSONNIÈRES.

7 00 2611 Autumn Day near Bordeaux.
10 00 2612 River near Bordeaux.
17 00 2613 Corneille (Pierre), after Le Brun. Parchment.
50 00 2614 Le Calvados. Parchment.

TISSOT (J. J.).

14 00 2615 First Pair of Breeches. Only 100 Printed.
23 00 2616 The Two Friends. " " "
12 00 2617 The Elder Sister. " " "
16 00 2618 The Quarrel. " " "
23 00 2619 The Hammock. " " "

VAN ELTEN.

15 00 2620 Winnockie Creek, N. J.

WALTNER.

2621 Harmony, after F. Dicksee. *$57 50*

2622 Mlle. P. M., " Dubois. *17 00*

2623 Lost Bird, " Marcus Stone. *23 00*

2624 Christ before Pilate, after Munkacsy. Proof before the Plate was steeled. *80 00*

2625 L'Angelus, after Millet. *415 00*

2626 Le Doreur, " Rembrandt. *37 00*

WEBER.

2627 Scotch Cattle. *5 00*

2628 LES CENT CHEF D'ŒUVRES: 100 of the finest Etchings of the Modern School. Text in French, folio, satin covers. Paris, 1884. *115 00*

www.ingramcontent.com/pod-product-compliance
Lightning Source LLC
Chambersburg PA
CBHW031403270326
41929CB00010BA/1310
* 9 7 8 3 7 4 4 6 7 3 2 1 1 *